THOMAS HARDY: LANDSCAPES OF THE MIND

THOMAS HARDY: LANDSCAPES OF THE MIND

Andrew Enstice

First published 1979 by
THE MACMILLAN PRESS LTD
London and Basingstoke
Associated companies in Delhi
Dublin Hong Kong Johannesburg Lagos
Melbourne New York Singapore Tokyo

Printed in Great Britain by
LOWE AND BRYDONE PRINTERS LTD
Thetford, Norfolk

British Library Cataloguing in Publication Data

Enstice, Andrew
    Thomas Hardy
    1. Hardy, Thomas, b.1840 – Homes
    and haunts – England – Wessex
    823.8   PR4754

ISBN 0–333–25593–3

Zoo whether 'tis the humpy ground
That wer a battle viel',
Or mossy house, all ivy-bound,
An' vallen down piece-meal;
Or if 'tis but a scraggy tree,
Where beauty smil'd o' wold, o,
How dearly I do like to zee
The pleace a tale's a-twold o'.

(William Barnes)

Contents

List of Maps

Introduction

It has been my intention in this book to analyse the relationship between 19th-century southern England and its literary image in Hardy's Wessex. I have traced the changing perception of his landscapes through the major novels, and tried to discover what he achieves by the changes in his own attitude to basically similar settings.

Hardy's perception of Wessex demanded its geographical visualisation, and therefore its identification with southern England. Yet the emphasis on actual place varies from novel to novel, from scene to scene. Casterbridge is closely identifiable with Dorchester, Tess's Marlott completely unidentifiable except for its location on a Wessex map.

The maps and close descriptions give a firm base for the communities of the novels, but they tend also to confine the major characters, and this becomes apparent as Hardy moves from close description towards the more general. *Tess* becomes scenic and characterised and *Jude* personalised and variable where similar geographical settings previously only varied (except in detail) from novel to novel.

Of course, as in the pastoral *Far from the Madding Crowd* or elegiac *Woodlanders*, the settings are also literary in a more general sense. But I have traced the development from particular towards flexible landscapes, and looked at the characters as elements of their settings. The first five novels are grouped as enclosed landscapes and, taken together, they show clearly Hardy's dependence on his Wessex homeland, and indicate the strongly regional nature of his earlier work. Of course *The Mayor of Casterbridge* and *The Return of the Native*, as their titles suggest, centre quite strongly on individuals. It is, however, only in *Tess* and *Jude* that the individual clearly emerges as independent of the community, and therefore as the focus of landscape, rather than a part of it, and the importance of this when the novels are seen as a whole lies in Hardy's growing rejection of the narrower aspects of regionalism.

I have taken *The Mayor of Casterbridge* as the anchorstone of my argument, largely because it represents the zenith in Hardy's work of what I have called the 'enclosed' landscape—that is, a world self-sufficient and self-centred, in which all characters, buildings and events are chosen and described for their close dependence on each other. Like the mediaeval town which Hardy's first description evokes, Casterbridge is a complete world, one in which roads arrive without leaving, coaches come but never seem to go, and people drift by, are caught in the fine web of human relationships, hopelessly enmeshed, and remain. The country around focuses on the market town, and nothing that could detract physically from that clear centre of attention is included in the novel. The cosmopolitan nature of Dorchester in the 1840s and 1850s (the period of the novel − Hardy, as I shall demonstrate, was at some pains to recreate his setting in terms of the Dorchester of more than thirty years before his novel was written) is consigned to literary oblivion in the construction of a world dominated by the living organism that pulses with human life at its centre.

'Landscape' in *The Mayor of Casterbridge* means not merely the visual aspect of the area, but all things pertaining to the world of Casterbridge. Just as the 18th-century art of landscaping involved a careful reconstruction of the existing scene, with a close attention to the necessary relationships of beauty, economy and harmony, so Hardy's art involves the reconstruction of the diverse Dorchester scene, organising and controlling our experience of it. The essential beauty, economy and harmony of the setting are translated, through the author's pen, into something recognisably similar, yet easier to comprehend. A world that would take a man his lifetime to understand has been ordered and simplified so that all may appreciate its structure.

It is the same kind of authorial landscaping that dominates Hardy's portrayal of the Wessex scene in *Under the Greenwood Tree*, *Far from the Madding Crowd*, *The Return of the Native*, and *The Woodlanders*. As the name of each novel suggests, the focus of attention is the community or place. Even *The Mayor of Casterbridge*, with its powerful examination of Henchard's tragedy, focuses not only on the man but on the town and his place in it. 'The Mayor', in the context of the title, is the current representative of the mayoralty, Henchard or Farfrae, 'two-hundredth odd' of the line. In *Under the Greenwood Tree* it is the human relationships within the village community which dominate, and the characters themselves form the physical bulk of the novel's 'landscape'. In *Far from the Madding Crowd* it is the farming community, working in partnership with nature, which dominates, and all its elements—fields, animals, buildings, men and the agricultural seasons—are parts of its 'landscape' structure. *The Return of the Native* concentrates on the balanced struggle of men and heath, within its exclusive heathland world, while *The Woodlanders* turns to orchards and woods and man's close relationship with them for its 'landscape'.

In all these novels, my work turns on Hardy's translation of the setting into the literary 'landscape'. Nature, visual, economic and aural, figures large in each, as do the rural characters of each setting; buildings and local features vary in prominence. Notably, all except *The Woodlanders* represent settings within a few miles of Hardy's childhood home at Stinsford (and even that novel reflects certain elements of the Stinsford area, although geographically based elsewhere), and all concentrate on their own 'landscapes' to the exclusion of others.

However, an enclosed landscape by its very nature imposes severe restrictions on the author and on his major characters. Henchard's rebellion against his life focuses, of necessity, on his position in Casterbridge, and it is that world alone which accepts the full weight of his frustrated criticism. In trying to loose himself from some of the restrictions of these enclosed worlds Hardy looked farther afield, amongst new settings and new ideas. *The Woodlanders* is located ten or twelve miles from the Stinsford area, and the ideas are wider, of love, marriage, divorce, social mobility and the need for intellectual fulfilment; but the method is still basically one of enclosed landscaping, and the community is our focus. In *Tess* the limits are changed and the 'landscapes' change with them. The individual is now the focus, moving from community to community, growing, exploring and discovering as she goes.

It is in *Jude*, however, that the enclosed landscape is finally abandoned, relegated to an almost undescribed undercurrent of characters and thought, welling up only occasionally in little eddies of cruelty and pettiness—the slaughtered pig, the quack Vilbert, or the self-righteous citizens of Aldbrickham. In this novel, the settings to be translated into a literary landscape exist only in the mind—of the author or the characters, or even the audience—and the difficulty of definition becomes one of determining the 'reality' of any given perception. Christminster cannot be defined, as Casterbridge can, as a 'landscape' of itself. It is seen through Jude's dream-misted eyes, and through the second-hand eyes of the tranter's boot-boy friend, and through Hardy's critical eyes, and through the eyes of the reader, seeing Jude's later disillusion before it has really become apparent to him. Each aspect is one feature of the new landscape – a landscape which I now call a 'landscape of the mind', not as representing any particular definable mind, but rather a perceived amalgam of many ways of looking at the same thing. It is in this light that we follow Jude on his travels round the anonymous towns of Wessex, watching him take up and discard ideal after ideal, maturing and changing all the time in his attitude to and perception of Christminster itself.

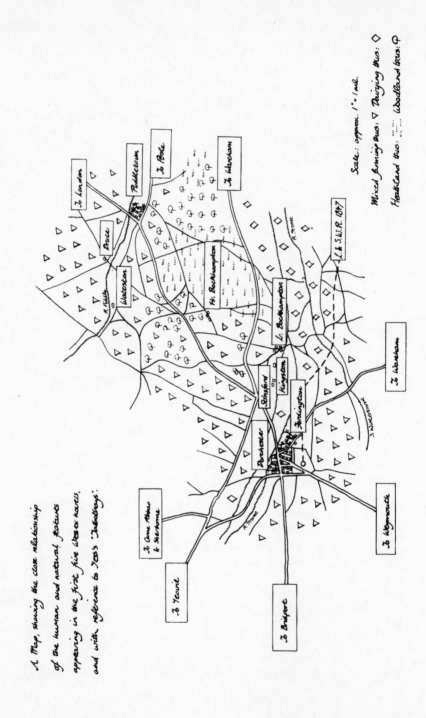

A Map, showing the close relationship of the human and natural features appearing in the first five Wessex novels, and with reference to Toss's Industrys.

To London

Puddletown

To Poole

Brice

Warebeam

Watercom

Hr. Beckhampton

Lr. Beckhampton

L. & S.W.R. 1847

Stinsford

Kingston

Fonington

Porchester

To Casterbridge & Sherborne

To Yeovil

To Bridport

To Weymouth

R. Frome

R. Piddle

R. Stour

R. Wintercook

Scale: approx. 1" = 1 mile.

Mixed farming thus: ▽   Dairying thus: ◇

Heathland thus: ·····   Woodland thus: ♀

1 Townscape: *The Mayor of Casterbridge*

I.

In this chapter it is my intention to establish an anchorstone for my argument, by looking in some detail at the way Hardy treats the town of Dorchester in translating it into his fictitious 'Casterbridge'. This translation can be taken as the clearest of all in Hardy's Wessex. Many of his settings can be identified only by assumption or by their location on his Wessex maps, but Casterbridge corresponds too closely to the real Dorchester of the mid-nineteenth century to be seen as anything but an artistic interpretation of that town.

Beginning with the panoramic views which welcome Susan and Elizabeth-Jane to the 'ancient borough', and following through the ancient stone and brick streets, through market days, harvests and festivities, through churches, inns and public buildings, through rich dwellings and slums, almost every detail described can be checked against records, maps, pictures, histories and surviving buildings. It is against this background of landscape manipulation that the first signs of the fundamental conflict in Hardy's work appear – the town's perfection of independence, embodying men as a part of itself, time out of mind, and encompassing men as disparate as Henchard and Farfrae within its succession of 200-odd mayors, also traps the free spirit of man. Henchard's struggle against circumstance is the tale of one man who could not accept his defined role in the Casterbridge world – the precursor of Tess and Jude, and successor to Troy and Clym. *The Mayor of Casterbridge* is one novel in a developing line; but it is notable both for the perfection of its form – the form that traps – and for the fact that it marks the end of the novel of harmonious landscape. As with the Wessex novels before it, it is the greater harmony that dominates, reducing the warring figures of Henchard and Farfrae to their place within the mayoral structure, and the timeless borough. After the less successful *Woodlanders*, Hardy turned finally to the struggle of the individual to free him (or her) self from the smothering Wessex landscapes, and *Tess of the d'Urbervilles* and *Jude the Obscure* reflect in their titles this new dominant interest. But it is in *The Mayor of Casterbridge* that Wessex attains its zenith. The reasons for this are both complex and subtle, and the following outline will demonstrate how Hardy interwove reality and imagination to produce Casterbridge.

2.

Thomas Hardy was born on June 2nd, 1840, in a cottage at Higher Bockhampton, on the very edge of the heath he was to make famous in *The Return of the Native*. The spot is much the same today, lonely only if you find that physical isolation impels loneliness, dark only if your imagination finds darkness in trees. By the time Hardy was born, the cottage was already at the head of a number of lifehold cottages which bordered the lane leading up to the woods and the heath, and the connection of his father and grandfather with the church choir at Stinsford parish church, over a mile distant, had forged strong bonds between these outlying families and the main body of the village (itself divided into Bockhampton and Stinsford). In addition, Hardy's father carried on a thriving stone-mason's business, employing a number of men (census returns show 2, Hardy says 25), and their neighbour, William Keats,[1] ran a successful haulage business (already, two of Hardy's characters for *Under the Greenwood Tree* are visible, with elements of later figures, such as Jude). In such a situation, it can be assumed that Hardy was in no way cut off from ordinary social intercourse, while enjoying all the advantages peace and solitude bring to the imagination.

Certainly, whatever his early character, Hardy's mother saw in her son a potential far greater than the scope afforded by a stonemason's business, however thriving, could ever fulfil. She might well have been guided in her thinking, of course, by the knowledge that her husband's was the last of the three lives on which the cottage was held; in a period when lifeholds were increasingly being taken in hand, rather than renewed on customary payment of the fine, there could be little hope of advancement for the son of a third 'life', as long as his skills were those which required the inheritance of house and land to allow him to prosper.[2] The opening of a village school in 1848 provided some scope for the boy, but too little for the liking of his mother, and a year later he was sent to a day-school in Dorchester, walking the 2 ½ miles in each direction every day. (The move was less approved by Mrs. Martin, of Kingston House, who had paid for the new school, and took a great interest in education among the villagers; Hardy was her particular favourite.) He remained at this school until he was sixteen, continuing the daily walk even when it was removed to premises with space for boarders. Here he learnt Latin and Greek, and for a while taught at the Sunday School, until in 1856 his father articled him to John Hicks, a local architect (this choice was dictated by Thomas Hardy senior's own profession; had Hardy been allowed to follow his early inclinations without the necessity of finding a career, he would probably have pursued the Classics, in which he was extremely proficient). While studying under Hicks he read Greek authors and began to explore the theories of paedo-baptism, in discussions with his fellow-pupil, Bastow. Hicks and Horace Moule, newly returned to Dorchester, also entered academic discussions with Hardy, and William Barnes' school, next door to the architect's office, was a fruitful field for advice. Hardy's own words, dictated for the *Life* to Florence Emily, his second wife, suggest what effect this background must have been having on a still very young man:

> Owing to the accident of his being an architect's pupil in a county-town of assizes and aldermen, which had advanced to railways and telegraphs and daily London papers; yet not living there, but walking in every day from a world of shepherds and ploughmen in a hamlet three miles off, where modern improvements were still regarded as wonders, he saw rustic and borough doings in a juxtaposition peculiarly close. To these externals may be added the peculiarities of his inner life, which might almost have been called academic – a triple existence unusual for a young man – what he used to call, in looking back, a life twisted of three strands – the professional life, the scholar's life, and the rustic life, combined in the twenty-four hours of one day, as it was with him through these years.[3]

It is interesting to note here two points relevant to the later discussion of *The Mayor of Casterbridge*: the reference to the advanced state of Dorchester in the later 1850s (the novel, according to internal dating evidence, is set mainly in the 1840s and 1850s, but notably lacks the above-mentioned advances); and the romantic vagueness of the chosen comparative, 'a world of shepherds and ploughmen'. We are forewarned to be wary of Hardy's fictitious settings, and of his apparently factual assertions (whether in the Prefaces or elsewhere). Like the *Life*, all his writings are potentially coloured by his fertile imagination.

From 1862 to 1867 Hardy lived in London, working for the architect Arthur Blomfield (his original move being that of the young man setting out to seek his fortune, with two letters of introduction and limited funds). It was while there that he began to write seriously, though his first novel, *The Poor Man and the Lady*, was not begun until his return to Dorchester and Bockhampton in the late summer of 1867. He continued to work on it during 1868, his increased status as an architect allowing him to work less regularly at Hicks' office in the town, and it was while he was on a short visit to London that winter (to discuss the manuscript with George Meredith, for Chapman & Hall) that he heard of the death of Hicks, and the purchase of his business by G. R. Crickmay of Weymouth. Hardy worked on much the same basis with Crickmay, dividing his time between writing at Bockhampton and architectural work at Weymouth, until the long commission at St. Juliot's in Cornwall, where he met his future bride. For the next thirteen years, even after their marriage, he lived in lodgings in Dorset and in London, until in 1883 the couple returned to Dorchester, where their first (and only) permanent home, Max Gate, was built. *The Mayor of Casterbridge* was the first novel to be published after this move. After the early 1900s, Hardy rarely ventured out of his rural retreat, other than on bicycle (later car) trips around Dorset itself.

There can be no doubt, then, that Hardy knew Dorchester extremely well. He knew it as a child at school, as an articled pupil, as a scholar, an architect, a writer and a resident. He also knew it as a villager from outside its ancient walls. Few men can have known it as well as he.

But if we are to discover some policy of deliberate distortion in Hardy's literary portrayal of the town, it is useless merely to establish that he knew Dorchester so intimately, unless we can also confirm that *The Mayor of Casterbridge* is set at some period within his lifetime: in other words, that he knew the reality of the Dorchester on which he drew, and was not altering it merely to create a sense of historical distance.

The period in which Hardy set the novel is quite closely defined in the Preface:

The incidents narrated arise mainly out of three events, which chanced to range themselves in the order and at or about the intervals of time here given, in the real history of the town called Casterbridge and the neighbouring country. They were the sale of a wife by her husband, the uncertain harvests which immediately preceded the repeal of the Corn Laws, and the visit of a Royal personage to the aforesaid part of England.

The 'uncertain harvests' occurred in 1848 (the year of Repeal); and the 'Royal personage' (Prince Albert) passed through Dorchester in 1849, on his way to inaugurate the new Portland breakwater (it was at this period that Portland became the most formidable naval harbour in England). We can therefore assume that the main body of action in the novel takes place during the later 1840s, ending probably just after the half-century – the very time when the young Hardy would first have come to know intimately the borough of Dorchester as he traversed its streets and alleys on his daily walk to and from school.

But what was Dorchester like in the late 1840s, to a young boy seeing it for the first time from Stinsford Hill, the same vantage point as the weary Susan and Elizabeth-Jane?

For Elizabeth-Jane it was 'an old-fashioned place . . . huddled all together; and . . . shut in by a square wall of trees, like a plot of garden ground by a box-edging.'[4] With this assessment Hardy, as author, agrees:

> Its squareness was, indeed, the characteristic which most struck the eye in this antiquated borough, the borough of Caster-bridge . . . It was compact as a box of dominoes. It had no suburbs – in the ordinary sense. Country and town met at a mathematical line. . . .
>
> To the level eye of humanity it stood as an indistinct mass behind a dense stockade of limes and chestnuts, set in the midst of miles of rotund down and concave field. . . .
>
> From the centre of each side of this tree-bound square ran avenues east, west, and south into the wide expanse of corn-land and coomb to the distance of a mile or so.[5]

It is this delightful picture that has also captured the imagination of generations of Dorchester residents and chroniclers.[6]

Yet the reality of the borough in the 1840's was very different.

There is no vantage point from which the whole town, and all its avenues, can be overlooked, since it spreads over the curving scarp of a hill cut into shallow cliffs by the River Frome, which runs close beneath the town walls (on the north at least). From the north-east, the direction from which Susan and Elizabeth-Jane, approaching from Weydon Priors, would have reached it, it gives, as it did more than a century ago, on its dominating height, an impression of spreading across much of the skyline. The chestnut walks of the Roman walls,[7] extending across the western and southern sides of the town, are seen as green patches of foliage beyond the low line of houses which skirts the river at the foot of the hill on which the town is built, while the trees on the northern wall extend perhaps a hundred yards eastwards, before the 'walk' ends at the natural defence of the river scarp. The river itself curves sharply round the base of the town, altering its direction of flow from east to south, before meandering into the open meadows running away eastward. From the point where the London road crosses the river to enter the town, cottages straggle away south-east, to merge into farm buildings on the slope of the hill south of the river. This part of the town is dominated by the square tower of St. George's Church, Fordington, and the short stretch of chestnut 'walk' marking the eastern wall is lost behind the houses of Fordington High Street.

When Elizabeth-Jane saw Casterbridge in the sunset 'The mass became gradually dissected by the vision into towers, gables, chimneys, and casements, the highest glazings shining bleared and bloodshot with the coppery fire they caught from the belt of sunlit cloud in the west.'[8] It is a romantic description, foreshadowing Jude's vision of Christminster — the promised city. Yet, curiously, this is the most accurate part of the whole passage: because the romantic view of Dorchester is one that fits well with Hardy's vision of a timeless 'mediaeval' borough, independent and self-centred, beckoning to the world around it. Already, in half a page of description, Hardy has begun to translate Dorchester into a physical form more suited to his vision of Casterbridge.

In fact, as Hardy well knew, Dorchester had always had a 'suburb', not perhaps 'in the modern sense', but certainly in the Roman.[9] The original town of Durnovaria, built to house the displaced population of Mai-dun, was constructed on the familiar square pattern, with advantage taken of the natural defences of the River Frome on the north-eastern sector of the site. The early earth ramparts were soon supplemented by a ditch and stockade, and later by a wall, within

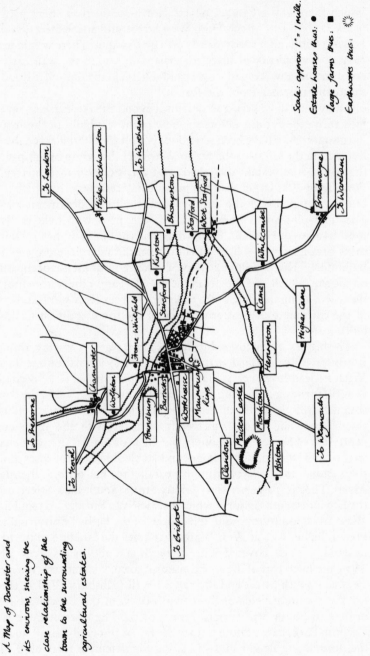

A Map of Dorchester and its environs, shewing the close relationship of the town to the surrounding agricultural estates.

Scale: approx. 1" = 1 mile.

Estate house thus: ●

Large farms thus: ■

Earthworks thus: ☼

To London

Higher Bockhampton

To Wareham

Bhcompton

Stafford

West Stafford

Broadmayne

To Wareham

Kingston

Whitcombe

Frome Whitfield

Stinsford

Came

Charminster

Higher Came

Wolfeton

Herrington

To Sherborne

Fordington

Barracks

Dorchester

Maumbury Rings

Monkton

To Weymouth

To Yeovil

Clandon

Maiden Castle

Ashton

To Bridport

which there was a basic east-west, north-south main street pattern
(today's High East Street /High West Street, and South Street /North
Square), with other roads mainly on a grid system. There would seem
to have been plenty of space for expansion within the walls, as was
common in new Roman towns, and several luxurious villas stood in
the corners farther from the forum.[10]

There may have been a settlement beyond the Roman site, on the
hills above the Frome, before the new town was built, or the area of
Fordington may have been settled by poorer local families, unable to
live within the safety of the walls. Whatever the origin of this part of
the town, it is certain that there was a large Roman cemetery at
Fordington, (far larger than the present-day cemetery, in which new
burials 'mingled with the dust of women who lay ornamented with
glass hair-pins and amber necklaces, and men who held in their
mouths coins of Hadrian, Posthumus, and the Constantines')[11] with,
in its later history, a Christian church on the site of the present-day
building.[12] There is also extensive evidence of domestic occupation
on the site, which stretches from the double-gate at the eastern foot of
the town, along the edge of the river, and curves away south and west
of the extreme south-eastern corner of the town walls (at Gallows
Hill).

The history of the town during the 'Dark Ages' is obscure, though
it was certainly occupied virtually continuously up to the present day.
What is clear, however, is that Fordington continued to be occupied
as well, forming a thriving agricultural community, while the town
shrank within its walls, to attain a shape characteristic of it well into
the second half of the nineteenth century, with the main concentration of houses strung out in the shape of a cross, along the main
streets, and with minor cottages and stable huddled together along
the various 'back streets', running parallel to, but behind, the main
streets. The open area between Trinity Street (South Back Street, until
the late nineteenth century, when it was driven through to join High
West Street almost opposite the church of the Holy Trinity) and the
line of the old wall at West Walks was, until the building of the new
hospital in 1836, covered with orchards and allotments; even after
1836, the main part of the area continued open, well into this century.
Between South Street and the eastern wall (Salisbury Walks), there
lay the common fields of the townsfolk, with the Bowling Green
nearest to South Street itself. North of the High Street there was
Colliton Park, bare of houses since the fall of Imperial Rome, and on
the dominating height midway along the defensive river bluff, the

site of the short-lived castle, empty until the construction of the prison in 1792. Below it, and to the east along the foot of the bluff, lay the remains of the priory, where only the old mill house stood intact, by the diverted mill stream which ran through this small plot of level ground.

There are other differences, too: the Marabout Barracks, built in 1795 and housing a large garrison; the Union Workhouse, built in 1836 (the same year that the County Hospital was begun); the L & SWR station of 1847; and that most Victorian of buildings, the gasworks (1833). The Barracks spread conspicuously across the land between the western wall and Poundbury, and the Workhouse (now a hospital) lies directly in the path of Farfrae and Lucetta as they go to join the harvest-helpers on the open land west of the town. The station was built between the South Walks and 'the Ring', while the gasworks marred the eastern wall of the town.

In short, Dorchester, even in the 1840s, was far from being a mathematical square where 'within the wall were packed the abodes of the burghers'. Nor was it 'at that time, recent as it was, untouched by the faintest sprinkle of modernism'.[13] Without any detailed consideration of the matter, we have seen the prominence and abundance of continuing modern works in this 'antiquated borough' (a point which will be discussed more fully). This does not, however, prevent Hardy using features of the real town to create his fictitious Casterbridge: the long gardens of all the major houses might, if any thought were given to the matter, seem strange in a town where the dwellings are 'packed' together. In the context of Dorchester's open spaces, of course, they are quite natural. The 'Durnover end of Casterbridge', on the other hand, is less uneasy in the general description of the town, though its high incidence of barns and ricks and dairies is more easily understandable as a village without the walls, where no shops other than those of agricultural dealers exist, because agriculture dictates a thriving high street, yet the inhabitants can walk into town for daily supplies.

3.

But all these changes made by Hardy affect only the general appearance of the town. What of the character he portrayed in his detailed descriptions? Here again, he is careful to omit any details that might prejudice his very particular conception of 'Casterbridge', while utilising others to their full. He paints with loving care the 'Three Mariners' inn (a real building of the period):

> This ancient house of accommodation for man and beast, now, unfortunately, pulled down, was built of mellow sandstone, with mullioned windows of the same material, markedly out of perpendicular from the settlement of foundations. The bay window projecting into the street, whose interior was so popular among the frequenters of the inn, was closed with shutters, in each of which appeared a heart-shaped aperture, somewhat more attenuated in the right and left ventricles than is seen in Nature. . . .
>
> A four-centred Tudor arch was over the entrance, and over the arch the signboard, now visible in the rays of an opposite lamp. Hereon the Mariners, who had been represented by the artist as persons of two dimensions only – in other words, flat as a shadow – were standing in a row in paralyzed attitudes. Being on the sunny side of the street the three comrades had suffered largely from warping, splitting, fading, and shrinkage, so that they were but a half-invisible film upon the reality of the grain, and knots, and nails, which composed the signboard.[14]

It is a sensuous description, lingering over details so long that the words conjure to our imagination impressions both tactile and visual, as though we stood with one hand upon the door-jamb, gazing in fascination at the ill-lit features of the inn. The age of the building and its sign weigh upon us more forcibly than any sense of their individuality; each feature seems to represent in itself all the undescribed details of this and other ancient buildings in the town, and to call so clearly for our attention that in the end we are unaware that, with all the rich imagery devoted to its appearance, we still have not discovered the shape and size of the Three Mariners, or with any accuracy located doors or windows, or even established whether it stands back from the street, and whether it joins its neighbours – and especially, whether those neighbours actually resemble it, or will be assumed to do so by default of any other mention. Compare this description with the treatment given the 'King's Arms' (again a real building) a few pages before:

> A spacious bow-window projected into the street over the main portico, and from the open sashes came the babble of voices, the jingle of glasses, and the drawing of corks. The blinds, moreover,

being left unclosed, the whole interior of this room could be surveyed from the top of a flight of stone steps to the road-waggon office opposite.[15]

It could be surveyed, but it is not. Here, it is the characters alone who interest Hardy, and not the physical appearance of the building. The bow-window having acted as a magnet and focus for our attention, we are immediately drawn to the room within (also undescribed), to enter the dinner conversation of the merchant princes of the town. The hotel, its purpose served, is cast aside without a second thought.

There is a similar contrast of treatment between the two houses which figure most largely in the novel; on the one hand, Henchard's (later Farfrae's) house is 'one of the best, faced with dull red-and-grey old brick'[16] while Lucetta's (a portrait of Colliton House, shifted from its true position at the north-west corner of the town, to a dramatically more effective site near the centre – the only instance in the novel where this is clearly done) is described in those same terms that arrested our attention at the Three Mariners – conveying impressions and details, without ever descending to mere architectural enumeration:

> The Hall, with its grey facade and parapet, was the only residence of its sort so near the centre of the town. It had, in the first place, the characteristics of a country mansion – birds' nests in its chimneys, damp nooks where fungi grew, and irregularities of surface direct from Nature's trowel. At night the forms of passengers were patterned by the lamps in black shadows upon the pale walls. . . . The house was entirely of stone, and formed an example of dignity without great size. . . . It was Palladian, and like most architecture erected since the Gothic age was a compilation rather than a design. But its reasonableness made it impressive.[17]

Churches, too, are not free from this process of selection. As with the inns, divided into high, middle and low (The King's Arms, the Three Mariners, Peter's Finger), the churches cater for differing social strata. But it is in the neutral social stance of our first impression that we meet St. Peter's,

> . . . a grizzled church, whose massive square tower rose unbroken into the darkening sky, the lower parts being illuminated by the

nearest lamps sufficiently to show how completely the mortar from the joints of the stonework had been nibbled out by time and weather, which had planted in the crevices thus made little tufts of stone-crop and grass almost as far up as the very battlements.[18]

Each type of building has one representative described, that description being then allowed to dominate any passing reference to others of a similar kind. (This process was first used in *Far from the Madding Crowd*, as will be seen in the discussion of that novel). More particularly, however, the representatives chosen reflect one characteristic of the town: age. The Georgian facades are barely mentioned, while the 'country mansion', tudor inn and grizzled church are described in warm detail, excluding even their outlines in the concentration on an overwhelming impression of age. It is the same method as is used in the general description of the town, playing down or ignoring certain elements, emphasising others; it becomes easy to assume that the whole town resembles these venerable buildings, as it is easy to assume that Durnover lies within the town walls, for want of direct evidence to the contrary.

In fact the town, in the 1840s, was a rich amalgam of styles and periods, ranging from sixteenth-century buildings to brand new houses and shops, in 'traditional' and Victorian designs. Despite its relatively small size, Dorchester had not remained static in architectural terms, and there was a good deal of money ready to erect imposing modern facades in place of such 'dilapidated' buildings as the Three Mariners. Besides the Hospital and the gasworks there were the new All Saints Parish Church (1843–5), almost opposite the King's Arms hotel (facade c. 1800), the new Corn Exchange (1847–8), replacing the building of 1792, spanning the entrance to North Square, which Hardy describes in the novel, and the 1815 facade on the Antelope Hotel (facing Cornhill, part of the old market place). The Almshouse clock that chimes in with the others at 8 p.m. on the day of Susan and Elizabeth-Jane's arrival was placed above the new facade of Napper's Mite when it was rebuilt in 1842, and imposing town houses of the 1840s gaze across High West Street.

But these are only the notable buildings most recently altered or built when Hardy's characters were acting out their tragedy. The classical facade of Shire Hall (where the Tolpuddle Martyrs had so recently met their fate) dominates High West Street, and seventeenth and eighteenth century houses jostle side-by-side above shop-fronts ranging from mere tudor windows, through elegant Georgian

A Map of Dorchester and Fordington, shewing the continuing architectural development of the borough.

Scale: approx. 6" = 1 mile.

L.S.S.W.R

1 Barracks 1795
2 Workhouse 1836
3 Station 1847
4 Colliton House 17th c.
5 Prison 1790-2
6 All Saints Church 1843-5
7 Wollaston House 1786
8 Napper's Mite 1616
9 Gasworks 1833
10 Hospital 1839
11 Shire Hall 1795-7
12 South Lodge 1760
13 Fordington House 18th c.
14 Corn Exchange 1847-8
15 17th c. buildings
16 18th c. buildings
17 19th c. buildings

ranges, to ornate emporia. Those apartments above the china shop which were the only suitable ones in town for the new arrivals were probably the legacy of the experimental Wessex Theatre, which housed Edmund Kean for a few brief years in the 1830s before it failed.

The mere physical appearance of the town is not, however, all that Hardy so very carefully alters. He portrays Casterbridge as a place almost as unchanging in its manners and society as it is in its physical presence. 'Casterbridge announced old Rome in every street, alley, and precinct. It looked Roman, bespoke the art of Rome, concealed dead men of Rome.'[19] Yet this past is detached from everyday life in a way that suggests Casterbridge to be an entity in time almost as much as in space, ancient, yet without any conscious sense of its own history. 'They had lived so long ago, their time was so unlike the present, their hopes and motives were so widely removed from ours, that between them and the living there seemed to stretch a gulf too wide for even a spirit to pass.'[20]

Actual history becomes garbled into the folk-tales of the Bloody Assize ('in Roman times') and the burning of Mary Channing, where 'not one of those ten thousand people ever cared particularly for hot roast after that',[21] while Farfrae's position as 'two-hundredth odd' of the elected mayors serves to emphasise permanence rather than the passage of time. As with the physical appearance of the town, all suggestion of continuing change has been eliminated. Even contemporary historical events are couched in terms that rob them of any significance except as triggers for 'traditional' celebrations. ' . . . a day of public rejoicing was suggested to the country at large in celebration of a national event that had recently taken place.'[22] And 'A Royal Personage was about to pass through the borough on his course further west, to inaugurate an immense engineering work out that way.'[23]

Dorchester at this period, however, was far from being a timeless focus for the Dorset countryside. Though the town's Roman past would have been as commonplace as Hardy portrays it, and the more recent past as garbled,[24] there were changes so new and so relevant that no man in a position such as Henchard's could have overlooked them. In 1835, Parliament had amended the ancient boundaries of the borough, and the long-disputed tything of Colliton Row, within the town walls but once a part of the Manor of Fordington, had been included within the new borough, as had Fordington itself. An ancient history of dispute between Dorchester and the manor which surrounded it had thus been settled, and the de facto situation of Fordington as a dormitory suburb for the richer town became legal truth. In addition, with the new franchise of the 1832 Reform Act, the old stranglehold of the Earl of Shaftesbury over the returning of Members of Parliament had been broken. The Court of Record was abolished by the 1835 Act, but the Quarter Sessions and Court Leet continued for some time. The posts of Bailiff and Capital Burgess were also abolished, and the town council reconstituted of the Mayor, four Aldermen, and twelve councillors.

All of this is most unobstrusively absent from Hardy's view of the ancient Borough of Casterbridge, as are the modern shops and houses, and all other features of change. We are left to assume (again, for want of evidence to the contrary) that, because the Mayor is the two-hundredth odd in line, the other features of the borough have also not changed.

And what of other aspects of town life, less obvious than buildings and less memorable than Borough reforms, but none the less important to everyday life? The 'two old constables' who escape their duty by thrusting their staffs up a convenient drainpipe are more reminiscent of the parish constables who enforced the bye-laws before 1835 (two from the Mayor's parish, one each from the other two parishes) than of the Dorchester Watch Committee of 1836, which appointed four watchmen (later constables) to patrol at night, and two by day. This was later changed to five at night, and one by day (the figure relevant during the 1840s). The fire precautions of the town were also brought up to date, this time by local agreement, with a general Committee of Management being appointed (1842) to supervise the parish engines. A new engine was bought in 1849.[25] There was a Post Office in the town from 1699 (or possibly even earlier), with local deliveries by messenger; the free delivery area was extended in 1836. In addition, there were coach services worthy of a town situated at the junction of turnpike roads between London and Exeter, Sherborne and Weymouth, and Wareham and Dorchester, with the Channel Islands traffic and local business as well. The Royal Mail ran daily between Dorchester and London (taking $13\frac{1}{2}$ hours), with its office at the King's Arms (this Hardy does mention, though only in Newsom's brief passing); also operating a daily service from that hotel was the Magnet, with the Herald working from the Antelope. The Royal Dorset coach ran between Dorchester (King's Arms) and Bristol, on alternate weekdays, and the Duke of Wellington provided a similar service to Bath (as did the John Bull, from the Antelope). The Emerald coach ran every weekday from the King's Arms to Southampton, and the Portsmouth coach on Tuesdays, Thursdays and Saturdays. The Independent ran from Portsmouth to Exeter, via the Antelope, every day, and the Royal George operated a Weymouth-Dorchester service daily, to connect with the London services at both hotels. All of these coaches faced decline and rapid extinction when, in 1847, the new L & SWR line to Dorchester was opened (to be joined by the GWR line between Weymouth and Yeovil, in 1857), no doubt with all due ceremony.

Yet of all this activity Hardy makes virtually no mention: the coaches might as well be a single weekly service for all the attention they receive (compare their brief appearances with the detailed and frequent description of local markets) and the railway, once its absence is explained, is abandoned, at the very time when its arrival would have been provoking the maximum of excitement and interest. Obviously, Hardy is making sure that Casterbridge seems more independent and 'old-fashioned' than such busy connections with the outside world would suggest. By omitting yet more details he is once again manipulating our vision of his town to his own ends.

But just as, in the case of the buildings, he emphasised the elements of pre-Georgian architecture, and magnified the importance of the walls, so now, with the daily life of the town, Hardy picks out a very few elements and portrays those in great detail. Before the action of the novel is allowed to proceed, with the arrival of Susan and Elizabeth-Jane, market-day is described with a precision that, to modern minds, must recall the directions for a television 'set':

> First the vans of the carriers in and out of Casterbridge, who hailed from Mellstock, Weatherbury, The Hintocks, Sherton – Abbas, Kingsbere, Overcombe, and many other towns and villages round. Their owners were numerous enough to be regarded as a tribe, and had almost distinctiveness enough to be regarded as a race. Their vans had just arrived, and were drawn up on each side of the street in close file, so as to form at places a wall between the pavement and the roadway. Moreover every shop pitched out half its contents upon trestles and boxes on the kerb, extending the display each week a little further and further into the roadway, despite the expostulations of the two feeble old constables, until there remained but a tortuous defile for carriages down the centre of the street, which afforded fine opportunities for skill with the reins. Over the pavement on the sunny side of the way

hung shop-blinds so constructed as to give the passenger's hat a smart buffet off his head, as from the unseen hands of Cranstoun's Goblin Page, celebrated in romantic lore.

Horses for sale were tied in rows, their forelegs on the pavement, their hind legs in the street, in which position they occasionally nipped little boys by the shoulder who were passing to school. And any inviting recess in front of a house that had been modestly kept back from the general line was utilised by pig-dealers as a pen for their stock.[26]

It is as vivid as if we had been a companion of the young Hardy, as he was nipped by the shoulder on his way to school of a market morning. The child's impression of detached involvement − of being a part of this way of life, while yet not directly concerned − is intense, and a reminder of that curious many-stranded thread of understanding which characterises Hardy's portrayal of his native 'Wessex'. However, the passage is not wantonly expanded: it is exactly this kind of wondering semi-involvement that must have been the reaction of newcomers such as Susan and Elizabeth-Jane, and of ourselves as we follow them into what is, for us, a new world. This one passage occupies, in its entirety, nearly three pages, and Hardy returns to the subject at pp. 179−180, pp. 187−188, p. 196, p. 325, and at several other places in the novel. The market is given an importance equalled only by Hardy's repeated emphases on the appearance of the town as a square set into its rural background. The rural entity is given a commercial existence, its emphasis evolving from that first long, lingering gaze, as the first description of the Three Mariners led us on to the sense of age in the buildings of the town.

The importance attached to the market in *The Mayor of Caster-bridge* is, however, scarcely an exaggeration. Defoe, on his visit to Dorchester more than a century before, wrote 'The downs round this town are exceeding pleasant, and come up on every side, even to the very street's end; and here it was that they told me, that there were 600 thousand sheep fed on the downs, within six miles of the town.'[27] In addition to the local trade created by the vast flocks of sheep still pastured in the 1840s to north and south of the town, there was a thriving corn trade, and as the county town and natural focus for agriculture for the whole of Dorset, Dorchester's bi-weekly markets and frequent fairs attracted enormous business. At this period the markets were still held in the town itself and, there being no market place proper, spilled over into the side streets, dividing into specialised sections in each alley or lane. Little of the town was unaffected, so great were the numbers of traders and livestock, and until the revival of road haulage in the present century, sheep and cattle continued to be driven down even from Wiltshire and Somerset.

In *The Mayor of Casterbridge*, then, Hardy manipulates the reality of Dorchester, emphasising some aspects and playing down others, in order to create a very particular imaginative view of Casterbridge. All of this, including his one serious distortion of fact, the picturing of the town as a square set in the rolling downland fields, tends towards a view of Casterbridge as a place independent of life beyond the bounds of South Wessex, almost independent of time itself; 'Thus Casterbridge was in most respects but the pole, focus, or nerve-knot of the surrounding country life.'[28]

The ancient borough becomes an entity beyond all question of distance and change. Returning to the evidence in more detail, we can recall that first, most startling assertion: that Dorchester stood, and always had stood, proudly alone on its open hills, with no company but that of the fields outside its walls. Fordington, the Workhouse, the Barracks, all are ignored, though the first has an important role to play in the novel, and the last two figured in *Far from the Madding Crowd*, published twelve years earlier. There is no secret as to why Hardy is doing this: he states, again and again, that Casterbridge is a body complementing its rural situation, not imposing upon it. The question to be asked is, what is he achieving by portraying the town thus? The answer is readily provided, by the Royal Commission upon whose advice, in the Municipal Corporations Act of 1835, the village of Fordington was finally gathered within the borough of Dorchester:

The town of Dorchester is in a thriving and flourishing condition. The buildings have improved very much in late years and it is perhaps fortunate that they have not extended beyond the old limits of the town,[29] as we find in other places. There has been therefore less speculation; but the trade of the place is steady, and no appearance of decline or decay is anywhere visible. It is true, that from the narrow confines of the town, and the want of small houses within its bounds, the greater part of the population which would naturally belong to the town of Dorchester are settled in the adjoining village of Fordington. The poverty of Fordington ought, therefore, to be taken into account when estimating the real prosperity of Dorchester, and the two should in reason be considered as a single town. A considerable number of the inhabitants of Fordington are parishioners of Dorchester, and many of the others inhabiting the village gain a livelihood by working in the town. This connexion between the borough and its suburb seems to make it reasonable and indeed desirable that they should be united for all purposes.

Hardy, in Casterbridge, is portraying the relationship of Dorchester and Fordington as it was, in every sense but the narrowly physical; he joins the two into a definable entity which has elements of both, within those visible confines which had never been the limit of Dorchester, but which grip the imagination more strongly than any line on a map is able to do. No matter that, since the seventeenth century, the walls had been under piecemeal attack, until only fragments of them remained by the 1840s: they were as clearly defined imaginatively (and, for most of their length, by the tree-lined walks which had replaced them) as ever, providing the perfect boundaries for Casterbridge. (As a less definable bonus, the idea of a walled town, set into miles of rolling country, the complement of its rural surroundings, is strongly suggestive of the mediaeval heart which, by descriptive emphasis, Hardy portrays in his town). Within these walls, the scattered houses of Dorchester are padded out, to become the mass 'gradually dissected by the vision into towers, gables, chimneys and casements'[30] which packs out the acres within. It is as necessary to the imagination to have the whole space of the town occupied by streets as it is to bring Fordington within the walls; only in this way can the entity of Dorchester and Fordington be effectively portrayed for those who have no conception of its spirit. Only in this way can Hardy effectively create a picture of a town complementary to its rural environment, and bridge the gap between those who know such a town, and those to whom a town with urban sprawl, however ancient, is either a parasite upon the land, or the fulfilment of heaven upon earth (in each case, a place divorced from its immediate surroundings). Hardy knew London and its middle-class society well from the age of 22 onwards; he knew the concept of 'town' as 'London', and 'country' as a place to which such people could retire for a brief rest from labours of civilisation and Empire. The two were different worlds, and he must also have known, by 1884, that his novels were valued by most people for their portrayal of that 'other world'. Casterbridge was the only town he ever showed in any depth, and he took good care that the relationship of Dorchester and

Fordington with their surroundings should be firmly established in the reader's mind.

However, he has also altered the reality of the visual 'character' of the town, and with this he achieves something which operates much more subtly than the hammer-blows of concrete description. He freezes the town, robbing it of a changing past and present, suggesting no future, but only a timeless 'is'. The houses are old, but there is no chance given for the imagination to play with concepts of 'periods' in style. In every case, architectural definitions are minor, carefully robbed of all but a visual effect, and secondary to the atmospheric descriptions which take precedence:

> The front doors of the private houses were mostly left open at this warm autumn time, no thought of umbrella stealers disturbing the minds of the placid burgesses. Hence, through the long, straight, entrance passages thus unclosed could be seen, as through tunnels, the mossy gardens at the back, glowing with nasturtiums, fuchsias, scarlet geraniums, 'bloody warriors', snap-dragons, and dahlias, this floral blaze being backed by crusted grey stone-work remaining from a yet remoter Casterbridge than the venerable one visible in the street. The old-fashioned fronts of these houses, which had older than old-fashioned backs, rose sheer from the pavement, into which the bow-windows protruded like bastions, necessitating a pleasing chassez-dechassez movement to the time-pressed pedestrian at every few yards. He was bound also to evolve other Terpsichorean figures in respect of door-steps, scrapers, cellar-hatches, church buttresses, and the overhanging angles of walls which, originally unobstrusive, had become bow-legged and knock-kneed. [31]

There is the same wealth of detail, but lack of definition, that so enriches the descriptions of the Three Mariners, St. Peter's Church, High Place Hall, and the market itself. There is a sense of 'old' about the whole town, but we are too delighted with the material offered to stop and ask ourselves what this means. Try to define the buildings within the town as clearly as the town itself, and you discover that Hardy has given you nothing precise to work with, only a 'feeling'. He has no intention of destroying that physical unity he was at such pains to create, only of illuminating its character yet more clearly.

It is as part of this process that the history of the town becomes channelled into the separate Roman past, and the 'folk-tales' of outstanding local events. It is exactly the same process of characterising by ignoring major features that governs the refusal of admittance to important historical facts: Dorchester, as a part of English history, becomes the independent Casterbridge, in which events outside the town have no existence, those inside no meaning in historical terms. The borough reforms have never occurred, there is no parliament to which Shaftesbury's friends can be elected: there is no Shaftesbury. The bustling present of Dorchester, with its technological advances and busy coming and going of, first coaches, then trains, vanishes. Such things become as incidental as architectural styles, and are made to seem as timeless as the town itself. By underplaying the coaches, Hardy makes them a minor part of timeless town life; by omitting to mention the arrival of the railway, he even gives that most modern of events an insignificance that can be born only of long familiarity. Once more, he alters our perception by the careful balance of detail.

4.

All the alterations so far discussed have been designed, by one means or another, to present Casterbridge to us as an entity which has life in a world where time has no meaning, and roads arrive, but never seem to depart. With the next stage in the creation of a distinctive character for his town, Hardy turns to the focus of town and country life, the market. The atmosphere of age melts imperceptibly into the vivid impressions of stalls, traders, livestock and, above all, movement, which introduce us to the market. And that in its turn flows without break into a fascinated observation of the people who are the lifeblood in this pulsating heart, set in the green body of Wessex:

> The yeomen, farmers, dairymen, and townsfolk, who came to transact business in these ancient streets, spoke in other ways than by articulation. Not to hear the words of your interlocutor in metropolitan centres is to know nothing of his meaning. Here the face, the arms, the hat, the stick, the body throughout spoke equally with the tongue. To express satisfaction the Casterbridge market-man added to his utterance a broadening of the cheeks, a crevicing of the eyes, a throwing back of the shoulders, which was intelligible from the other end of the street. If he wondered, though all Henchard's carts and waggons were rattling past him, you knew

it from perceiving the inside of his crimson mouth, and a target-like circling of his eyes. Deliberation caused sundry attacks on the moss of adjoining walls with the end of his stick, a change of his hat from the horizontal to the less so; a sense of tediousness announced itself in a lowering of the person by spreading the knees to a lozenge-shaped aperture and contorting the arms.[32]

The description is couched in the same detailed yet imprecise fashion that marked the description of the buildings; and the figures selected – 'yeomen, farmers, dairymen, and townsfolk' – are as carefully chosen. There are no gentry, no passing travellers (en route to Exeter or the Channel Islands), no tourists or outsiders, no uninvolved characters of any kind or standing. Only the people who actively contribute to the economic and social life of the town have a place here – this is the raw material of the personality of Casterbridge.

A picture of Dorchester in its everyday social and economic context in the 1840s can be obtained from the introductory remarks to *Pigot's Commercial Directory of Doresetshire* for 1842, in the section devoted to Dorchester:

> The spinning of worsted yarn, and the manufacture of woollen goods, formerly ranked as the staple here; but these branches have greatly declined, if they are not entirely lost – a little blanketting and linsey being the only articles now manufactured. Dorchester ale has long been famed, and it still maintains a superior character; the mutton of this district is likewise held in great and general estimation.

It is a factual guide-book style easily recognisable today, and presents a picture startlingly broad and simple when compared with the close involvement of Hardy's description. There is an impersonality about it which makes us realise that simple description does not necessarily convey the true character of a place.

But continuing for a moment with the purely factual, the Directory entries reveal that the character of the three main streets – High East Street, High West Street, and South Street – has changed little in the past 130 years; the first contained, even then, the lesser elements of trade, with few 'gentry' or notable tradespeople, the second held many of the gentry and the professions, the last was the major trading street. Hardy makes no such divisions. For him, once again, it is important that the town should have a central, unified character. The description of High East Street on the market-day walk from the Three Mariners to Henchard's house is in fact an amalgam of all three streets (the bulk of the market ran through Cornhill, the part of South Street nearest the centre, into North Square; the sheep market, until shortly before the date of the novel, used to run up Pease Lane), though only those elements Hardy considers relevant are included:

> The agricultural and pastoral character of the people upon whom the town depended for its existence was shown by the class of objects displayed in the shop windows. Scythes, reap-hooks, sheep-shears, bill-hooks, spades, mattocks, and hoes at the ironmonger's; bee-hives, butter-firkins, churns, milking stools and pails, hay-rakes, field-flagons, and seed-lips at the cooper's; cart-ropes and plough-harness at the saddler's; carts, wheel-barrows, and mill-gear at the wheelwright's and machinist's; horse-embrocations at the chemist's; at the glover's and leather-cutter's, hedging gloves, thatchers' knee-caps, ploughmen's leggings, villagers' pattens and clogs.[33]

All of this is doubtless quite accurate; but it is only a part of the truth. To take High East Steet, for example (since it is, ostensibly at least, the one described in greatest detail); in 1842 there were indeed a number of boot and shoemakers – Charles Crocker, James Fox & Son, Robert Nutt, William Stoodley – and there was the carpentry, building and stonemasonry firm of George and William Slade. There were the ironmonger's shops of John Galpin, Thomas Wood and Hooper Tolbort (the last also came under the heading of 'Painters, plumbers and glaziers', and was agent for the Eagle Fire Insurance Company in Dorchester; quite a number of the town's tradesmen seem to have turned their hands to various occupations), and the saddler's shop of George Greening. But what of the shops needed for day-to-day town life? Thomas Style, the chemist whose horse embrocation was so prominently featured, was also a grocer and tea-dealer. There were no fewer than four other similar grocer's shops in High East Street, one of which, John Ensor's, also made cement. There were two baker's and confectioner's shops, two butcher's, a draper's and a milliner's, two perfumier's and hairdresser's, two dealers in groceries and sundries, a fruiterer/seedshop/grocer's, a nursery shop, a tailor's, a toyshop and two clock and watch makers (whose only mention in Hardy's novel is in the description of chiming clocks at curfew; this use of sound without reference to a corresponding visual reality is an aspect of the 'atmosphere-building' already mentioned). There were also those taverns which brewed the famous Dorchester ale, reduced for the purposes of the novel to three; the King's Arms, the Three Mariners, and Peter's Finger. The Antelope is mentioned in passing, as a posting inn, but is carefully avoided otherwise. Yet besides the King's Arms and the Three Mariners, in High East Street, there were also the Chequers, the Mailcoach, and the White Hart, William Symes' beershop, and four brewers and maltsters, one of which, George Galpin's, was also a cooper's, and another, William Hodges and Son, a wine and spirit merchant (and West of England Fire agent). There was a cabinet-maker and a gun and fishing rod maker, two surgeons, Richard Poynter's school, William Hawkins the auctioneer's, and two attorney's offices, one the registrar of births, deaths and marriages, the other the superintendent registrar.

It all shows a much broader picture than that in *The Mayor of Casterbridge*, and when the still more varied businesses and professions of the other streets are added, it makes Hardy's cursory description of the shops seem far from the reality. Yet, in the same way as the physical character of the town, Hardy has isolated the agricultural heart of the town's trade, and in one brief paragraph he sets out its essential features far more effectively than accurate description could do, and by including this passage in a generally descriptive one he merges buildings and trade as carefully as, in the description of the market, he merges buildings and people. Necessary as a perfumer's and hairdresser's may have been to town life in 1842, the effects of its intrusion upon Hardy's idyllic town-world would hardly have been in keeping with his picture of a rugged rural centre.

In this context of selection and emphasis, it has been noticeable that Hardy has selected not only for certain characteristics of the town, but also for the professions and statuses of those within its walls. Most obvious by their absence are the gentry, both those of the elegant town houses in High West Street and South Street, and those of the large houses around Dorchester and Fordington (Wolfeton, Frome Whitfield, Kingston Maurward, Stafford, Came, Herringston, and Monkton, to mention only the nearest). Hardy makes brief acknowledgement of the special relationship between the town and the big estates around it:

They entered into the troubles and joys which moved the

aristocratic families ten miles round . . . And even at the dinner-parties of the professional families the subjects of discussion were corn, cattle-disease, sowing and reaping, fencing and planting; while politics were viewed by them less from their own standpoint of burgesses with rights and privileges than from the standpoint of their county neighbours.[34]

There are clear echoes of that first dinner-party at Middlemarch. Yet here there will be no discussion of Reform Acts or Corn Laws or agricultural improvements; there is to be no further mention of those agricultural estates and their aristocratic owners (or crown tenants – much of the land around Dorchester was – and still is – the property of the Duchy of Cornwall); the professional families are to reappear as mere names in the background of the town council, during the period of Farfrae's rise to the mayoralty, and their politics are of outstanding irrelevance, as are any politics in the novel. There is no sign of aristocratic privilege and influence, and no intrigues behind the throne of power. Only the embittered Jopp comes anywhere near a real sense of dishonesty.

In short, there are to be no characters or incidents which might detract from the image of Casterbridge as 'the pole, focus, or nerve-knot of the surrounding country life'. The town must stand unchallenged as the most powerful element in the novel.

In all levels of society, Hardy selects a 'representative' group, as he selected certain buildings; indeed, the three inns chosen represent his choice of social levels in concrete form, as he makes clear:

> The inn called Peter's Finger was the church of Mixen Lane. It was centrally situate, as such places should be, and bore about the same social relation to the Three Mariners as the latter bore to the King's Arms. . . . The company at the Three Mariners were persons of quality in comparison with the company which gathered here; though it must be admitted that the lowest fringe of the Mariners' party touched the crest of Peter's at points.[35]

As was clear in Farfrae's and Henchard's visits to the latter pub, there was a similar contact between the Mariners and the King's Arms. The three groups are also given a careful 'religious' grading. The Peter's Finger frequenters have no established religion – the inn is their 'church'. For the other two social groups there are the 'high' and 'low' churches – both Church of England, but with a physical relationship in the sloping High Street which suggests a difference of creed, and a consequent social difference – which are Hardy's shorthand for the internal divisions of the established church, built up over 200 years or more, but by the 1840s hardened into social rather than religious differences. (Dorchester looked back, to eighteenth century religion, rather than forward, to the Oxford movement. A third church, higher still in both religion and status – and in the High Street – served the rich parish of Holy Trinity, where most of the town's gentry lived. Its exclusion here is another sign of Hardy's selection process.) In a few short sentences Hardy dismisses the theological attitudes of the Victorian Church, with an indifference bordering on contempt:

> On the afternoon of every Sunday a large contingent of the Casterbridge journeymen – steady church-goers and sedate characters – having attended service, filed from the church doors across the way to the Three Mariners Inn. The rear was usually brought up by the choir, with their bass-viols, fiddles, and flutes under their arms.[36]

(This church, All Saints, which Hardy does not describe, was one of the newest buildings in Dorchester at the time).

> Chancing to look out of the window at that moment he saw a flock of people passing by, and perceived them to be the congregation of the upper church, now just dismissed, their sermon having been a longer one than that the lower parish was favoured with. Among the rest of the leading inhabitants walked Mr. Councillor Farfrae with Lucetta upon his arm, the observed and imitated of all the smaller tradesmen's womankind.[37]

Religion is a social definition, as clearly as the public houses, and, for Hardy's Casterbridge, as empty of deep human involvement. The fervent discussions of paedo-baptism of his youth, and the Baptist, Independent, Unitarian and Wesleyan chapel congregations, are all relegated to the oblivion of irrelevant details in the world of human problems Hardy envisages. That empty concern of the nineteen eligible young ladies which fell upon Farfrae in his rise to power and eminence[38] is echoed in the cynical image of the 'flock' disgorged from the upper church: not the flock of Christianity, but the empty-headed flock of fashion-following women. No matter how much the other factors of town life in Casterbridge might be dictated by the expedience of creating an image, the established church is one thing on which Hardy admits no compromise, casting out its social hypocrisies with a restraint which shows his opinion of how highly they figure in the true nature of human society. Compare his treatment of the Victorian Sunday with his treatment of the real depths of the human soul in Elizabeth-Jane, sitting up with her dying mother:

> To learn to take the universe seriously there is no quicker way than to watch – to be a 'waker' as the country-people call it. Between the hours at which the last toss-pot went by and the first sparrow shook himself, the silence in Casterbridge – barring the rare sound of the watchman – was broken in Elizabeth's ear only by the timepiece in the bedroom ticking frantically against the clock on the stairs; ticking harder and harder till it seemed to clang like a gong; and all this while the subtle-souled girl asking herself why she was born, why sitting in a room, and blinking at the candle; why things around her had taken the shape they wore in preference to every other possible shape. Why they stared at her so helplessly, as if waiting for the touch of some wand that should release them from terrestrial constraint; what that chaos called consciousness, which spun in her at this moment like a top, tended to, and began in.[39]

The words beat upon us, gathering strength like the tick of the clocks, until our heads are ready to burst with the sheer awareness of existence. Concrete and abstract seem to mingle and dissolve into one overwhelming perception, and in this brief passage the startling awareness that has characterised our view of the town and its people is distilled into a feeling of the immensity of simply being alive. This, and not religion, characterises Hardy's perception of human existence. He includes only that which has a direct bearing on Casterbridge as it works in everyday life: from the slums of Mixen Lane, through the honest small dealers – Buzzford, Coney and their ilk – who congregate at the Three Mariners, to the powerful traders who seem to control the destinies of the town.

Yet it is none of these who actually directs the town, in more than the most cursory way; they are its lifeblood but, as Hardy has taken great trouble to emphasise, the town is an entity, complete in itself, independent of what lies beyond the bounds of Wessex, of what lies beyond the bounds of its own present. No one character, or group of characters, can be more than a passing element in the Casterbridge scene. The displaced liviers and criminal elements who inhabit Mixen Lane are described in a manner that makes them totally a part of the world in which they live:

> The lane and its surrounding thicket of thatched cottages stretched out like a spit into the moist and misty lowland. Much that was sad, much that was low, some things that were baneful, could be seen in Mixen Lane . . .
> Yet this mildewed leaf in the sturdy and flourishing Caster-bridge plant lay close to the open country; not a hundred yards from a row of noble elms, and commanding a view across the moor of airy uplands and corn-fields, and mansions of the great. A brook divided the moor from the tenements, and to outward view there was no way across it — no way to the houses but round about by the road. But under every householder's stairs there was kept a mysterious plank nine inches wide; which plank was a secret bridge.
> If you, as one of those refugee householders, came in from business after dark — and this was the business time here — you stealthily crossed the moor, approached the border of the aforesaid brook, and whistled opposite the house to which you belonged. A shape thereupon made its appearance on the other side bearing the bridge on end against the sky; it was lowered; you crossed, and a hand helped you to land yourself, together with the pheasants and hares gathered from neighbouring manors. . . .
> Walking along the lane at dusk the stranger was struck by two or three peculiar features therein. One was an intermittent rumbling from the back premises of the inn half-way up; this meant a skittle alley. Another was the extensive prevalence of whistling in the various domiciles — a piped note of some kind coming from nearly every open door. Another was the frequency of white aprons over dingy gowns among the women around the doorways. A white apron is a suspicious vesture in situations where spotlessness is difficult; moreover, the industry and cleanliness which the white apron expressed were belied by the postures and gaits of the women who wore it — their knuckles being mostly on their hips (an attitude which lent them the aspect of two-handled mugs), and their shoulders against doorposts; while there was a curious alacrity in the turn of each honest woman's head upon her neck and in the

twirl of her honest eyes, at any noise resembling a masculine footfall along the lane.[40]

Like those anonymous figures described in the first market, there is an imperceptible amalgam between these people and their surroundings. The lane has the character of the people, and they have the character of the lane: sounds emerge from buildings and bring human life unseen to the lane; the women stand like signs by the doors of the mud-walled houses; the plank bridges emerge from the darkness as though the lane itself were reaching out to the poacher. But it is the lane which is the permanent feature, not any individual within it.

A similar treatment is applied to the next group up the social scale, the honest traders and journeymen. Once more we are introduced to them as a part of their inn, the attention focused on the building itself merging imperceptibly into the scene within, then picking up once more the details without, until we scarcely know where stone and wood end, and humans begin (if such a division can be made):

> Inside these illuminated holes, at a distance of about three inches, were ranged at this hour, as every passer knew, the ruddy polls of Billy Wills the glazier, Smart the shoemaker, Buzzford the general dealer, and others of a secondary set of worthies, of a grade somewhat below that of the diners at the King's Arms, each with his yard of clay.
>
> A four-centred Tudor arch was over the entrance, and over the arch the signboard, now visible in the rays of an opposite lamp. Hereon the Mariners . . . Being on the sunny side of the street the three comrades had suffered largely from warping, splitting, fading, and shrinkage, so that they were but a half-invisible film upon the reality of the grain, and knots, and nails, which composed the signboard.[41]

The passage of individual lives in Casterbridge is the same as the thin film of paint upon the Three Mariners' signboard; the features of the town show through into each man's life, as he becomes a part of the town's history, is absorbed into its entity. Each shape at the shutter is only a cypher of those who have gone before, and those who will follow, his individuality that of some house in a corner of the town, altered by each generation, repainted afresh, yet never changing in substance or form. The climax of events for those in Peter's Finger is the skimmington, but Hardy's images of its ending are those of transient (and recurring) features in nature: 'The roars of sarcastic laughter went off in ripples, and the trampling died out like the rustle of a spent wind.' 'The lamp flames waved, the Walk trees soughed, a few loungers stood about with their hands in their pockets. Everything was as usual.' And Jopp's words to the constable: 'Now I've noticed, come to think o't, that the wind in the Walk trees makes a peculiar poetical-like murmur tonight, sir; more than common; so perhaps 'twas that?'[42]

The human beings, and all the tremendous events of the night, are no more than the wind ruffling the trees of the town; they will come again, with the permanence of nature, but in new shapes, with nature's transience. What other form could the blood pulsing within the heart of man's natural environment possibly take? To ascribe strong personality to these characters would unbalance this delicate creation as surely as would the slavish description of the physical realities of Dorchester.

5.

Into this self-centred, self-supporting world of Casterbridge Hardy introduces the characters of his drama. Newson is an outsider, no more than a trigger for the action of the plot, and Hardy's treatment of him is as cursory as that of the other minor characters. Susan, coming to the town towards the end of her life, does little more than find a home for her daughter, a place for herself to die. Her death is an occasion for Hardy to emphasise the transience and unimportance of individual human lives, through the discussions of Mother Cuxsom, Christopher Coney, and Solomon Longways, and the last-named's action in digging up the four pennies used to weight Susan's eyelids. 'Why should death rob life o'fourpence?'[43] Her final purpose is to highlight the closeness of Roman past and Victorian present, as she is laid to rest next to 'men who held in their mouths coins of Hadrian, Posthumus, and the Constantines.'[44] The main interest is centred on the quartet of Elizabeth-Jane, Lucetta, Farfrae and Henchard.

Elizabeth-Jane has already been partially introduced, through the philosophical musings which I compared with Hardy's treatment of the Victorian Sunday, and in fact the major feature of her personality is her philosophical approach to life. She accepts every vicissitude with a stoicism born, not of the timid acceptance of her mother, but of a reasoned belief that little she could do would affect the course of her life. And in this context of Casterbridge's permanence, and human transience, it might seem that she was right in this belief. However, it is her own background that impels her towards such a view; in Casterbridge she is only beginning to feel her way as a part of the community. She has grown up in circumstances which have forced an independence of mind upon her at an early age:

. . . she had been taken off to Canada, where they had lived several years without any great worldly success, though she worked as hard as any woman could to keep their cottage cheerful and well-provided. When Elizabeth-Jane was about twelve years old the three returned to England, and settled at Falmouth, where Newson made a living for a few years as boatman and general handy shoreman. . . .

Elizabeth-Jane developed early into womanliness. Her face, though somewhat wan and incomplete, possessed the raw materials of beauty in a promising degree. There was an under-handsomeness in it, struggling to reveal itself through the provisional curves of immaturity, and the casual disfigurements that resulted from the straitened circumstances of their lives. She was handsome in the bone, hardly as yet handsome in the flesh. She possibly might never be fully handsome, unless the carking accidents of her daily existence could be evaded before the mobile parts of her countenance had settled to their final mould.[45]

This is the life of the poor woman, the same situation that Tess faces, where the death of the father cannot even be given the philosophical considerations later accorded to Susan; his death means, above all, poverty. The trek to Casterbridge, following in the tracks of Henchard, is a last desperate hope, and the two women could easily have joined the displaced liviers of Mixen Lane, or died of exposure beneath a hedgerow. Life at this level was pitiless, and Elizabeth-Jane's mind could not but be conditioned by it, unprotected even by the working hands of her father.

But the mind, like the countenance, is amenable to changing circumstance, if that change comes soon enough; with her knowledge of what lies close behind to urge her on, Elizabeth takes the opportunity afforded by her new status with Henchard, not to become a fashionable figure, but to learn – Latin, Greek, history, accounts; things which are on a practical level in her new world, as was her net-seining before – for she is too well aware of the transience of fortune, at any level of society. Her arrangements are well-proved when she leaves Henchard for Lucetta, and later when she leaves the latter and returns to net-making for a living. Her next move is to rejoin Henchard in his fallen state, and once more she adjusts to circumstance. She sees the faint gleam of hope of Donald Farfrae's interest vanish in his marriage with Lucetta. By the time she too becomes his bride, the admired of all the townswomen, she has indeed no cause to be other than wary of the future:

> Her position was, indeed, to a marked degree one that, in the common phrase, afforded much to be thankful for. That she was not demonstratively thankful was no fault of hers. Her experience had been of a kind to teach her, rightly or wrongly, that the doubtful honour of a brief transit through a sorry world hardly called for effusiveness, even when the path was suddenly irradiated at some half-way point by daybeams rich as hers. [46]

This kind of stoicism is by no means a general representation of attitudes in Casterbridge. It is very much a result of uncertainty in an individual's life, rather than an element of the eternal town which she enters.

Lucetta shows a totally different kind of life. Born into a poor branch of a 'gentle' family, when she appears in Casterbridge it is as the inheritor of wealth and position. She is the only prominent reminder of the existence of the gentry in this working world; but it is only through her relationships with Henchard and Farfrae that she appears at all; 'Lucetta as a young girl would hardly have looked at a tradesman. But her ups and downs, capped by her indiscretions with Henchard, had made her uncritical as to station.'[47] For Hardy, such an attitude as that of the young Lucetta merely indicated the complete lack of reality in such a social situation − country landowners he knew to have a distinctive place in the life of the rural world; town-based gentry who contributed nothing but their names had not − and he ignores such people. Like Susan before her, Lucetta becomes more of a dramatic trigger to events than a character in her own right. The competition of the two established rivals for her hand helps to widen the rift to unbridgeable proportions; and her death, when it comes, is caused by a traditional expression of the town's disapproval at such a disruptive influence − the skimmington. Her disturbing presence is absorbed into the daily existence of the town, in a process begun when she married Farfrae, and became part of his mayoral status, 'two-hundredth odd of a series forming an elective dynasty dating back to the days of Charles I.'[48] Her death, when it comes, is as unimportant as was Susan's.

For his part, Farfrae is no such disturbing element. From the very beginning of his life in Casterbridge he is working in the same pattern that made Henchard mayor before him. Casterbridge is not a last hope, nor a place of personal connection, but a chance opportunity, of the kind that will eventually arise for men of the enterprising mould of Farfrae and Henchard: 'I said to myself, "Never a one of the prizes of life will I come by unless I undertake it!" and I decided to go.'[49]

But there are great differences between the two, even in their basic approach to problems. When Farfrae comes to Casterbridge, he is on his way to Bristol, and thence to America, to seek his fortune. His immediate past is obscure, though he was obviously not coming directly from Scotland, and he also knew enough about the corn trade, despite his youth, to impress Henchard at once. His direct attack on the latter's books shows that he was well versed in the theoretical as well as the practical side of the hay and seed business. With this grounding, and a warm mixture of the romantic and commercial in his character, and an honest approach to others, Farfrae takes his chance in the town. He begins with a good situation, and a good friend, and it is inevitable that with all these factors in his favour, in a town where trade and honesty combine to prosper business, he should advance:

> Just when I sold the markets went lower, and I bought up the corn of those who had been holding back at less price than my first purchases. And then . . . I sold it a few weeks after, when it happened to go up again! And so, by contenting mysel' with small profits frequently repeated, I soon made five hundred pounds . . . while the others by keeping theirs in hand made nothing at all![50]

The formula is that of the successful businessman since time began. In the same astute manner, Farfrae sees the commercial benefit of modern methods — well tried and tested, of course — and introduces Casterbridge to its first seed drill.[51]

But it would be a mistake to assume merely from this contrast in his character with Henchard's that Farfrae represents the irresistible force of modernism overtaking the town. Hardy has omitted from the novel any reference to the machines that were already in use on local farms, and to the water-meadow experiments outside the town that, the century before, led European agriculture forward – it is another aspect of his creation of an 'ageless' character for the town – but he makes no more play of this new machine than of Farfrae's accurate measures and hard-headed wage accounts. It is all a part of the contrast in character between the two men, and Farfrae, perfectly suited to the Casterbridge climate, is within a year or two as much a part of the town as any man born there, heading the local business community, sitting on the bench of magistrates, financing local celebrations, occupying a prestigious town house, marrying into the local families, and generally acting, not as guide and mentor of the town, but simply the latest manifestation of the town's commercial success. Every phase of the rivalry between him and Henchard is rooted, not in an opposition of modern and ancient, but a timeless struggle for power in this self-sufficient world. Marriages are dynastic, and the prizes basic – position, wealth and power, first for Henchard, then for Farfrae, as each occupies in his turn the trappings of local supremacy.

Henchard, though also an outsider and a self-made man, displays a very different background from his rival. Like Farfrae, he is a reminder that, enclosed as the town is, it is constantly changing, renewing itself, absorbing new blood and new ideas from without, and altering imperceptibly, so that the entity remains, but flourishes. It is a natural process, which can take account of such differing individuals as Farfrae and Henchard. The latter's skills as a hay-trusser are of little relevance to the world of business, and he has no other training. He works by intuition, rule of thumb, and a forthright honesty. He came to the town alone, and worked himself up over eighteen years, without the initial advantage of friend or position, and the consequent advantages of money and status. His rise was far less assured than that of Farfrae, though his tenacious and forceful personality would have been of great assistance: we can envisage such a man, faced by the alternatives of a Mixen Lane existence or a fight to advance, struggling each painful step of the way along the road to fortune. Even more than Elizabeth-Jane, he had reason to be wary of sudden changes around him.

But with advancement came friends and respect, and time made up for initial disadvantages. Both men are essentially a part of the community of Casterbridge. However they rose, their success is merely a repetition of successes down the preceding centuries, and a precursor of others to come. Henchard's failure is merely one of a long line that is equally continuous:

> These bridges had speaking countenances. Every projection in each was worn down to obtuseness, partly by weather, more by friction from generations of loungers, whose toes and heels had from year to year made restless movements against these parapets, as they had stood there meditating on the aspect of affairs. In the case of the more friable bricks and stones even the flat faces were worn into hollows by the same mixed mechanism. The masonry of the top was clamped with iron at each joint; since it had been no uncommon thing for desperate men to wrench the coping off and throw it down the river, in reckless defiance of the magistrates. . . .
>
> The miserables who would pause on the remoter bridge were of a politer stamp. They included bankrupts, hypochondriacs, persons who were what is called 'out of a situation' from fault or lucklessness, the inefficient of the professional class – shabby-genteel men, who did not know how to get rid of the weary time between dinner and dark. The eyes of this species were mostly directed over the parapet upon the running water below. . . .
>
> To this bridge came Henchard, as other unfortunates had come before him.[52]

The description moves as surely as the earlier, pleasanter, scenes: from the town, through the people who pass anonymously, each making his slight mark, to Henchard – simply the latest in a very long line. His bankruptcy may be the result of personal misjudgement, but it is no new thing in Casterbridge.

It is, of course, much more a question of character that enters into the final phase of Henchard's self-destruction. The same quality that saw him well on his way to fortune, also contributes, in the outrageous conditions of one harvest, to his downfall – 'the momentum of his character knew no patience'.[53] Henchard, conditioned by his life's experience, is too inflexible to adjust, as Farfrae does, to the sudden alteration, and falls. And having fallen, he is too old and inflexible to accept circumstance as Elizabeth does; and how can a man whose life is built upon pride of character possibly attempt to rebuild in a place that has seen him fall? 'He had no wish to make an arena a second time of a world that had become a mere painted scene to him.'[54] Farfrae takes over quite naturally from the old master, and as naturally Henchard's mind cannot accept such a situation. In the circumstances of his emotional bereavement — the loss of Elizabeth-Jane — all incentive dies, and he ceases to have any future. He has been destroyed by the very character that made him a success. His bitter affirmation of total personal destruction, his 'will', is no more than a confirmation of the actual situation: 'that no man remember me'.[55] He will be remembered no more than Susan or Lucetta, and all who have gone before. They are all fading paint upon the sign.

2 The Village Community: *Under the Greenwood Tree*

Under the Greenwood Tree has perhaps the best-known setting of all Hardy's novels, the parish of Stinsford, where the scattered houses of Stinsford, Bockhampton and Higher Bockhampton make up the village of 'Mellstock'.

It also contains the most accurate transcription of topographical reality in any of Hardy's novels: ' "Half a mile from this (Lower Mellstock) were the church and the vicarage." Measuring the distance from Bockhampton Post Office to the church at Stinsford (Mellstock) we find in reality the distance is just about 1,000 yards.'[1] Compared with the strained topographical reality of *The Mayor of Casterbridge*, the adherence to reality here is startling.

In fact, the only departure from a reality of place came in the manuscript and first edition of the novel. The Dewys' cottage, based on Hardy's own at Higher Bockhampton, is described as having a 'thatched pyramidal roof' and 'single chimney standing in the midst'. In subsequent editions, it was 'a long low cottage with a hipped roof of thatch, having dormer windows breaking up into the eaves, a chimney standing in the middle of the ridge and another at each end.'[2] The latter description is exactly that of the Hardys' home.

This was where Hardy lived until he was sixteen, the place where several of his novels were written, and on which the majority of his experience of Dorset village life was based. It was here that his imagination first grasped the concept of the village as a community, and stretched out for what lay beyond. Imaginatively, this is the nearest to an ideal to be found in any of his works: it is the imperfect human paradise from which his characters are cast out, to take their solitary way through the Victorian economic reality of the nineteenth century.

With all this, however, the novel is not an accurate picture of Stinsford life in the 1840s.[3] Even before leaving the topographical detail aside, this becomes apparent: Hardy tells more by what he omits than by what he includes. The location of the buildings mentioned is accurate, and brief but graphic descriptions are given of most; but only a very few of the parish's buildings are mentioned at all, and no space is given to an overall 'village' picture.

The Dewys' house is naturally given precedence, both as home of the central figures, and as a basic 'type' for all the cottages of the parish:

> The window-shutters were not yet closed, and the fire- and candle-light within radiated forth upon the thick bushes of box and laurestinus growing in clumps outside, and upon the bare boughs of several codlin-trees hanging about in various distorted shapes, the result of early training as espaliers combined with careless climbing into their boughs in later years. The walls of the dwelling were for the most part covered with creepers, though these were rather beaten back from the doorway — a feature which was worn and scratched by much passing in and out, giving it by day the appearance of an old keyhole. Light streamed through the cracks and joints of outbuildings a little way from the cottage, a sight which nourished the fancy that the purpose of the erection must be rather to veil bright attractions than to shelter unsightly necessaries. The noise of a beetle and wedges and the splintering of wood was periodically heard from this direction; and at some little distance further a steady regular munching and the occasional scurr of a rope betokened a stable, and horses feeding within it.[4]

There is a rich and welcoming warmth about this description that establishes early the nature of such village homesteads. House and garden and outbuildings mingle in light and sound to suggest the inseparable functions of home and work in the setting; the warmly personal nature of Henchard's house in *The Mayor of Casterbridge* gives way to the present necessities of village life here represented. This is the heart of the village landscape, as distinct from that of the town. The generations of the family meet here with others of the village, with the evidence of the artisan all around; it is very different from the sharp social divisions of the public houses in Casterbridge. It is the heart of a community.

The other house that figures largely in the novel is Geoffrey Day's Lodge. But in keeping with the avoidance of superfluous description elsewhere applied, Hardy devotes little time to the exterior appearance of the Lodge, concentrating instead on its function as a base for Fanny's marriage:

> The most striking point about the room was the furniture. This was a repetition upon inanimate objects of the old principle introduced by Noah, consisting for the most part of two articles of every sort. The duplicate system of furnishing owed its existence to the forethought of Fancy's mother, exercised from the date of Fancy's birthday onwards. The arrangement spoke for itself: nobody who knew the tone of the household could look at the goods without being aware that the second set was a provision for Fancy when she should marry and have a house of her own.[5]

Hardy goes on to describe the furniture in some detail – the practical nature of 'kitchen dressers', 'Cups, dishes, and plates' and so on, is obvious – before returning to a description of the chimney-corner, the social focus of the house (here, the Lodge is complementing the Dewys' cottage, in much the way marriage brings individuals together).

Both cottages are stamped with something beside their functions, however; just as Mixen Lane seems of a one with the people who live in it, so here the houses take on the personality of their occupants. The sociability and involvement of the Dewys in the village is marked by the cottage doorway, 'a feature which was worn and scratched by much passing in and out', while the lonely life of the keeper is reflected in the more ordered patterns of his house:

> The ceiling was carried by a beam traversing its midst, from the side of which projected a large nail, used solely and constantly as a peg for Geoffrey's hat; the nail was arched by a rainbow-shaped stain, imprinted by the brim of the said hat when it was hung there dripping wet.[6]

Personality also provides the reason for the only mention of farming in this novel, in Shiner's house:

> Farmer Shiner's was a queer lump of a house, standing at the corner of a lane that ran into the principal thoroughfare. The upper windows were much wider than they were high, and this feature, together with a broad bay-window where the door might have been expected, gave it by day the aspect of a human countenance turned askance, and wearing a sly and wicked leer.[7]

The building is not referred to again, and its only function seems to be to prejudice us against its occupant. The harmony of man and his creation, so notable a feature in both *The Mayor of Casterbridge* and *Under the Greenwood Tree*, seems to be directed towards establishing in the reader an irrational objection to Shiner:[8] he is, like the house, a member in good standing of the community, but there is something unfortunately different, and repellent, about them. (If this view needs any more support, consider the fact that this is the only unidentifiable building Hardy describes in the novel; it has been included, apparently, for only this purpose.)

Beyond these three houses, the only other place described is, in similar manner to the selected buildings described in *The Mayor of Casterbridge*, representative of a type. Mr. Penny's house is a type for all the artisans' houses, and the manner of its description, with man and house almost undistinguishable, a pattern for all such places:

> Mr. Penny's was the last house in that part of the parish, and stood in a hollow by the roadside; so that cartwheels and horses' legs were about level with the sill of his shop-window. This was low and wide, and was open from morning till evening, Mr. Penny himself being invariably seen working inside like a framed portrait of a shoemaker by some modern Moroni. He sat facing the road, with a boot on his knees and the awl in his hand, only looking up for a moment as he stretched out his arms and bent forward at the pull, when his spectacles flashed in the passer's face with a shine of flat whiteness, and then returned again to the boot as usual. Rows of lasts, small and large, stout and slender, covered the wall which formed the background, in the extreme shadow of which a kind of dummy was seen sitting, in the shape of an apprentice with a string tied round his hair . . . Outside the window the upper-leather of a Wellington-boot was usually hung, pegged to a board as if to dry.[9]

Mr. Penny sits framed and defined by the open window, his appearance one with the tools of his trade, while the background contains, with equal emphasis, the lasts for local shoes and the dummy-like apprentice. Men and materials merge into a larger picture, and are drawn out of the frame, into the life of the village, by the Wellington upper which breaks the artistic limits of the scene and links it to the men passing outside.

No other buildings are described in any detail, the manor-house, church and vicarage being noticeably excluded, their only function

A Map of the Parish of Stinsford,
with particular reference to those
features included in Hardy's
'Under the Greenwood Tree'.

Scale: approx. 2½" = 1 mile.

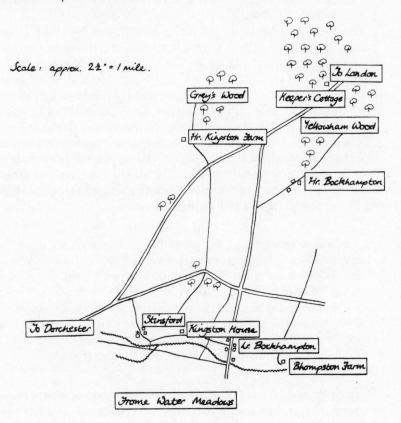

Grey's Wood

Keeper's Cottage

To London

Yellowham Wood

Hr. Kingston Farm

Hr. Bockhampton

To Dorchester

Stinsford

Kingston House

Lr. Bockhampton

Bhompston Farm

Frome Water Meadows

being with regard to the choir or the wooing; the outlying farmsteads are only mentioned as a part of the choir's Christmas rounds, and Budmouth and Casterbridge have no special connection at all with the events of the novel. Just as *The Mayor of Casterbridge* deals only with the mercantile life of the town, so *Under the Greenwood Tree* portrays only the artisan community of the village, excluding even the more general 'street-scenes' which might have been expected of a novel set so firmly in the heart of the community (the school, built in the most densely-populated part of Stinsford parish, where cottages line both sides of the road, might almost have stood alone, from all we can gather in Hardy's descriptions.)

More important than the exclusion of buildings, however, is the exclusion of nature. Where are the open fields portrayed in *Far from the Madding Crowd*, the heath of *The Return of the Native*, and the water-meadows of *The Mayor of Casterbridge*? All these, so close-set around the parish, and all closely-observed by Hardy, might never have existed. Even the rich meadows of Tess's 'Talbothays' have no mention here, despite their proximity to the main village.

The reason for the exclusion of all these aspects of the area lies, as before, in the bias of the novel. In *The Mayor of Casterbridge* nature appears at one remove, in its relation to the social and economic life of the town; here, nature becomes a backcloth to the village life, seen in its domestic aspects and in its simple proximity:

> It was a morning of the latter summer-time; a morning of lingering dews, when the grass is never dry in the shade. Fuchsias and dahlias were laden till eleven o'clock with small drops and dashes of water, changing the colour of their sparkle at every movement of the air; and elsewhere hanging on twigs like small silver fruit. The threads of garden-spiders appeared thick and polished. In the dry and sunny places dozens of long-legged crane-flies whizzed off the grass at every step the passer took.[10]

Simple personal pleasure in the beauty of the morning is here more important than any functional aspect of Nature. Dew, flowers, colour, spiders' webs and crane-flies hold the attention, rather than thoughts of the benefits to the farmer's pocket of such a morning. It is the codlin-trees and Geoffrey Day's hives which press most upon our attention, in their roles of domestic economy. The few references to nature which step outside this sphere are the passing observations of men concerned more with the effect of rain upon their own persons, than with its effect upon crops and livelihood:

> A single vast gray cloud covered the country, from which the small rain and mist had just begun to blow down in wavy sheets, alternately thick and thin. The trees of the fields and plantations writhed like miserable men as the air wound its way swiftly among them: the lowest portions of their trunks, that had hardly ever been known to move, were visibly rocked by the fiercer gusts, distressing the mind by its painful unwontedness, as when a strong man is seen to shed tears. Low-hanging boughs went up and down; high and erect boughs went to and fro; the blasts being so irregular, and divided into so many cross-currents, that neighbouring branches of the same tree swept the skies in independent motions, crossed each other, or became entangled.[11]

The description is detailed, accurate and effective, moving the reader close to the experience of actually standing in such rain, but it lacks the leaden despair of crop-failures in *The Mayor of Casterbridge*, and displays none of the emotional involvement of the raging thunderstorm in *Far from the Madding Crowd*. Emotion appears as a personal attribution of anthropomorphism to the writhing trees – a very different matter from the anxious watchers of the sky whose bank balances depend on the crop around Casterbridge,[12] or even from the hard-headed monetary calculations of Gabriel Oak as he fights to save the storm-threatened ricks.[13] This is autumn seen through the eyes of men secure from its immediate effects.

Having established that neither buildings nor nature occupy a position of supreme importance in the novel, the point arises, what does? What, if anything, gives *Under the Greenwood Tree* the same cohesion and form as *The Mayor of Casterbridge*?

The answer lies with the people of the novel. Where Henchard and Farfrae were functions of an ancient town, the characters of *Under the Greenwood Tree* have an independence and personality unusual in any of Hardy's work. It is not that they are more closely observed, or better drawn, than the characters of the other novels (indeed, they are sketchy by comparison with Hardy's other major characters); but their lives revolve around relationships with each other, not dependence upon some more permanent object. It is the sophisticated web of relationships, built up over centuries of village life and adapted by each succeeding generation that gives the depth needed in the novel. The subtle relationship of man and stone, seen in Casterbridge, is here replaced by the subtle relationships of men. It is an ambitious attempt on Hardy's part, to look for material in such insubstantial areas: the simple framework of four seasons and the dual plot provide structure without obscuring the details described. (*Under the Green-wood Tree*, seen like this, is less of a rural idyll, more a key to help us unlock the deeper secrets of the other novels.)

The importance of the characters is established early in the novel. An opening sequence similar to that of *The Woodlanders* suggests we are to see man emerging as a part of the natural landscape, but in fact the descriptions which do arise suggest far more the human than the natural element:

> . . . he could now be seen rising against the sky, his profile appearing on the light background like the portrait of a gentleman in black cardboard. It assumed the form of a low-crowned hat, and ordinary-shaped nose, an ordinary chin, an ordinary neck, and ordinary shoulders. What he consisted of further down was invisible from lack of sky low enough to picture him on.

> Shuffling, halting, irregular footsteps of various kinds were now heard coming up the hill, and presently there emerged from the shade severally five men of different ages and gaits, all of them working villagers of the parish of Mellstock. They, too, had lost their rotundity with the daylight, and advanced against the sky in flat outlines, which suggested some processional design on Greek or Etruscan pottery.[14]

The images are of a half-length silhouette and a classical pottery design – the night sky is nothing more than a backcloth to the man-made pictures. It lacks even the power of the assumed emotion in the storm-tossed trees. Compare this description with that of the maltster, in *Far from the Madding Crowd* (a similar situation and grouping of characters in each case), 'his frosty white hair and beard overgrowing his gnarled figure like the grey moss and lichen upon a leafless apple-tree'.[15] Even making allowance for the development of Hardy's style, the contrast is remarkable.

I have already quoted the description of Mr. Penny at work, wherein he emerges from the craft of his shop, a human extension of his trade. The other example of this type of description is Old James, whose appearance is that of his work (in both cases the characters have an extended existence, in the village's social life, but it is established early that their work is essentially part of their nature, not to be left behind in their spare time):

> Being by trade a mason, he wore a long linen apron reaching almost to his toes, corduroy breeches and gaiters, which, together with his boots, graduated in tints of whitish-brown by constant friction against lime and stone. He also wore a very stiff fustian coat, having folds at the elbows and shoulders as unvarying in their arrangement as those in a pair of bellows: the ridges and the projecting parts of the coat collectively exhibiting a shade different from that of the hollows, which were lined with small ditch-like accumulations of stone and mortar-dust. The extremely large side-pockets, sheltered beneath wide flaps, bulged out convexly whether empty or full; and· as he was often engaged to work at buildings far away . . . he carried in these pockets a small . . . canister of tea, a paper of salt, and a paper of pepper; the bread, cheese and meat, forming the substance of his meals, hanging up behind him in his basket among the hammers and chisels.[16]

The telling point of this description, however, is its similarity to the descriptions of buildings in *The Mayor of Casterbridge*. The full and detailed examination of Old James, lingering carefully over each aspect of his clothing, noting the stains and weathering of the coat, establishing the permanence of folds and bulging pockets, and so casually linking his meal with the tools of trade that supply it, suggests a permanence about his appearance much akin to the permanence of the Casterbridge structures.

However, the description is of a man as part of his trade. The personal aspects of Old James are dealt with in the lines, 'he lived in a cottage by himself, and many people considered him a miser; some, rather slovenly in his habits.'[17] In fact, even this sees him from the point of view of others; he becomes almost entirely a function of his relationships with other people, through work and social communion. William Dewy (in a passage that foreshadows the description of Gabriel Oak in *Far from the Madding Crowd*[18]) personifies this attitude towards the characters. He alters according to the mood of others:

> His was a humorous and kindly nature, not unmixed with a frequent melancholy; and he had a firm religious faith. But to his

neighbours he had no character in particular. If they saw him pass
by their windows when they had been bottling off old mead, or
when they had just been called long-headed men who might do
anything in the world if they chose, they thought concerning him,
'Ah, there's that good-hearted man – open as a child!' If they saw
him just after losing a shilling or half-a-crown, or accidentally
letting fall a piece of crockery, they thought, 'There's that poor
weak-minded man Dewy again! Ah, he's never done much in the
world either!' If he passed when fortune neither smiled nor
frowned on them, they merely thought him old William Dewy.[19]

Essentially, then, as Henchard and Farfrae in *The Mayor of
Casterbridge* represent through their tragedy the fall, and rise, of many
others before and since, so James and William, while having
individual characteristics, represent others who have lived and
worked for generations before in the village, and others who would
follow. The solid structures of Casterbridge life are here translated
into the solid presence of individual representatives of past and future,
who are the foundation for the minor alterations of the present.

In keeping with this function, the other characters, beside their
roles in the immediate drama, represent some permanent aspect of the
human relationships of the village. This is one reason why so many
'minor' characters occupy such prominent positions in this novel;
essentially, all have some role to fulfil, and their relevance or
otherwise to the issues of marriage and choir is secondary to this role,
in terms of emphasis in the text. Hence the weight given to Old
James, who plays no other part in the novel, and the relative
prominence of Leaf, whose parallels in other novels – Joseph Poor-
grass, in *Far from the Madding Crowd*, Abel Whittle in *The Mayor of
Casterbridge*, Christian Cantle in *The Return of the Native* – are given
only slight attention. There are the vicar, the churchwarden and the
schoolmistress; the skilled workers and the keeper; the wives, both
efficient (Mrs. Dewy) and self-centred (Mrs. Day). And Elizabeth
Endorfield holds the key of superstition and ancient remedies, while
Leaf trembles for all the less-than-efficient menfolk of the village.
There is the sociable welcome of the Dewys, and the wise
detachment of Geoffrey Day, and the peaceable neutrality of William
Dewey; even the hermit-like meanness of Old James. At every turn
we find the characters of the novel representing something more than
mere personality – something above the laws of time by which
human lives are bound; something on which real trust can be placed,

as a foundation as permanent as anything to be found in this impermanent world. They hold the key to the deepest structure of the rural community, upon which depends the whole of man's ability to construct from nature a more permanent world for himself; it is the structure whose bones are visible in Henchard and Farfrae as mayors, and similar characters in the later novels – Oak, Venn, Winterborne – but which is obscured by other considerations in those novels. Only here, in *Under the Greenwood Tree*, is it met directly, and some attempt made to explore its complexities in print.

3 The Farming Community: *Far from the Madding Crowd*

The setting of *Far from the Madding Crowd* is the valley of the River Piddle, just upstream of Puddletown. (The latter spelling is a Victorian emendation.[1]) The area was well-known to Hardy as a child, and features in his work throughout his life. His mother's younger sister, Martha, was married to a Puddletown man, John Brereton Sharpe (supposed to be the model for Troy), and the Hand family (related through Hardy's maternal grandmother, Elizabeth Hand) counted numerous Puddletown members: James Sparkes, a cabinet-maker, and the three uncles, all bricklayers, Henery, William and Christopher, as well as John Antell, the cobbler. Hardy paid frequent visits to his Puddletown relatives, at first in company with his mother, and later by himself, walking across the heath road between the village and his own home. He had no direct connection with the farms on which the main action of *Far from the Madding Crowd* is based, but must often have wandered along the line of the Ridgeway overlooking the Piddle valley, and watched the everyday life of the mixed farms below. He would have met the workers in the village itself, tired after a day's hard field work, cold from winter fencing and maintenance, or relaxing in times of ease. Animals seem to have become as familiar as people to him, but crops are treated sketchily in the novels, indicating that he never came to know man's plants as well as his creatures. Perhaps this comes from his early familiarity with a different kind of farming, that of the heath's-edge and the Frome valley. Apple and vegetable crops he knew, as also the dairy cattle of Lower Bockhampton (they are featured largely in *Tess of the d'Urbervilles*). He knew the trees and wild creatures of the heath, and encountered sheep in the sparse fields between Puddletown and Higher Bockhampton,[2] but crops such as wheat and barley were confined to the richer soils north and south of his home, coming no nearer than Druce Farm, or the outlying fields of Higher Kingston, beyond the main London road. They seem to have impressed him more in the mass, as qualities of tone or movement ('the ground was melodious with ripples, and the sky with larks'[3]) — it was this characteristic that enabled Gustav Holst, many years later, to create such an evocative musical portrait of Egdon Heath [4] — and as functions of economic necessity (as when Oak calculates the value of the threatened ricks) than as individual plants. They serve as a reminder that all of Hardy's descriptions of nature and man are subservient to the landscape of general effect in his Wessex novels; nothing is included which is superfluous to that effect.

The detailed reality of the Puddletown Hardy knew is tempered in *Far from the Madding Crowd* by this artistic function. The basis of existence for the community is shifted, from the ancient square of Casterbridge's enclosed trading world, to the wider sphere of agriculture. The need for a concrete image of the community is changed, too, from buildings to fields, and the men and their actions alike take colour and life from the new landscape.

Although buildings are of minor importance in the novel, they do have a function, in agricultural terms. They are described in detail only when necessary, the necessity being dictated by the need to circumscribe certain functions of the agricultural community. In Norcombe, before the action shifts to Weatherbury, the only building given attention is the cow-byre on the slope of the down (the hut is more an extension of simple hurdle shelters than a building). It is the agricultural side of Bathsheba's life that is emphasised, even Oak's courtship visit centring on the lamb, not the interior of the cottage. At Weatherbury itself, where the world to be encompassed is that of the mixed farm (the artisans, dairymen, journeymen, woodsmen and other rural figures being variously dealt with in other novels), a very limited range of buildings is described, each serving a particular function of life on the farm. Bathsheba's farmhouse is a type for the decayed properties bequeathed to tenant farmers by landlords whose estates are grown too large to manage personally:

By daylight (it) presented itself as a hoary building, of the early stage of Classical Renaissance as regards its architecture, and of a proportion which told at a glance that, as is so frequently the case, it had once been the manorial hall upon a small estate around it, now altogether effaced as a distinct property, and merged in the vast

tract of a non-resident landlord, which comprised several such
modest demesnes.

Fluted pilasters, worked from the solid stone, decorated its front,
and above the roof the chimneys were panelled or columnar, some
coped gables with finials and like features still retaining traces of
their Gothic extraction. Soft brown mosses, like faded velveteen,
formed cushions upon the stone tiling, and tufts of the houseleek or
sengreen sprouted from the eaves of the low surrounding buildings. A gravel walk leading from the door to the road in front was
encrusted at the sides with more moss – here it was a silver-green
variety, the nut-brown of the gravel being visible to the width of
only a foot or two in the centre. This circumstance, and the
generally sleepy air of the whole prospect here, together with the
animated and contrasting style of the reverse facade, suggested to
the imagination that on the adaptation of the building for farming
purposes the vital principle of the house had turned round inside its
body to face the other way.[5]

The description is subtly different from those employed in *The
Mayor of Casterbridge*, where buildings in the aggregate suggest age
and continuity. Here there is continuity, but of a kind that reminds us
of the vagaries of the rural world, based not on trade but on nature
and the sweat of man's brow. The simple affirmation of the house's
changed status might have been enough to place the thing in an
economic and social context, but Hardy's essential union, of man and
nature, dictates that mere social vagaries are not enough. The weight
and bulk of description are given to features which bespeak the
harmony of the building with its role – a harmony born, not of
design, but of necessary adaptation. As centre of a small agricultural
estate, the building had purpose; as the farmhouse of a tenant farmer,
it still has purpose, although altered. Nature and time adjust what
man has made, as long as the creation has a function in harmony with
nature. The mosses and sengreen become symbols of the acceptance
by nature of something that has a place in the rural world.

Bathsheba's farmhouse having been described, Boldwood's, which
is of a similar status, is given the most cursory treatment. We are told
it 'stood recessed from the road'.[6] In a similar fashion, only one
representative of the building most associated with farmwork is
detailed – Bathsheba's barn:

The vast porches at the sides, lofty enough to admit a waggon

laden to its highest with corn in the sheaf, were spanned by heavy-
pointed arches of stone, broadly and boldly cut, whose very
simplicity was the origin of a grandeur not apparent in erections
where more ornament has been attempted. The dusky, filmed,
chestnut roof, braced and tied in by huge collars, curves and
diagonals, was far nobler in design, because more wealthy in
material, than nine-tenths of those in our modern churches. Along
each side wall was a range of striding buttresses, throwing deep
shadows on the spaces between them, which were perforated by
lancet openings, combining in their proportions the precise
requirements both of beauty and ventilation. . . .

The lanceolate windows, the time-eaten arch-stones and cham-
fers, the orientation of the axis, the misty chestnut work of the
rafters, referred to no exploded fortifying art or worn-out religious
creed. The defence and salvation of the body by daily bread is still a
study, a religion, and a desire. [7]

Here, there is even more emphasis given to function and continuity,
in a world of changing economic, social and spiritual values. This is
the very heart of the farm world, and is made as concrete as possible,
while fortifying the knowledge that it is as a symbol of function that it
exists, not by its own right. Once again, the interior is given full
treatment (something accorded only to the three main buildings of
the novel – the farmhouse, the barn and the malthouse).

The porches are designed to admit fully-laden wagons, the roof is
noble in its perfect interpretation of the simple necessity of protecting
the food of man and beast for the winter, and buttresses and windows
stand mute testimony to the balance between beauty and function –
between art and simple survival – that, in *Far from the Madding
Crowd*, is the study and joy of author and characters alike. In this
novel, more than in any other, Hardy expresses his sheer (and short-
lived) pleasure at the harmonies of man's agricultural partnership
with nature.

The third member of the inanimate trio is Warren's Malthouse.
Where the farmhouse bore in itself the harmony of natural adaptation
and change, and the barn the rich beauty of continuing function, the
malthouse radiates warmth and comfort, the symbol of man's
continuing need to relax from his work, and commune with his
fellow men:

There was no window in front; but a square hole in the door was

glazed with a single pane, through which red, comfortable rays
now stretched out upon the ivied wall in front. Voices were to be
heard inside. . . .

The room inside was lighted only by the ruddy glow from the
kiln mouth, which shone over the floor with the streaming
horizontality of the setting sun, and threw upwards the shadows of
all facial irregularities in those assembled around. The stone-flag
floor was worn into a path from the doorway to the kiln, and into
undulations everywhere.[8]

Each building, as description progresses, is associated with men; they
emerge from it as they emerge from the fields, a part of the landscape.
But in the malthouse, the involvement of men with its atmosphere of
hospitable warmth is so essential that their features are as naturally a
part of its functional character as the undulations of a floor, worn by
generations of malters stoking the kiln. The other two buildings
retain their function and feeling even without immediate reference to
men; the malthouse is virtually an extension of the men themselves, a
shell of warmth emanating from their own companionship.

The farm life has been centred around farmhouse and barn, the
companionship of the workers around the malthouse; the main social
action takes place almost entirely in the open air. There remain, in
terms of function, only the community's links with the trading
community at Casterbridge to be rendered in physical form (cottages
are virtually ignored, as having no more direct function to the
community than shelters; the Buck's Head at Roytown and other
buildings mentioned in Casterbridge and elsewhere are given cursory
treatment, being introduced only for reasons of plot).[9] This final
building is the Corn Exchange at Casterbridge, where the scattered
farming communities meet in economic need, and it is notable
because it is given such concrete treatment while yet being hardly
delineated. It receives the force of the same function and nature which
brought men into the description of the malthouse; the actual
appearance of the building matters less than the atmosphere it
conveys, which is here associated with the coming-together of men in
business, rather than companionship. The words devoted to the
material of the building are few, but when its occupants are
extensions of its function, the final effect is considerable:

The low though extensive hall, supported by beams and pillars,
and latterly dignified by the name of Corn Exchange, was

thronged with hot men who talked among each other in twos and threes, the speaker of the minute looking sideways into his auditor's face and concentrating his argument by a contraction of one eyelid during delivery. The greater number carried in their hands ground-ash saplings, using them partly as walking-sticks and partly for poking up pigs, sheep, neighbours with their backs turned, and restful things in general, which seemed to require such treatment in the course of their peregrinations. During conversations each subjected his sapling to great varieties of usage — bending it round his back, forming an arch of it between his hands . . . or perhaps it was hastily tucked under the arm whilst the sample-bag was pulled forth and a handful of corn poured into the palm, which, after criticism, was flung upon the floor.[10]

The treatment of material here is reminiscent of the market-scenes in *The Mayor of Casterbridge*, but the detached objectivity of those street scenes has been altered, the men becoming living embodiments of the town's trading relationship with its rural neighbours. The mechanics of exchange are more important than the surroundings.

These are the only buildings which have a major function in the novel, and in keeping with this limited use of them, their physical position is of little relevance to the development of the novel. Where, in *The Mayor of Casterbridge*, physical reality is altered to create the landscape of the market-town, here the main work of this landscape-creation lies with natural features. In keeping with the idea that the farm community has a peripheral contact with Weatherbury, through the maltster's, the two farms are shifted about a mile from their true position, bringing into a single area of focus the river, the farms, the valley-edges with the bracken-fringed heath beyond, and the highway between Casterbridge and Weatherbury. However, no emphasis is given to this area as a unit, other than the slight emphasis on the single nature of the agriculture. The heath and woodland touch the edges of the community, but have little place in its life.

The community of *Far from the Madding Crowd* is, then, only loosely circumscribed, with a few limited poles of physical emphasis. How is it given the depth and continuity of a place as identifiable as Casterbridge? The answer lies in nature: nature in its agricultural aspect, and man's involvement with it.

To step back for a moment to a comparison with *The Mayor of Casterbridge*; in that novel, the natural scene outside the town is extremely limited in scope. It is the town itself which is used to create

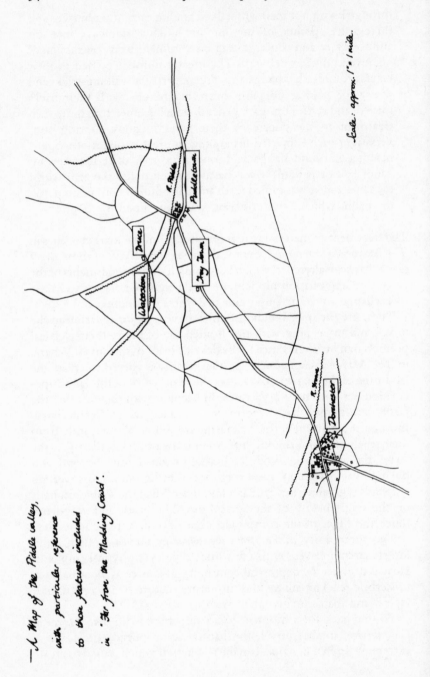

—A Map of the Riddle valley, with particular reference to those features included in "Far from the Madding Crowd".

Scale: approx. 1" = 1 mile.

the appropriate scene and atmosphere, the landscape of rural trade. In keeping with this function, it is the town at a distance which first occupies Hardy's descriptive powers, and all else leads on from there. So, too, in *Under the Greenwood Tree* we first meet Dick and the band-members as figures on a backdrop of nature, before being introduced to their characters and roles. Equally in keeping with the different character of *Far from the Madding Crowd*, it is nature seen at a distance, before our close involvement with it, which first demands full descriptive attention:

> The hill was covered on its northern side by an ancient and decaying plantation of beeches, whose upper verge formed a line over the crest, fringing its arched curve against the sky, like a mane. To-night these trees sheltered the southern slope from the keenest blasts, which smote the wood and floundered through it with a sound as of grumbling, or gushed over its crowning boughs in a weakened moan. . . . Between this half-wooded, half-naked hill, and the vague, still horizon that its summit indistinctly commanded, was a mysterious sheet of fathomless shade — the sounds from which suggested that what it concealed bore some reduced resemblance to features here. . . . The sky was clear — remarkably clear — and the twinkling of all the stars seemed to be but throbs of one body, timed by a common pulse.[11]

In Casterbridge, the town was the heart of a rural body, with men its blood; in Mellstock, the community was the living entity; here, on the windswept hillside, the whole of creation throbs as one being. Men are a small part of that whole.

Passing through this general scene, we emerge into a world of agricultural seasons and activities. Life is defined as accurately at each stage of this novel by firm descriptions of the natural surroundings as it is by streets and walls in Casterbridge and people in Mellstock. Boldwood's emotional reaction to Bathsheba's valentine card is set into the late snow of the season as naturally, for such a man, as it would have been in a drawing room for most Victorian readers:

> Over the west hung the wasting moon, now dull and greenish-yellow, like tarnished brass. Boldwood was listlessly noting how the frost had hardened and glazed the surface of the snow, till it shone in the red eastern light with the polish of marble; how, in some portions of the slope, withered grass bents, encased in icicles,

bristled through the smooth wan coverlet in the twisted and curved shapes of old Venetian glass.[12]

The images, of brass, marble and Venetian glass, are taken from the Victorian drawing room, as befits 'the nearest approach to aristocracy that this remoter quarter of the parish could boast of', but the scene is entirely natural, Boldwood's perception of it that of long familiarity.

In contrast with the coldness of this portrait, the sheep-dip is hemmed about with Spring until the season is almost tangible:

> The grass about the margin at this season was a sight to remember long . . . Its activity in sucking the moisture from the rich damp sod was almost a process observable by the eye. The outskirts of this level water-meadow were diversified by rounded and hollow pastures, where just now every flower that was not a buttercup was a daisy. . . . To the north of the mead were trees, the leaves of which were new, soft, and moist, not yet having stiffened and darkened under summer sun and drought . . . From the recesses of this knot of foliage the loud notes of three cuckoos were resounding through the still air.[13]

This detailed description of the surroundings, when they might seem not to warrant such comprehensive treatment, is carried throughout the novel, expanding and emphasising the agricultural world in which the story is set, just as the descriptions of the town are repeated and expanded in *The Mayor of Casterbridge*, and the characters of *Under the Greenwood Tree* are illuminated in cohesive vignettes. Here, however, such passages have a second purpose, allowing nature to reflect and magnify human emotions. We glimpse it in the cold harmony of the winter scene with Boldwood's mood — each frozen into a brief moment of listless indecision — but it shows most clearly in Bathsheba's situation after her flight from Troy:

> Up the sides of this depression grew sheaves of the common rush, and here and there a peculiar species of flag, the blades of which glistened in the emerging sun, like scythes. But the general aspect of the swamp was malignant. From its moist and poisonous coat seemed to be exhaled the essences of evil things in the earth and in the waters under the earth. The fungi grew in all manner of positions from rotting leaves and tree stumps, some exhibiting to her listless gaze their clammy tops, others their oozing gills.[14]

Malignancy lurks in nature just as in human affairs — and in both it is a natural part of life. This association of the surroundings with the participants in the drama of life is part of the process by which Hardy builds his world. He gives it breadth and scope by concentrating on agriculture, and defines limits that are ones of character, not space, adjusted to the functional poles of the main buildings, and the man-made concepts they embody. Now he peoples this world, drawing forth men from it as though he were a deity drawing the plastic of men's bodies from the earth, before breathing life into his creations. Oak, described in the same easy, non-committal terms at the very opening of the novel that characterised the description of Old James in *Under the Greenwood Tree*, becomes a reality when the general landscape of nature is permeated by his individuality:

. . . an unexpected series of sounds began to be heard in this place up against the sky. They had a clearness which was to be found nowhere in the wind, and a sequence which was to be found nowhere in nature. They were the notes of Farmer Oak's flute.[15]

Man, forming new patterns from Nature, casts the clarity of his mind upon the regulated confusion of the untamed world. We are drawn inexorably in upon the sound of the flute, to expand again within the new world; we are inside the things described before, and are launched upon an exploration of possibilities from within.

The first part of the novel, dealing with the development of the relationship between Oak and Bathsheba, is bound closely to their roles as young farmer and country girl who might have been a governess 'only she was too wild'.[16] Events revolve around their respective farming roles, the two human figures as apparently unchangeable as the other elements of the natural scene. One juxtaposition, curious at first to ears unused to rural priorities, is reminiscent of John Clare's attempts to display man's indissoluble connection with the natural world by substituting simple reality for elegant logic: 'By making enquiries he found that the girl's name was Bathsheba Everdene, and that the cow would go dry in about seven days. He dreaded the eighth day.'[17]

Semantically, the two facts are inelegant together in the one sentence. Realistically, there is nothing more reasonable than that the two should be taken in conjunction, in such a situation. By interrupting the flow of prose with this juxtaposition, Hardy forces our whole attention onto the necessarily close relationship between the courtship of this couple and their everyday agricultural lives.

Similarly, the description of Oak the suitor is constructed on the same lines as descriptions of other natural objects:

> He . . . put on the light waistcoat patterned all over with sprigs of an elegant flower uniting the beauties of both rose and lily without the defects of either, and used all the hair-oil he possessed upon his usually dry, sandy, and inextricably curly hair, till he had deepened it to a splendidly novel colour, between that of guano and Roman cement, making it stick to his head like mace round a nutmeg, or wet seaweed round a boulder after the ebb.[18]

It is hardly the mannered human vision of much Victorian literature, and the contrast is made the greater by the use of very similar terms to portray one of Oak's sheepdogs:

> George, the elder, exhibited an ebony-tipped nose, surrounded by a narrow margin of pink flesh, and a coat marked in random splotches approximating in colour to white and slaty grey; but the grey, after years of sun and rain, had been scorched and washed out of the more prominent locks, leaving them of a reddish brown, as if the blue component of the grey had faded, like the indigo from the same kind of colour in Turner's pictures. In substance it had originally been hair, but long contact with sheep seemed to be turning it by degrees into wool of a poor quality and staple.[19]

All the elements of involvement in the hard life of agriculture are evident in this nondescript dog (apparently largely of Old English strain, but as far removed from the modern collie as is the present Italian sheepdog, which may be of any convenient mixture of breeds). The weight given to picturing such a minor 'character' in the novel reminds us once more of man's relative stature in the farming world, reliant as he is at this period upon Nature's day-to-day organisation to make his own work prosper. Another image – a favourite of Hardy's – emphasises the harmony of man with his natural surroundings, and also his individual unimportance, as transient as the leaves on a tree; 'We thought we heard a hand pawing about the door for the bobbin, but weren't sure 'twere not a dead leave blowed across.'[20]

This gentle reminder of man's transience, unobtrusive in the early part of the novel, marks Oak's changed character, saddened and wiser from the force of circumstance. He is aware now of his own frailty, and also of the strength he draws from his close association with nature. When we see him with Boldwood's eyes, the sunrise after St. Valentine's Day, he seems, as a representative of Man, both to draw from and give to Nature: ' . . . on the ridge, up against the blazing sky, a figure was visible, like snuff in the midst of a candle-flame.'[21] It is an idea developed more fully in *The Return of the Native*,[22] but even here the sense of a perfect union between Man and Nature is very strong. Man casts the light of his understanding on the world, but to do so he must draw from Nature the fuel of that understanding.

The same glow goes on to touch Warren's malthouse,[23] suggesting the same rooted harmony with nature as is given explicitly to the man; and the other major buildings in the novel share in this involvement as they are variously involved with men in their natural roles.

These roles come to life vividly in the most powerfully described event in the whole novel – the thunderstorm after harvest supper. Oak's weather-reading skills, like his ability in deciphering the stars, are evidence of the harmonious existence of such a community in nature. The landscape of fields and farm comes alive in detail, and acts in close harmony with the man whose life is a part of the same landscape. Even at the height of the storm, Oak merges perfectly into the scene illuminated by each flash of lightning: ' . . . the rick suddenly brightened with the brazen glare of shining majolica – every knot in every straw was visible. On the slope in front of him appeared two human shapes, black as jet. The rick lost is sheen – the shapes vanished.'[24]

When the rain at last comes on in earnest he becomes as one with the sky and the earth. 'The rain stretched obliquely through the dull atmosphere in liquid spines, unbroken in continuity between their beginnings in the clouds and their points in him.'[25] It is not a struggle to oppose the elements, but to harmonise with them, taking their strength and using it, and turning aside their destruction when it comes. Oak is a focus for all that is best and most skilled in Man's efforts to achieve a perfect harmony in life. He has been through the personal tragedies that bring the realisation of weakness, and can temper the pride of ability with awareness. In him, Hardy displays all the qualities which combine to make the farming community function. Other characters are, by comparison, sketchy in treatment, since in them Hardy can concentrate on other aspects – of character, circumstance and function — which combine with Oak's skills to portray as fully as possible the whole community.

Bathsheba herself is in every way a farm girl, born into a family of yeoman stock, and too taken up with the rather wild existence she has led in the country to be concerned with advancing herself. 'She's so good-looking, and an excellent scholar besides — she was going to be a governess once, you know, only she was too wild.'[26]

When she takes over her uncle's farm, it is only her sex that raises doubts as to her ability to run it herself, and those doubts she soon dispels by an obviously competent management of affairs (her dismissal of Oak, and subsequent re-hiring, are the result of emotional involvement rather than evidence of lack of foresight in farm matters). Throughout the novel, no matter how violent or complicated her private affairs, she is able to recognise the paramount needs of her farm. In the event, it is she, helping Oak to save the ricks, who proves more reliably agricultural in mood than the unfortunate Boldwood, who loses most of his crop in the thunderstorm. Others rise and fall about her, but she, the perfect successor to her uncle, maintains the steady middle course. Images of her, though fewer and less prominent than those involving Oak, are nevertheless entirely to do with Nature. Like Oak, she is a dead leaf upon the wind: 'He heard what seemed to be the flitting of a dead leaf upon the breeze, and looked. She had gone away.'[27] In her passage through the woods on horseback, 'The rapidity of her glide into this position was that of a kingfisher — its noiselessness that of a hawk.'[28] And when courted by the brilliant Troy 'No christmas robin detained by a window-pane ever pulsed as did Bathsheba now.'[29]

In many ways, she is the perfect counterpart to Oak. Her emotional uncertainty, her forwardness, her apparent recklessness, are all tempered by an inborn respect for the way of life she leads, and an instinctive knowledge of how far she can bend the day-to-day rules of the farm. Mistakes, when she makes them, are personal; in business matters she takes no decision that is irreversible. (The one mistake that might have harmed the farm, her marriage to Troy, is prevented from large-scale damage by circumstance. It can be argued that it would have led to disaster eventually, but in the context of the novel the question does not arise.)

Boldwood receives even less attention from imagery than Bathsheba, his place in the community being implied rather than stated. His farm, scarcely mentioned, is apparently successful (though he is only a tenant), since he is described by Liddy as 'a gentleman-farmer at Little Weatherbury',[30] and the occasion of his neglect of the ricks occasions much comment locally, being produced as evidence of his temporary insanity in the appeal to the Home Secretary after the killing of Troy. Occasional images seem to reflect the comfortable union of the farming and genteel ways of life; 'Boldwood went meditating down the slopes with his eyes on his boots, which the yellow pollen from the buttercups had bronzed in artistic gradations.'[31] In the passage describing his impression of the frozen morning, images of the drawing room combine easily and naturally with images of the farm. His standing is rather like that of the successful Henchard in *The Mayor of Casterbridge*, at the highest social level which still admits of personal involvement in a working community.

Other, less important, characters also centre on Oak as the symbol of farm life, drawing a personal involvement with nature from occasional strong images. ' . . . his frosty white hair and beard overgrowing his gnarled figure like the grey moss and lichen upon a leafless apple-tree'[32] describes the maltster at our first meeting with him. As with the images of Bathsheba (of wild birds) and Boldwood (the juxtaposition of farm and drawing room) the images are suited to the character, being of old apple trees, the staple of his involvement with the community. Fanny, fleeing to meet Troy, is compared to the lambs of the farm on which she worked: 'He had frequently felt the same quick, hard beat in the femoral artery of his lambs when overdriven.'[33] Like them, she is a victim of circumstance, whose brief span of years is soon terminated by the harsher realities of life in the rural world.

More happily, the minor characters appear together at the shearing supper, and twilight touches the revellers with a soft light that emphasises the utter harmony of their celebrations with a natural world that provides the bounty they celebrate:

> The sun had crept round the tree as a last effort before death, and then began to sink, the shearers' lower parts becoming steeped in embrowning twilight, whilst their heads and shoulders were still enjoying day, touched with a yellow of self-sustained brilliancy that seemed inherent rather than acquired.[34]

Troy is locally supposed to be the illegitimate son of the Earl of Severn, but born into the family of a poor doctor. As with all the major characters except Boldwood (whose long standing in the community seems to serve as sufficient local connection), great care is taken to emphasise his family links with the area. Bathsheba's deceased uncle is discussed at length at the malthouse (her parents are mentioned, but are of considerably less importance, having died early), as also are the close connections of Oak's family with the maltster's, a circumstance which confers on him familiarity by association.

Hardy is working here to establish something of that 'class of stationary cottagers' on whom this farming world is stated to depend, in the Preface. So too, when he describes the ancient barn, he is at pains to point out the static nature of rural society:

> The citizen's *Then* is the rustic's *Now*. In London, twenty or thirty years ago are old times; in Paris ten years, or five; in Weatherbury three or four score years were included in the mere present, and nothing less than a century set a mark on its face or tone. Five decades hardly modified the cut of a gaiter, the embroidery of a smock-frock, by the breadth of a hair. Ten generations failed to alter the turn of a single phrase.[35]

However, having demonstrated the element of continuing change which kept Casterbridge pulsing with life, it seems unlikely that Hardy would have been so insensitive to the more familiar farm world, even allowing for his relative literary immaturity. The Preface seems, by its bland contradiction of the reality of the novel, to be more of a sop for the Victorian reading public, who could comprehend a rustic idyll, but not a working rural community.

A dating for *Far from the Madding Crowd* depends solely on the internal evidence of Farmer Boldwood. Aged about forty at the time of these events, he is described in *The Mayor of Casterbridge*, at the time of Henchard's bankruptcy, as 'a silent, reserved young farmer.' Oak, twenty eight years old, is at that age when men cease to preface 'man' with 'young' in their description of him; it is therefore reasonable to suppose that about fifteen years have elapsed since Henchard's bankruptcy, setting this novel firmly in the 1860s. (This link between the two novels seems the kind likely to appeal to regular Victorian readers of Hardy's work, who can feel they have some kind of 'local' status by their recognition of a local man. Certainly there seems little reason otherwise for this entirely fortuitous mention of one of Henchard's anonymous creditors, in the later novel.) The

Casterbridge of *Far from the Madding Crowd* contains the same Corn Exchange that figures in *The Mayor*, fifteen years earlier (the Exchange actually demolished in Dorchester in 1848) and the Union Workhouse (1836, but absent from *The Mayor*). It avoids reference to the railways (a second line, the Great Western, was opened in 1857) or other modern innovations. Above all, the main London highway becomes the Casterbridge — Weatherbury road, as deserted as the turnpike must have been in these years of the railway boom (all the main coach routes in this area had been closed by the 1850s).

In short, Hardy has selected his material very carefully, where it is identifiable, to negate any impression of period. Dating, based on such evidence, is impossible — in keeping with the assertion in the text of a kind of rural limbo in time.

Yet even this assertion, considered carefully, does not deny the possibility of change. Three or four score years may be the present, but what of the fifth, sixth and seventh score years?

In fact, just as the later *Mayor of Casterbridge* actually comes alive by the operation of perennial change, and fills out the stated rigidity of the community to a more flexible reality, so in *Far from the Madding Crowd* the stated fixity of rural life is brought alive by a process of natural change and development. Those 'stationary cottagers' are rather poorly represented, since the entire novel concentrates, not on a complete community, with married couples, social roles and hours of work and leisure, but a working farm world, where characters are seen largely through their roles on the farm. Oak is of course the clearest example, combining as he does the skills of modern shepherding with ancient knowledge and practical ability. And far from being stationary, he is very much in the mould of Henchard, seeking his fortune anew at Weatherbury. In fact, many of the characters are very mobile indeed: Bathsheba comes from Norcombe Down, where she had apparently arrived not long before; the maltster's family is divided between Norcombe and Weatherbury, while his account of his own travels takes him over most of Dorset; Troy necessarily travels a great deal in the army, and later even reaches America; and poor Fanny drifts around the county apparently aimlessly.

In fact, Oak's similarity to Henchard is quite marked. Both are men of strong character, skilled in their own ways, and succeeding by ability and personality. Yet Oak also contains something of Farfrae, being open to modern ideas, and young enough to adjust to force of circumstance:

He had passed through an ordeal of wretchedness which had given him more than it had taken away. He had sunk from his modest elevation as pastoral king into the very slime-pits of Siddim; but there was left to him a dignified calm he had never before known, and that indifference to fate which, though it often makes a villain of a man, is the basis of his sublimity when it does not.[36]

At every turn, Oak accepts his lot, and works to make the best of it. He is proud, but not too proud, forceful, but not too much so. Boldwood falls, and he is offered the tenancy in his stead; then comes Bathsheba, and he accepts her hand, and farm, as a happy alternative to emigration. Permanent as he may be, and permanent as is the world he represents, there is nothing stationary in him or it.

2.

The skills of Gabriel Oak are many, and are given greater weight than any other aspect of practical life in this novel. Like the descriptions of the markets and fairs in *The Mayor of Casterbridge*, which established the county mercantile nature of the novel, Oak's lore crops up again and again throughout the novel, with equally impressive emphasis on every occasion:

The Dog-star and Aldebaran, pointing to the restless Pleiades, were half-way up the Southern sky, and between them hung Orion, which gorgeous constellation never burnt more vividly than now, as it soared forth above the rim of the landscape. Castor and Pollux with their quiet shine were almost on the meridian: the barren and gloomy Square of Pegasus was creeping round to the north-west; far away through the plantation Vega sparkled like a lamp suspended amid the leafless trees, and Cassiopeia's chair stood daintily poised on the uppermost boughs.

'One o'clock,' said Gabriel.[37]

Gabriel was already among the turgid, prostrate forms. He had flung off his coat, rolled up his shirt-sleeves, and taken from his pocket the instrument of salvation. It was a small tube or trochar, with a lance passing down the inside; and Gabriel began to use it with a dexterity that would have graced a hospital-surgeon.

Passing his hand over the sheep's left flank, and selecting the proper point, he punctured the skin and rumen with the lance as it stood in the tube; then he suddenly withdrew the lance, retaining the tube in its place. A current of air rushed up the tube, forcible enough to have extinguished a candle held at the orifice.[38]

The impending storm is portended by wild and domestic creatures:

> Every voice in Nature was unanimous in bespeaking change. But two distinct translations attached to these dumb expressions. Apparently there was to be a thunder-storm, and afterwards a cold continuous rain. The creeping things seemed to know all about the later rain, but little of the interpolated thunderstorm; whilst the sheep knew all about the thunder-storm and nothing of the later rain.[39]

And this is followed by a very prosaic rending of the ricks into pounds sterling at risk.

Oak is described as 'a man who clung persistently to old habits and usages, simply because they were old'.[40] But the skills which lead him at last to the tenancy of Little Weatherbury are a mixture of old and new — the trochar, and the moveable hut, and the mathematical calculations, mixed with the knowledge of stars and weather — which arises solely from the desire to work most efficiently at his job. It is this, like the respective merits of Henchard and Farfrae in their landscape, which dictates the emphasis given to certain 'traditional' aspects of the work. Purely gratuitous 'colour' has no place in the world of Oak's farming. It is verbal lore that comes out in the forefront of everyday life. This is the continual affirmation that Oak's traditional skills are not his alone, but a mere example of similar attributes amongst the other workers in the agricultural landscape. 'Crooked folk will last a long while.'[41] ''Tis well to say "Friend" outwardly, though you say "Troublehouse" within.'[42] '"Twill be a gallant life, but may bring some trouble between the mirth.'[43] 'New lords, new laws'.[44] '"Tis clane dirt; and we all know what that is.'[45] 'She've a few soft corners to her mind, though I've never been able to get into one, the devil's in't.'[46] 'You'll come to a bit o'bread.' 'From pillar to post.' 'In black and white'. 'Better wed over the mixen than over the moor.' 'Pride and vanity have ruined many a cobbler's dog. Dear, dear, when I think o'it, I sorrows like a man in travel!'[47] 'Well, I hope Providence won't be in a way with me for my doings. . . . Your next world is your next world, and not to be squandered offhand.'[58]

Compared with this flood of sayings, some well-known, others not, but all connected with ways of making rural life on the farm an easier thing for all, there is one reference to the Weatherbury stocks, and the few references to hiring and sheep fairs, and the market — this compared with the weight given, in *The Mayor*, to these latter. And quite noticeably there is no weight given to the 'meeting of rural lives' theme that predominates in *The Mayor of Casterbridge* market and fair scenes. In *Far from the Madding Crowd* it is the actual mechanics of being hired, or selling corn, or moving sheep, that come to the fore — examples of the mercantile side of farming, where it touches upon the very different world of Casterbridge.

But where Oak embodies all the virtues of this adaptable world, Troy, by contrast with the harmonies of image and circumstance displayed in the other characters, comes on the scene like a bolt of lightning. But, like the lightning, he is only the agent of destruction; he is not inherently evil. Born and brought up in Weatherbury, and spoiling good prospects by enlisting, he is in many respects similar to Bathsheba. His emotional skirmishes, too, are stormy but sincere. Where Troy differs from other characters is in his attitude to the farming community. To him, the old farmhouse is not a symbol of harmonious adaptation, but 'a rambling, gloomy house'. 'My notion is that sash-windows should be put throughout, and these old wainscoted walls brightened up a bit; or the oak cleared quite away, and the walls papered.'[49] He is the agent for potential destruction whose actions force Gabriel's last-minute intervention to save the ricks. And where Gabriel calculated the loss of £750 'in the divinest form that money can wear — that of necessary food for man and beast',[50] Troy bemoans the loss of £200 on a horse bogged down in the wet going following the storm.[51] Even in his decision to leave Bathsheba and the farm, the image is of gaming. 'He simply threw up his cards and forswore his game for that time and always.'[52]

Yet, despite his apparently ill-atuned character, Troy is a part of this life. Like the storm, he is something upredictable, potentially damaging, and unwelcome; yet he is also dazzling, splendid, and a brilliant image of man's power, as the storm is of nature's. 'His sudden appearance was to darkness what the sound of a trumpet is to silence. Gloom, the genius loci at all times hitherto, was now totally overthrown, less by the lantern-light than by what the lantern lighted.'[53] At times, he almost seems to share in nature's power, in a manner purer and more striking than Oak, whose life is one of harmony and partnership. The scarlet-coated figure seems to equal the power of nature, and complement her: 'The soldier turned a little towards the east, and the sun kindled his scarlet coat to an orange glow.'[54] Henchard, Tess and Jude can all look back to a common root in this first of Hardy's characters to display impatience or dissatisfaction with a world that, for all its beauty of structure, conspired to deny the free spirit of man its path to self-discovery. For a moment, in Troy, the meteoric brilliance of Man seems to rival the very universe:

> Beams of light caught from the low sun's rays, above, around, in front of her, well-nigh shut out earth and heaven – all emitted in the marvellous evolutions of Troy's reflecting blade, which seemed everywhere at once, and yet nowhere specially. These circling gleams were accompanied by a keen rush that was almost a whistling – also springing from all sides of her at once. In short, she was enclosed in a firmament of light, and of sharp hisses, resembling a sky-full of meteors close at hand.[55]

But meteors of course burn themselves out, and it is to the world of Gabriel Oak and Bathsheba Everdene that *Far from the Madding Crowd* owes its success.

4 The Landscapes of 'The Great Heath': *The Return of the Native*

I.

The 'Great Heath' of Hardy's Wessex stretches from Dorchester to Poole, spreading its inhospitable arms south to the Purbeck hills and north to the valleys of the north Winterborne and the Stour. It is a well established precept that *The Return of the Native* is based on certain places and features, well known to Hardy by their proximity to his childhood home, which have been removed to imagined sites somewhere in the centre of this heath.

It can be argued, perhaps more forcibly with *The Return of the Native* than with any other of Hardy's novels, that it is the imaginative sweep of the landscape which concerns us, not the narrow reality. This is a reasonable criticism with relation to the novel's intended effect, but if a topographical reality exists it must be explored as fully as possible before we can understand how Hardy has used his departures from the reality, and how he has used his adherence to it. It may initially offend the imagination to limit the bounds of the novel, but it will take little study of the area actually defined to realise the true scope it provides for a panorama of the mind. There is, after all, little reason why our acceptance of the limited geographical scope of the other novels discussed, which does not detract from the largeness of their effect, should be denied to *The Return of the Native*.

Hardy himself created the myth of a vast heathland, and executed his portrayal of it so skilfully that, as in the case of Casterbridge, even local people can recognise their surroundings in his atmospheric portrait. In the Preface to the novel he says:

> Under the general name of 'Egdon Heath' . . . are united or

typified heaths of various real names, to the number of at least a dozen, these being virtually one in character and aspect, though their original unity, or partial unity, is now somewhat disguised by intrusive strips and slices brought under the plough with varying degrees of success, or planted to woodland.

Seventeen years later, in his postscript to the same novel, Hardy added:

. . . certain topographical features resembling those delineated really lie on the margin of the waste, several miles to the westward of the centre. In some other respects also there has been a bringing together of scattered characteristics.

As with the Preface to *Far from the Madding Crowd*, Hardy's direct statements of intent and action need to be treated with circumspection. His now well-established desire to edit his life and work before public perusal, evidenced by his self-authorship of the *Life*, and the destruction of most of his notes and papers, casts some doubt on well-known assertions.

The first passage hints at the reality by the word 'typified', but goes on to suggest that the heath was more extensive in Hardy's childhood (the period of the story is stated in the Preface to be between 1840 & 1850). In fact, the northern ridge of heath (which is the only part portrayed in *The Return of the Native*) was already, when the novel was written, little more than a spine of rough land between the Frome and Piddle valleys, dissected by woods and pastures and crossed by several roads. For the most part it was little more than half a mile at its widest, this wild land.

However, in one part the heath did still stand unmolested: Puddletown Heath, totally isolated from the low spine of heaths to its east, embattled by woods, meadows, and arable farms, and bordered by two turnpikes and a well-used track, lay almost untouched. Two miles by one and a half miles, the nearest heaths of comparable size lay south, between Woodsford and Moreton, and east, north of Wool and Wareham; the one lay two and a half miles away as the crow flies, across the rich Frome watermeadows, and the others nearly five and over eight miles respectively, beyond the pastures of Tincleton and Affpuddle. In the second passage Hardy suggests that the topographical 'coincidences' of *The Return of the Native* with Puddletown Heath do not detract from the representative nature of his Egdon Heath. Yet

A Map of the heathlands
from Dorchester to Poole,
showing the differing
characteristics of each.

Scale: approx. ½" = 1 mile

Puddletown

Dorchester

R. Frome

Hills thus:

Upland heaths thus:

Sandy heaths (New Forest type) thus:

Other sandy heaths thus:

Marshy heaths thus:

the Moreton heath lies in a low, marshy area of country, where stunted trees rise on the low hummocks of land which manage to push their heads above the reed-beds and dark, acid soil. This is a featureless landscape, crossed by raised tracks which wend their way between the treacherous levels, and relieved only by the occasional field reclaimed from the grudging soil. It is the farther limit of the heathland behind Poole Harbour, and doubtless once covered the whole swampy floor of the Frome valley, as far as the cliffs of Dorchester.

The heath above Affpuddle is of similar character to Puddletown Heath, but so attenuated as to be little more than a strip of uncultivated land, with fertile valleys stretching away to the north and the south. It connects with Wool heath, which briefly seems to resemble Puddletown Heath, but soon opens out into wide, sandy levels, with a clear view across to the Purbecks and Poole Harbour. Wareham Heath, farther east, resembles closely the New Forest, of which it is a detached portion: open areas give way to stunted woods, and farmsteads huddle in small enclosures of rough pasture hacked from the gently undulating land. Away to the south lies the vast sweep of Arne, similar at first to Moreton Heath, but pierced by the innumerable channels and estuaries of Poole Harbour. The older alluvial deposits of Moreton are here replaced by fresh sand (this heath has been deposited in the mouth of the Frome since Roman times, when Wareham was a flourishing port.)

But this is not the landscape of *The Return of the Native*. After his magnificent opening chapter, Hardy tells us that 'the above-mentioned highway traversed the lower levels of the heath from one horizon to another.'[1] The lower levels. Hardy's Egdon Heath, after that one romantic defnition of 'Bruaria', is confined to an upland world, of valleys and steep heights, heather and furze, and wild ponies cropping the rough plants. It is the haunt of the great bustard, a bird of the open upland, and in summer the bracken clothes its slopes in the profusion of gravel soil.[2] 'Egdon Heath' and Puddletown Heath are not only topographically synonomous, but imaginatively synonomous. They are one and the same.

Of course, I have so far only argued the particular and, by Hardy's time, virtually unique character of Puddletown Heath, and suggested the similarity of Hardy's 'Egdon'. There remains the topographical accuracy of the imagined landscape, when compared with the real, to be discussed. Is it, as Hardy states, no more than a use of places in a generalised setting, or is it more concrete than this?

In fact, we are coming now to a process already seen in Hardy's novels, as he adjusts his landscape to suit each atmosphere or theme. The mercantile world of Casterbridge; the world of social village life in Mellstock; the agricultural world of the Weatherbury farms; and now the world of the open heath. In the other novels, the mere fact of geographical proximity has not been allowed by Hardy to colour the purity of each vision with the character of its neighbour: each world carefully excludes all mention of the others, except in a context allied to itself. And each world carefully excludes the physical proximity of Egdon. Farfrae and Elizabeth-Jane have to drive beyond Weatherbury to reach their 'Egdon'; Troy and Bathsheba meet for a demonstration of swordplay in a ferny hollow on the very northern edge of the heath, where it spreads across the sky – but it is not mentioned; and the Mellstock villagers go blithely about their business with the heath stretching contentedly across their whole eastern skyline – they mention Blooms-End – yet never have occasion to notice it. Why, when all Hardy requires of his settings is that they overlook unwanted features, should it be necessary for him in this novel to pick up the setting of Egdon and move it, ponies, furze, bustards and all, to a point some miles away? All he need do is overlook the existence of features unwanted in the atmosphere of *The Return of the Native*; and indeed, this is all he does.

His description of Puddletown Heath is so accurate that the characters of the novel can be followed, step by step, as they cross its soaring heights and deep-cut valleys. Each journey from Rainbarrow to the 'Quiet Woman'; each excursion under Rainbarrow's high shoulder to Mistover Knap; each passage of a vehicle up the Mistover track, or onto the Anglebury turnpike; the 'quag' that Diggory and Thomasin encounter before that last fateful climax; the valley where Thomasin plays with her baby, can all be identified and followed as though we walked with them. The natural landscape of Puddletown Heath is reproduced with an accuracy as great as that devoted to the representation of Stinsford in 'Mellstock'.

Other features, however, are less definable. The 'Quiet Woman' inn, based on an inn whose walls now shelter only cows, is placed with some accuracy on the Anglebury turnpike (the Wareham-Dorchester road), and Blooms-End nestles at the foot of a last outcrop of heath, facing up a small valley.[3] Yet the distance between the two, never mentioned, seems in the novel to be greater than the reality of a mile. Thomasin is not allowed by Wildeve to walk it every day; her anguish during the final storm is increased by the knowledge that

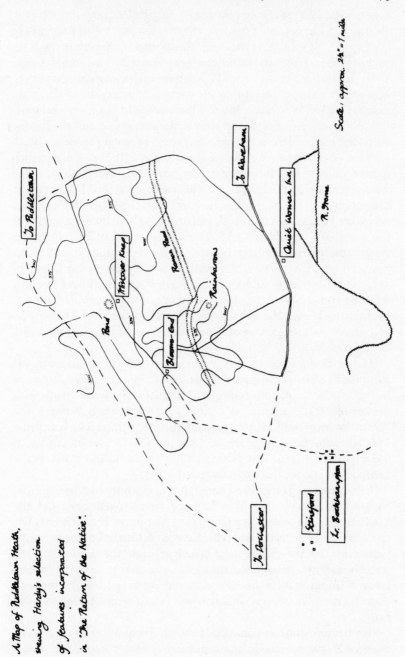

A Map of Puddletown Heath,
showing Hardy's selection
of features incorporated
in 'The Return of the Native'.

To Puddletown

To Wareham

To Dorchester

Stinsford

Lr. Bockhampton

Quiet Woman Inn

R. Frome

Mistover Knap

Roman Road

Rainbarrow

Blooms-End

Road

Scale: approx. 2½" = 1 mile

Clym will not have reached the inn during the 'considerable interval' she waits. [4] The turnpike road, so clear by the inn, seems suddenly to vanish, as Blooms-End has no mentioned connection with it: journeys to and from the farmhouse are all carefully undefined, unlike those to and from the inn. The cottages of the lesser characters, apparently grouped on the heath without connection to the main houses, suddenly draw closer when needed – Fairway becomes Clym's neighbour; Thomasin runs to the cottage nearest the inn for help after the incident at the weir. But they are never precisely placed.

North of Rainbarrow, the lonely house at Mistover Knap, which existed only in Hardy's imagination, shimmers indefinably on the ridge overlooking the broad valley below Rainbarrow. It is not in the exact centre of the heath, but to stand atop the ridge and gaze out across the Frome valley to south and east is easily to imagine oneself at the heart of a desolate world. There is no sight of Dorchester or Puddletown from here, and the farms of the river valley are lost in the haze. Nearer, the folds of the heath itself disgorge rising shreds of mist, and the great shoulder of Rainbarrow, actually lower than the Mistover ridge, seems to loom up and cut off the horizon. It is here, near the track from Hardy's cottage to Puddletown, where he must so often have walked, that we can come closest to the imaginative reality of 'Egdon'. [5]

The track itself becomes the circuitous vehicle route from the turnpike to Mistover (the part which leads to Puddletown vanishes, as does the other end, connecting with the Bockhampton road). This mysterious track, cutting as it does across the heath between the 'Quiet Woman' and Mistover, would brighten the trackless expanse of heather and furze which reaches out towards the distant cottage at 'Alderworth' – were it not for its ability to vanish as easily as the turnpike to the south, when the need arises.

These features having been noted, it remains only to point out that Yellowham woods, the Weatherbury farms, Mellstock, and the London road, all vanish as though they had never been, there is but one road, and one track, and these have no definable course or limits. Gone, too, are the rough fields which separate the heath from the water-meadows: though the meadows, as a distant haze, do appear. Gone is Ilsington Wood to the east, and the easy turnpike route to Alderworth. All beyond Puddletown Heath seems never to have existed.

But having gone beyond Puddletown Heath, and having mentioned Alderworth, the location and reality of this second area needs to be established. Taking Lea's work as the basis, it is reasonably well-established that Alderworth is a cottage which lies on the small patch of upland heath between Affpuddle and the Frome valley, dominated by a huge knoll ('The Devil's Bellows'). 'East Egdon' is supposed to be Affpuddle, and the other places named – Throope Corner, Throope Great Pond, Rimsmoor Pond, and Oker's Pool – are all taken direct from the life. What Lea does not mention is that, while these places are named, their relationship to one another is far from that one might expect, and the relationship of the area to the previously-described main body of Egdon even more curious.

The approach to the cottage is described accurately, and the ponds, when they appear, are given positions close to the real; but Throop Corner moves to the west of the cottage (its real position is eastward), and Affpuddle, if it is indeed the basis for East Egdon, is moved from a position one mile north-west of the cottage, to somewhere two miles to the west. There is a road between the cottage and the two villages mentioned (is Briantspuddle, really only half a mile north, not one mile east, the basis for the other village?), which apparently connects somehow with the turnpike; yet no-one ever walks it.

As far as the distance between the cottage and the main body of the heath is concerned, the estimate varies. It is six miles when Clym sets out, four by the later stages of the book and variable between. Diggory, walking from Throop Corner (at this stage, west of the cottage) reaches the inn in half an hour. Johnny Nunsuch, wandering overfar from home, plays at Throop Great Pond (on the map, a good seven mile walk).

And what of the intervening landscape? According to the novel, it is simply open heath. The reality is that it would take a very perverse man to avoid the many roads and tracks available on the ridge for the convenience of the walker; and the relation between this 'corridor' of heath and 'Egdon' is as carefully altered. Where is the Mistover track? And where is Rainbarrow, when Clym lays his mother down only a mile from the Blooms-End cottages (neighbouring Blooms-End itself), in a spot that must be in the shadow of the Rainbarrow ridge?

Quite simply, Hardy has created a very concrete landscape, in describing Puddletown Heath, but has had to overcome the problem of extending his story beyond the real heath, to create a sense of space, without destroying the atmosphere of the untamed heathland. Instead of simply ignoring the areas that do not fit his plan, he has allowed the character of Egdon to stand for the new setting as well, whilst so jumbling features and distances that we cannot attempt to step outside his created landscape. The definable features which give form to Egdon might also limit it, unless they are in their turn overlooked when space is needed in preference to form. This general principle applies to all places mentioned outside the heath. Try to find any of the churches at which marriages take place in *The Return of the Native*, and you will discover that the details given cannot be transferred to a map. Nor, despite references to them, are we given any hint of the whereabouts of Budmouth, Casterbridge or Weatherbury. Having taken such trouble to establish an atmosphere of limitless heath, Hardy is very careful not to provide any opportunity for us to find limits, however vague.

What emerges most obviously through this search for a 'real' Egdon heath is that there is only one clearly-defined feature in the novel: the heath itself. In the same way that Casterbridge is given life through the physical nature of the town, so the scattered community of the heath comes alive as part of the landscape of place. But each aspect of the Stinsford area with which Hardy deals is given its own particular treatment, according to its nature. Casterbridge has the sheer physical bulk of buildings; the farms have their poles of major functional buildings, with broad masses of landscape as the background; Mellstock relies on its people for its depth. Now, the heath is given precedence with a clear definition of its character and shape, yet without any outer limits. It has the definition of Casterbridge, combined with the fluidity of the farms.

The evidence of this central role given to nature is strengthened by the lack of prominence given to buildings. Comparing this novel with *The Mayor of Casterbridge*, *Under the Greenwood Tree* and *Far from the Madding Crowd*, the mixed roles of the buildings in those three – as bulk and focus, as extensions of their inhabitants, and as poles – are replaced by something far less prominent, yet just as important; they are foci for the three groups of characters who act out the tragedy of the novel. The heath is the landscape, but the ephemeral human features upon it are the mode of access to the human drama in which it plays its part.

In keeping with their simple role as definable places without individual character, the three houses – Mistover Knap, Blooms-End, and the Quiet Woman – are never fully or lengthily described, inside or out. Their features are illuminated as needed, in very similar fashion throughout. The inn appears first:

The front of the house was towards the heath and Rainbarrow, whose dark shape seemed to threaten it from the sky . . . The garden was at the back, and behind this ran a still deep stream, forming the margin of the heath in that direction . . . But the thick obscurity permitted only sky-lines to be visible of any scene at present.[6]

Next is Mistover Knap:

A white mast, fitted up with spars and other nautical tackle, could be seen rising against the dark clouds . . . Within was a paddock in an uncultivated state, though bearing evidence of having once been tilled; but the heath and fern had insidiously crept in, and were reasserting their old supremacy. Further ahead were dimly visible an irregular dwelling-house, garden and outbuildings, backed by a clump of firs.[7]

And finally, Blooms-End:

Beyond the irregular carpet of grass was a row of white palings, which marked the verge of the heath in this latitude. They showed upon the dusky scene that they bordered as distinctly as white lace on velvet. Behind the white palings was a little garden; behind the garden an old, irregular, thatched house, facing the heath, and commanding a full view of the valley.[8]

Clym's cottage, which figures briefly as a human focus, is given a treatment as cursory, though it also bears the only reference to a domestic garden:

From her elevated position the exhausted woman could perceive the roof of the house below, and the garden and the whole enclosure of the little domicile . . . There lay the cat asleep on the bare gravel of the path, as if beds, rugs, and carpets were unendurable. The leaves of the hollyhocks hung like half-closed umbrellas, the sap almost simmered in the stems, and foliage with a smooth surface glared like metallic mirrors. A small apple tree, of the sort called Ratheripe, grew just inside the gate, the only one which throve in the garden, by reason of the lightness of the soil.[9]

In every case, most emphasis is given to what lies around the houses, and the slight differences between them allow only enough scope to build up a composite picture of a representative heath dwelling. The picture is of a low, rambling, thatched house, surrounded — almost in defiance of the heath — by a sparse garden, and with ramshackle outbuildings and paddock. Even the inn, which might be regarded as a focus for human social life, shares this function equally with the other dwellings, the mummers' play being rehearsed at Mistover, and the Christmas party and later wedding celebrations taking place at Blooms-End. Most strikingly, however, all the descriptions suggest a human habitation crouching at bay before the heath, unassertive in an environment that could so easily overwhelm it, yet maintaining its position only by an act of defiance.

But beyond this sketching of the houses, Hardy elaborates little (adding equally imprecise pictures of the outbuildings), with the one exception that each of the three main houses is seen inside, in its chimney-corner (a point of some relevance later in the discussion). While the physical details of the heath are precise, we are never given the exact location of any of the houses. Were it not for the identification of the 'Quiet Woman' with Duck Dairy, and of Blooms-End with Hardy's cottage there would be no way of establishing their positions more closely than that of Mistover Knap, which could occupy any spot along a crescent of ridge several hundred yards long. Like their separate appearances, precise location is not important to the function of these houses. The cottages which are grouped near each house remain steadfastly undelineated, with no clear position in relation to their neighbours; and the other human features on the heath — track, road, paths, churches and villages — are no more than barely mentioned.

By contrast with its man-made features, the heath itself is treated with a depth and forcefulness reminiscent of the descriptions of house and barn in *Far from the Madding Crowd*, but with the continuing emphasis given to the town in *The Mayor of Casterbridge*. The opening chapter of the novel contains probably the most famous of all Hardy's descriptive prose:

> A Saturday afternoon in November was approaching the time of twilight, and the vast tract of unenclosed wild known as Egdon Heath embrowned itself moment by moment. Overhead the hollow stretch of whitish cloud shutting out the sky was as a tent which had the whole heath for its floor.[10]

It is the 'Titanic form' of the area, a picture in contrasts and masses, the concept of great sweeps of open land and sky, dark and light, without differentiation of shape or form, or any acknowledgement of detail. It is the view of a man who sees the overall landscape, and temporarily forgets what lies at his feet.

This aspect of the heath is quite similar to the qualites of landscape in *Far from the Madding Crowd*, although starker, more pure in its treatment of the subject. What comes later, with Eustacia on Rainbarrow, is something new to Hardy – the sound of his landscape. The voices of nature, mentioned in other novels, here become a central part of the atmosphere of the heath:

> Gusts in innumerable series followed each other from the north-west, and when each one of them raced past the sound of its progress resolved into three. Treble, tenor, and bass notes were to be found therein. The general ricochet of the whole over pits and prominences had the gravest pitch of the chime. Next there could be heard the baritone buzz of a holly tree. Below these in force, above them in pitch, a dwindled voice strove hard at a husky tune. . . . It was a worn whisper, dry and papery, and it brushed so distinctly across the ear that, by the accustomed, the material minutiae in which it originated could be realised as by touch. . . . They were the mummified heath-bells of the past summer, originally tender and purple, now washed colourless by Michaelmas rains, and dried to dead skins by October suns.[11]

This, the voice of the heath, is reiterated during the novel, in much the same way that the market scenes in *The Mayor of Casterbridge* are reiterated. Hearing supplies those innumerable gaps in our knowledge of the scene, while opening up an appreciation of what lies beyond the immediately perceptible. Just as the visual images of country men engaged in animated business suggest the colourful tapestry of Casterbridge's economic life, so the aural images of the heath suggest the curiously harsh harmonies of Nature, the seasons sweeping over vegetation that strives for individual survival only so far as it promotes the survival of an entire species. The sound gives us a far clearer picture of the heath in its natural perspective than does the visual detail which surrounds characters who venture into it.

The second mode of visual portrayal derives from the human need to find points of reference in a landscape. We see the grand harmony of a titanic scene, but must ask more, discover the minutiae that are its building blocks:

The pool . . . which seemed as dead and desolate as ever . . . would gradually disclose a state of great animation when silently watched awhile. A timid animal world had come to life for the season. Little tadpoles and efts began to bubble up through the water, and to race along beneath it; toads made noises like very young ducks, and advanced to the margin in twos and threes; overhead, bumble-bees flew hither and thither in the thickening light, their drone coming and going like the sound of a gong.[12]

Eustacia lies among tall ferns and watches the lizards. Mrs. Yeobright lies out on the shephered's thyme and watches the ants. Clym's solitary night walk is marked by other creatures of the heath:

In almost every one of the isolated and stunted thorns which grew here and there a nighthawk revealed his presence by whirring like the clack of a mill as long as he could hold his breath, then stopping, flapping his wings, wheeling round the bush, alighting, and after a silent interval of listening beginning to whirr again. At each brushing of Clym's feet white miller-moths flew into the air just high enough to catch up on their dusty wings the mellowed light from the west.[13]

And the reddleman focuses the creatures of the day:

Though these shaggy hills were apparently so solitary, several keen round eyes were always ready on such a wintry morning as this to converge upon a passer-by. . . . A bustard haunted the spot . . . Marsh-harriers looked up from the valley by Wildeve's. A cream-coloured courser had used to visit this hill . . . Here in front of him was a wild mallard — just arrived from the home of the north wind.[14]

It is only when men appear, or we see a house, or a distant lone heron, that some kind of definition in the normal sense is given to the landscape: for it is not the features which make Egdon. It is the heath itself, an entity which pulses with the life of myriad creatures and plants, and whose voice, through them, is the wind.

But where, in this self-contained landscape, does man have a place? It exists without need of his understanding or definition, yet, as the presence of the definable foci of the houses suggests, he has a more permanent relationship with this aspect of Nature than a mere pioneering venture into the wilderness.

Obviously there is no place here for the economic union of Man and Nature (*The Mayor of Casterbridge*), or the gentle domesticity of cottage gardens (*Under the Greenwood Tree*), or the harmony of agriculture (*Far from the Madding Crowd*). As the descriptions of the houses showed, there is a curious mixture of submissiveness and defiance in Man's life on the heath. In a land as harsh as this one is to outside elements, there must be harshness in Man's relationship with his surroundings:

> Wildeve's Patch (was) . . . a plot of land redeemed from the heath, and after long and laborious years brought into cultivation. The man who had discovered that it could be tilled died of the labour: the man who succeeded him in possession ruined himself in fertilising it. Wildeve came like Amerigo Vespucci, and received the honours due to those who had gone before.[15]

Man, by a process of attrition, wrests a living from the heath. But there is no victory. 'Within was a paddock in an uncultivated state, though bearing evidence of having once been tilled; but the heath and fern had insidiously crept in, and were reasserting their old supremacy.'[16] Elsewhere on the heath, Blooms-End dozes in a state of equilibrium, neither gaining nor losing; and men cut turf and furze from the hills, making as little permanent impression as the grazing ponies.

Clearly, the process is one of struggle and hardship, success and failure being as the blossoming and decease of the annual ferns. Men live in a natural balance as old as the heath itself:

> . . . its summit, hitherto the highest object in the whole prospect round, was surmounted by something higher. It rose from the semi-globular mound like a spike from a helmet. The first instinct of an imaginative stranger might have been to suppose it the person of one of the Celts who built the barrow, so far had all of modern date withdrawn from the scene.[17]

Rainbarrow is the only man-made object on the heath that seems to be in perfect harmony with its natural surroundings. It has the permanence of the creatures and plants which, dying each year, are always present; the individual human figures which, by their very individuality are made to seem impermanent, are thus given a timeless association with the heath (a timelessness not affected by the vague reference to 'Celts', as the Roman past was too distant and imprecise to limit Casterbridge).

> There the form stood, motionless as the hill beneath. Above the plain rose the hill, above the hill rose the barrow, and above the barrow rose the figure. Above the figure was nothing that could be mapped elsewhere than on a celestial globe.[18]

But there is something more than the simple association of another species with the heath. Living in a relationship of constant struggle with Nature, man is part of a unity that includes the whole of the natural universe:

> Such a perfect, delicate, and necessary finish did the figure give to the dark pile of hills that it seemed to be the only obvious justification of their outline . . . The scene was strangely homogeneous, in that the vale, the upland, the barrow, and the figure above it amounted only to unity. Looking at this or that member of the group was not observing a complete thing, but a fraction of a thing.[19]

The image is similar to one applied to Gabriel Oak, when Boldwood saw him as the snuff in the candle flame of the sun.[29] But it is here, in *The Return of the Native*, that Hardy gives the clearest exposition of the thread running through all his Wessex novels, of Man as part of a landscape. There is no justification of the situation, or philosophical abstraction of its relevance to Man; merely a statement of fact, that the earth has borne Man, and still bears him, in a harmony of past and present that needs no explanation. The past of the earth and the past of Man are inextricably interwoven, as are their present. Without Man, there would be no harmony of the scene; but without man, there would be none to perceive or care at its loss — 'the only obvious justification'.

This is why the gain and loss of cultivable land, and the attentions of furze and turf cutters, are balanced. There is an inherent equilibrium in such a landscape that cannot be disturbed by individual triumphs or failures.

Further evidence of this relationship between Man and Nature appears in one structural aspect of the novel that is taken directly from

the earlier *Far from the Madding Crowd*. In that novel, we are led into
the main action by way of Oak's flute, its patterned sound placing
order upon the magnificent wildness of Nature, and calming it for its
new role as partner with Man. Here, the ordered ways of agriculture
are of little use; Man places some recognisable stamp upon Nature,
while adjusting himself to cope with his unalterable environment.
' . . . though the gloom had increased sufficiently to confuse the
minor features of the heath, the white surface of the road remained
almost as clear as ever.'[21] We have been told that the road is almost a
part of the heath, rather than an imposition by Man; but it lays a
recognisable feature on the dark mass, and leads us to the first human
contact of the novel.

However, this first, visual lead takes us only as far as a prelude: the
story as it has occurred to the present. It remains for the second aspect
of the heath, its voice, to lead us into the main action of the novel:

> Suddenly, on the barrow, there mingled with all this wild
> rhetoric of night a sound which modulated so naturally into the
> rest that its beginning and ending were hardly to be distinguished.
> The bluffs, and the bushes, and the heather-bells had broken
> silence; at last, so did the woman; and her articulation was but as
> another phrase of the same discourse as theirs. Thrown out on the
> winds it became twined in with them, and with them it flew
> away.[22]

The sigh of Eustacia, borne with the wind, focuses our attention as
did Gabriel Oak's flute, and we are drawn from the vast expanse of
nature into the world of men upon the heath.

However, that 'prelude' deserves further explanation. It describes
for us the events that have led up to the drama about to be unfolded
on the heath; the troubled courtship of Wildeve and Thomasin, the
other aspects of which are soon to emerge. It also 'sets the scene',
preparing us for Clym's return, and establishing the antecedents of
the main characters. More than this, though, it prepares us for the
world of the heath, and creates an atmosphere of darkness and light,
cold and warmth and mingled sounds, which is to carry throughout
the novel. The basis for all this is the bonfire:

> It was as if these men and boys had suddenly dived into past ages,
> and fetched therefrom an hour and deed which had before been
> familiar with this spot. The ashes of the original British pyre which

blazed from that summit lay fresh and undisturbed in the barrow
beneath their tread. The flames from funeral piles long ago kindled
there had shone down upon the lowlands as these were shining
now. Festival fires to Thor and Woden had followed on the same
ground and duly had their day.[23]

Having established the harmony of Man and Nature in their
Universal context, Hardy now delves into its human aspect, to
portray the unity of past and present which is the foundation for the
harmony of all things of the moment. Here, in a blaze of light, the
same curious order that encompasses Man and Nature in all time, past
present and future, in Casterbridge, is brought to the apparently wild
and unencompassable heath. Each part of Hardy's world has its own
place and relation to all other parts. Nothing, not even the louring
heath, can stand entirely alone. ' . . . to light a fire is the instinctive
and resistant act of man when, at the winter ingress, the curfew is
sounded throughout Nature.'[24] It is the end of the old year, and the
commencement of a dark interregnum, a time of hardship and death
for all. By lighting their fire, these heath men show a coincidence of
understanding and practice with their distant forebears in their
relationship with Nature. The pattern is as old as Man himself.

It is apparent, however, that the relationship here described is not
the warm and patterned discipline of the farms to the west and north.
There are no lambs to bring hope to this gloom, as they did to Oak's;
this is the time of utter darkness. Life seems suspended in this
atmosphere; it is obvious that warmth, light and human company
mean more than the simple social conviviality of the maltster's room.
Men gather together because only in numbers can they find the
strength to defy the encroaching cold and darkness:

As the nimble flames towered, nodded, and swooped through
the surrounding air, the blots of shade and flakes of light upon the
countenances of the group changed shape and position endlessly.
All was unstable; quivering as leaves, evanescent as lightning. . . . Nostrils were dark wells; sinews in old necks were gilt
mouldings; . . . bright objects, such as the tip of a furze-hook one
of the men carried, were as glass; eyeballs glowed like little
lanterns. Those whom Nature had depicted as merely quaint
became grotesque, the grotesque became preternatural; for all was
in extremity.[25]

The leaping flames pick out human features as clearly as the details of buildings in *The Mayor of Casterbridge* or *Far from the Madding Crowd*, but there is nothing fixed or definite in these figures. None is a recognisable aspect of some person, but a line or shadow or gleam in the general mass, picked out from the all-pervading darkness. Individuals merge into a single human composite, with a new strength imparted to it, 'for all was in extremity'. When the crazy dance begins amidst the showering sparks of the dying fire, it is a terrifying travesty of those relatively ordered affairs in the other novels – but it is no less human or real for that. It is simply closer to the elemental reason for its existence, a pagan frenzy of defiance, just as Man is closer in every way on the heath to his elemental relationship with Nature. The sparks become an image of human life, doomed in the death of the single fire, yet annually enduring, rekindled from the ashes; they rely for their existence on the darkness all around, yet are in a state of constantly balanced opposition with it, wavering first to light, then to darkness, but never losing their overall equilibrium. The mercantile, domestic and agricultural harmonies of the other novels are replaced by a harmony of balanced dispute, dependent on each force, Man and Nature, striving with the other, yet never actually overcoming. Man defies the heath by his fiery gesture, yet the following spring he will once more rely on it for his living.

This image of Man and heath is picked up in the incidents and structure of the story, as events blaze up, die away and rekindle, their powerful descriptions being surrounded by and set into the constantly-recurring atmosphere of the heath. It is also, in more detail, taken up by the chimney-corners mentioned earlier: the only interiors given adequate description in the novel. The occasion and intensity of each description varies, but they are all based on a contrast of warmth and light within, cold and darkness without:

> The fire soon flared up the chimney, giving the room an appearance of comfort that was doubled by contrast with the drumming of the storm without, which snapped at the window-panes and breathed into the chimney strange low utterances that seemed to be the prologue to some tragedy.[26]

Yet each household, as has already been made clear, is imaginatively a part of the heath itself, a mere shell for human presence thereon, and the bronze burial-urns on the window-sill are the internal reminders of all that has been associated with Rainbarrow, the focus of Hardy's treatment of Man and Nature in this novel.

2.

The character most closely associated with the heath is, of course, Diggory Venn. He and his van emerge from it as though they were mere flickerings of its vital spirit:

> At length he discerned, a long distance in front of him, a moving spot, which appeared to be a vehicle, and it proved to be going the same way as that in which he himself was journeying. It was the single atom of life that the scene contained, and it only served to render the general loneliness more evident.[27]

He continues to haunt the action of the novel in much the same way as the heath, sometimes watching, sometimes listening, sometimes intervening, to good or ill effect. His position is as anomalous as that of Gabriel Oak, in *Far from the Madding Crowd*, but there is none of the shepherd's noble self-negation mixed with concerned involvement. The reddleman is a kind of the Shakespearian fool, the voice of conscience — but he is the voice of the heath, rather than of humanity, putting words to the 'strange low utterances' that the wind voices as the 'prologue to some tragedy'.[28] There is no overt moral assessment of his status, or of his curious determination to interfere in what are, after all, the affairs of others; his advancement of his own case is accepted readily, though he has no claim on Tamsin's affections. Oak offers advice, but little action; Diggory offers little advice, but much in the way of action.

Throughout the novel, the appearances of Diggory and his van are in remote quarters of the heath: 'Brambles, though churlish when handled, are kindly shelter in early winter, being the latest of the deciduous bushes to lose their leaves. The roof and chimney of Venn's caravan showed behind the tracery and tangles of the brake.'[29] Or, like some creature of the darkness, he emerges into the light that surrounds some human scene, to offer his help or hindrance: 'While he was closing the little horn door a figure rose from behind a neighbouring bush and came forward into the lantern light. It was the reddleman approaching.'[30] In fact, Diggory's relevance as a main character in the novel is minimal: he is much more of a trigger to the events in which others are caught up.

A more passive role is given to the minor characters – Grandfer and Christian Cantle, Timothy Fairway, Humphrey, Olly Dowden, Susan Nunsuch – who, singly or collectively, act as a chorus in the Greek fashion to the main events, involved but objective, and unable to alter the course of things. Their image, building and lighting the bonfire, is that of humanity on the heath in its state of uneasy equipoise with Nature. They go nowhere, alter nothing, and stir no more than the flying sparks from the fire; they are the enduring, unassuming human form. Their cottages are undescribed, and their home lives apparently non-existent (only Susan Nunsuch is seen beneath her own roof); they come alive in the novel only when they work to make a living from the heath, or when they are a background to the battles of men and Nature in which the major characters are involved.

Tomasin, nominally one of these major characters, is in fact the counterpart of the labourers, in a higher social context. She is the perfect middle-course of man upon the heath. 'A fair, sweet, and honest country face was revealed, reposing in a nest of wavy chestnut hair. It was between pretty and beautiful.'[31]

Always the innocent victim, she bends with each blow of fate, accepting and awaiting. Her character remains virtually unaltered throughout. Her reward is survival (by Hardy's preferred ending to the novel, no more than survival). Captain Vye and Mrs. Yeobright, too, are of little consequence as major characters. The good Captain is little more than a device to give suitable freedom of action to Eustacia in an age when no girl could safely indulge such eccentricity as hers without a sheltering wing. For Mrs Yeobright, her fate is to become a trigger for the conflict between Clym and Eustacia.

It is Eustacia herself who strikes us most forcibly, and her battle to overcome the encircling tentacles of the heath, to launch herself into her imaginedly ideal world, that involves others in a hopeless tangle of relationships. It is her sigh, mingling with the voice of the wind in the heather, that leads us into the dark world of the heath, and her image is one of blazing darkness. Where others live in neutral shades of harmony, fighting only to preserve a balance in their lives, she is unashamedly in opposition, to both the heath and the centres of light and warmth that contain its human elements.

She had Pagan eyes, full of nocturnal mysteries, and their light, as it came and went, and came again, was partially hampered by their oppressive lids and lashes; . . . Assuming that the souls of men and women were visible essences, you could fancy the colour of Eustacia's soul to be flame-like. The sparks from it that rose into her dark pupils gave the same impression . . . Egdon was her Hades, and since coming there she had imbibed much of what was dark in its tone, though inwardly and eternally unreconciled thereto.[32]

In many ways, she is similar to Troy, seeking always to change her situation or her surroundings in the search for a nebulous ideal. But where he blazes, meteor-like, across the ordered world of Weatherbury Farm, she smoulders with a passion barely restrained, that occasionally erupts in moments of flame. 'Her appearance accorded well with this smouldering rebelliousness, and the shady splendour of her beauty was the real surface of the sad and stifled warmth within her.'[33] Where other characters gather to strengthen themselves by the communal kindling of fire, or seek out light or hearth as the necessary focus of human survival on the heath, Eustacia walks alone, her light and warmth within her. The heath-croppers gather in curiosity round the lantern that lights the dice game; they flee from the lone figure of Eustacia.[34] But a more rational examination of her character begins, sadly, to reveal that the powerfully evocative passion of her nature is undirected, childish and, in the context of an Egdon that is never consonant with any man's mood, but a real force in its own right, quite pointless. In this sense it is Clym who dominates the novel. Although his name does not appear in the title, he is undoubtedly the returned Native whose idealistic struggles with the realities of the heath lead, at last, to his own evangelistic impotence. Where Eustacia represents the unthinking challenge to the heath, Clym represents a very clearly human intellectual challenge to a life that demands acquiescence. There is no doubt that the portrayal of two such very different personalities detracts from the strength of each, until neither impresses us as much as they are potentially able. Eustacia's undirected rebellion becomes the restless impatience of a spoilt child when compared with the idealism and thought of Clym's deliberate attempt to bring education to the heath. Yet that same idealism, seen in the context of the heath's realities, seems as childish and unconsidered as Eustacia's reaction. Eustacia, in her death, is magnificent, but pointless – to drown by accident is no ending of the tragic stature of Henchard's self-negation – but Clym's pathetic wanderings amongst people roused, not by his teaching, but by the curiosity of his own life, are scarcely more inspiring.

It is in the potential of Clym's life, however, that his real significance emerges. He is the first of Hardy's characters consciously to question the way of life around him, and although the return in *The Mayor* to less clearly-stated philosophies indicates Hardy's general failure to realise here a coherent attack upon the Wessex world of his early novels, the attempt foreshadows the clearly-worded assaults of *Tess* and *Jude*.

5 Transition:
The Woodlanders

Having designed his enclosed landscapes, almost accidentally in the first instance, and having brought them to perfection in *The Mayor of Casterbridge*, Hardy was in search of fresh vehicles for his ideas. To attempt merely to portray another type of landscape – perhaps woodland – as he had done to perfection with Casterbridge, would be to attempt no artistic advance, and even risk failure by comparison. In addition, having found the model of the tragic hero in the individuals who strive to impress their own personalities on these efficient landscapes, Hardy needed in future to look beyond the destructive social criticism of his early years, and apply his writing to the positive formation of ideas. In the last three Wessex novels, *The Woodlanders, Tess of the d'Urbervilles*, and *Jude the Obscure*, this is what he does.

In all the novels so far discussed, the setting has been – with minor excursions – the area around Stinsford. and Dorchester. In *The Woodlanders*, for the first time, the geographical location is elsewhere in Dorset. Exactly where the countryside of this novel is supposed to lie is a point open to discussion, and to differing interpretations. Hardy himself asserted that he used characterstics of a number of places, set generally into the real area around High Stoy in Dorset, but even this identification is complicated by the fact that in the first edition of the novel he refers to Bubb Down, also a real place, but ten miles farther west than High Stoy.

F. B. Pinion, in the *Thomas Hardy Year Book No. 2* (1971) examined the details of Hardy's amendments closely, coming to the conclusion that he originally set Little Hintock between Melbury Osmond and Bubb Down, but later shifted it east, to the High Stoy area, to prevent identification of Mrs. Charmond with any of the Ilchester family, whose residence was Melbury Sampford. Whatever the reasons for the shift of location, later editions reflect quite closely the landscape around High Stoy. It must be borne in mind here that the old

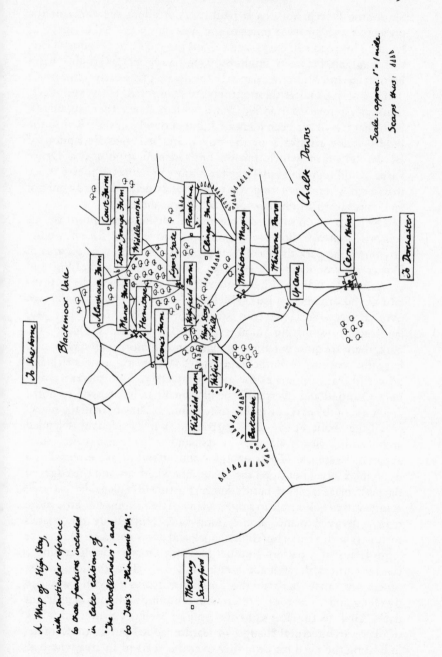

A Map of High Stoy, with particular reference to those features included in later editions of 'The Woodlanders', and to Tess's 'Flintcomb Ash'.

Sherborne-Dorchester coach road ran not along the route of the present A.352 but two miles to the west, by way of the village of Leigh. This road still exists, and rejoins the A.352 at Dogbury Gate, the windgap between High Stoy and Dogbury. On this basis, Hermitage and Minterne Magna fit the details given early in the novel quite closely, as far as their settings are concerned. However, if one thinks of *Far from the Madding Crowd*, with its detailed description of a barn that has never been identified, but certainly never stood in the Piddle valley landscape of the novel, and its brief description of Boldwood's farm which, but for Lea's identification of it as Druce Farm, could represent any large farmhouse in Dorset, it is easy to see that, even where the setting was more closely defined, Hardy did not feel constrained to describe only what was there.

The explanation of Hardy's choice of Melbury Sampford for his original landscape, however, is more tentative. One reason is quite obvious – the park there contains probably the largest single area in Dorset of woodland organised to be both visually pleasing and economically viable. Where other large Dorset houses have plantations and ornamental parks, Melbury Sampford combines the two over a large area – several square miles – with farmland (also landscaped) insinuating amongst the thickets and rides. Outside the park, there are quite extensive orchards (much more widespread until later this century). And the huge estate, with its immensely rich and powerful seat, dominates the area completely. Two places – Melbury Osmond and Evershot – lie like small satellite towns, to north and south of the park, guarding the entrances. They bear all the marks of villages built up by local patronage, with attractively-blended architecture, clearly-defined limits, and a size that belies their apparent sleepiness. Their energies and attention are directed not upon themselves but upon the estate. Elsewhere around the edges of the park, places that can hardly sustain the title of 'village' lie scattered at intervals of half a mile to a mile. Many of them consist of little more than a decayed manor house (long since eclipsed by the estate's fortunes) with a tiny church or chapel, and a few cottages. Others are large farms of a pattern unusual in south Dorset – built around a central courtyard, with the house flanked by its outbuildings. Yet others are farms built in the longhouse manner, with barn and dwelling under one roof – often with rambling additions of different dates. All show the clear signs of eclipse by Melbury Sampford: a lack of major architectural changes or features added purely to decorate, indicating the need for economy over the years in an area where all roads and riches tend to the fortune of the large house. There is an air of suspension in time, as though no regression had occurred, but equally no advance.

The buildings and society of *The Woodlanders* should be clearly enough recognisable in the description of this area; indeed, though it cannot be determined whether the place gave rise to the feeling, or the feeling to a search for the place, few other parts of Dorset so completely fit the nature of the book.[1] There should also be recognisable, however, the Stinsford area, with its large house (Kingston Maurward), the decayed manor (Waterston),[2] the ramshackle small farms and cottages (around Lower Bockhampton, mainly), the woodland and the orchards.

The opening paragraph of the novel describes, in fact, not so much the road that runs beside the Melbury Sampford Estate, or the old Sherborne /Dorchester high road below High Stoy, both of which were never so closely bounded by trees, but rather the main Dorchester /London road where it climbs Yellowham Hill (and where the footpath from Hardy's cottage to Waterston crosses Yellowham Wood), and the trees hang heavy on each side:

Here the trees, timber or fruit-bearing as the case may be, make the wayside hedges ragged by their drip and shade, their lower limbs stretching in level repose over the road, as though reclining on the insubstantial air. At one place . . . the leaves lie so thick in autumn as to completely bury the track.[3]

In this, the last of his detailed landscapes, Hardy is imaginatively turning once more to his Stinsford home for material. It is quite noticeable, in all his novels, that only this limited area provides the scope for his closely involved landscapes; all others — as the far-flung settings of *Tess* and *Jude* — are seen with the eye of artistic detachment.

One possible reason for Hardy's choice of a location elsewhere in Dorset when he was so obviously drawing on his Stinsford experiences may lie with this very detailed coverage of the area in his earlier Wessex novels. The logical setting of *The Woodlanders*, on the wooded estates of Kingston House, had already been mentioned in *Under the Greenwood Tree*, and if Hardy intended — as will seem clear — to isolate this landscape as thoroughly as his early Wessex settings, he could not afford to have it seen that it overlapped the village scenes of the earlier novel.

A Map of Melbury Sampford,
shewing the concentration
of decayed manors and
medium-sized farms around
the big estate.

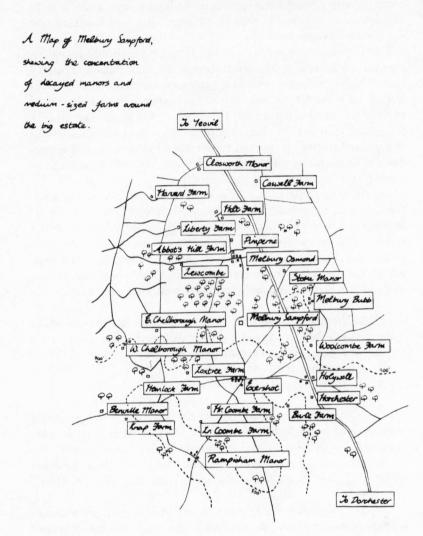

Scale: approx. 1" = 1 mile.

In fact, the topographical creation of *The Woodlanders* bears many similarities to *Far from the Madding Crowd*. There is the same location of the area in relation to a main road, with the same woolly indefinition of precise locations for houses and woods within the 'defined' setting. In much the same way as in *Far from the Madding Crowd*, people's lives are focused not on a precise entity (as in *The Mayor of Casterbridge* and, in different manner, in *The Return of the Native*) but on certain 'poles' of attention – the main individual buildings. The trees and the physical features are all there, but they have the same force as the farmland in *Far from the Madding Crowd*; they are atmospheric rather than precise. Precision in this novel is given to the focal buildings, and they too are not descriptive portraits of particular buildings but 'types' of the buildings they represent.

It is therefore much more difficult to attempt to discover how Hardy has 'landscaped' this novel.

There are in fact two levels to the setting. At the surface level Hardy describes in some detail the way of life of those engaged in the various aspects of the timber and cider trades; at a less obvious level there are recurrent indications of a wider economic life in the Hintock area.

The most obvious examples of the first level are the buildings. Marty South's cottage is the first to appear, perfunctorily described but fitted immediately into the overall pattern of gentle decay that marks most of the dwellings in Little Hintock:

> The next (cottage), which stood opposite a tall tree, was in an exceptional state of radiance, the flickering brightness from the inside shining up the chimney and making a luminous mist of the emerging smoke. . . . The house was rather large for a cottage, and the door, which opened immediately into the living-room, stood ajar, so that a riband of light fell through the opening into the dark atmosphere without.[4]

The light of human occupation suffuses the cottage, and lays its own characteristic pattern on the darkness without, bringing order to the natural world by linking it with man. And Marty herself is part of the cottage, at the lowest social and economic level of woodland life, as Giles sees her. ' . . . against the sky stood the thatched hip and solitary chimney of Marty's cottage, and (he) thought of her too, struggling bravely along under that humble shelter, among her spar-gads and pots and skimmers.'[5] The human being and her tools of trade and life stand inseparable beneath the sheltering thatch. Already, in the patterns of human light and the basic tools of human trade we can see themes from *The Return of the Native* and *Under the Greenwood Tree* reappearing in this final 'Stinsford' landscape.

Giles Winterborne's house, next up the social scale, also a lifehold, is apparently (from its very brief description) a larger, rambling version of Marty's cottage. Melbury's house, the most fully described of all — though still not given more than a general treatment — is a decayed manor, of the kind of Bathsheba's farmouse:

> It formed three sides of an open quadrangle, and consisted of all sorts of buildings, the largest and central one being the dwelling itself. The fourth side of the quadrangle was the public road.
> It was a dwelling-house of respectable, roomy, almost dignified aspect; which, taken with the fact that there were remains of other such buildings hereabout, indicated that Little Hintock had at some time or other been of greater importance than now.[6]

But it is much newer, closer to the present than the Jacobean farmhouse, and as such it exerts some of the controlled association of ideas which was so important in *The Mayor of Casterbridge*. In that novel, the Roman past was too remote to affect local inhabitants, while yet being an indissoluble part of their history, and therefore of their present lives; set against that, the buildings of the town spoke of a history recent enough to reflect the present in the past. Here, Melbury's house is old enough to be part of the landscape in imagination as well as reality, yet not old enough to lose contact with its human antecedents:

> The faces, dresses, passions, gratitudes, and revenges of the great-great-grandfathers and grandmothers who had been the first to gaze from those rectangular windows, and had stood under that keystoned doorway, could be divined and measured by homely standards of today. It was a house in whose reverberations queer old personal tales were yet audible if properly listened for; and not, as with those of the castle and cloister, silent beyond the possibility of echo.[7]

More than in any previous Wessex novel, Hardy unites the house and its occupants in a warm social intimacy of community and individual history. Even in its clearly described aspects the house is seen more as a working unit than as an entity in its own right. 'The building on the left of the inclosure was a long-backed erection, now used for spar-making, sawing, crib-farming, and copse-ware manufacture in general. Opposite were the wagon-sheds where Marty had deposited her spars.'[8] The emphasis has been shifted from the architectural details of Weatherbury Farm or High Place Hall to the atmosphere of immediate economic partnership based on long but not endless human acquaintance with the building.

A similar tendency to pass over physical details in favour of atmosphere applies to the description of Hintock House itself. The sketchy architectural aspects are swamped by the profusion of natural growth:

> The front of the house was an ordinary manorial presentation of Elizabethan windows, mullioned and hooded, worked in rich snuff-coloured freestone from Ham-hill quarries. The ashlar of the walls, where not overgrown with ivy and other creepers, was coated with lichen of every shade, intensifying its luxuriance with its nearness to the ground till, below the plinth, it merged in moss. Above the house to the back was a dense plantation, the roots of whose trees were above the level of the chimneys. . . . A few sheep lay about, which as they ruminated looked quitely into the bedroom windows. . . . It was vegetable nature's own home; a spot to inspire the painter and poet of still life – if they did not suffer too much from the relaxing atmosphere – and to draw groans from the gregariously disposed.[9]

A great deal of care has been exercised in painting the Hintock dwellings as places of character, without special individual note. They seem as crumbling representatives of a well-established past, sheltering a new generation as easily as a new summer, and as unconcerned at its passing. Each man leaves a mark, but the whole picture is basically unchanged.

In such a context it seems natural that social stances should be quite steady. Marty aspires to Giles, and works for him and Melbury. Giles aspires to Grace, and works for Melbury and Mrs. Charmond. Melbury seeks to put Grace into the company of Mrs. Charmond. And each looks to the level below: Mrs. Charmond deals with Melbury; Melbury deals with Winterborne; Winterborne with Marty. The only social fluidity comes, now as in the past, through love:

In addition to the sentimental relationship which arose from his father having been the first Mrs. Melbury's lover, Winterborne's aunt had married and emigrated with the brother of the timber-merchant many years before — an alliance that was sufficient to place Winterborne, though the poorer, on a footing of social intimacy with the Melburys. As in most villages so secluded as this, intermarriages were of Hapsburgian frequency among the inhabitants, and there were hardly two houses in Little Hintock unrelated by some matrimonial tie or other.[10]

There is a tendency in the characters, as in the buildings, to decay in importance: Fitzpiers, Melbury and South come from families once higher in social and economic status, and we watch Giles fall during the course of the novel. In fact, it is often assumed that the novel deals mainly with the decay of this type of society. Yet the signs of continuing change are all there to be seen. I have deliberately left, until now, one building undescribed. Fitzpiers' house

> . . . was small, box-like, and comparatively modern. . . . The cottage and its garden were so regular in their plan that they might have been laid out by a Dutch designer of the time of William and Mary. In a low, dense hedge was a door, over which the hedge formed an arch, and from the inside of the door a straight path, bordered with clipped box, ran up the slope of the garden to the porch, which was exactly in the middle of the house-front, with two windows on each side.[11]

Far from being representative of the modern Dr. Fitzpiers, encroaching upon the ancient community, this house is occupied by 'a retired farmer and his wife', symbols of the local community in every way. The building is a sign, not of drastic change in an unaltered community, but of permanent change, gradual in its effects, like the marks of people on the older dwellings; after all, Melbury himself is a successful timber merchant, where his forbears were holders of the manor of Little Hintock, then yeomen farmers; and the dying South's family once had their own copyhold land.

But the characters themselves give the lie most forcibly to the idea that Hintock faces drastic alteration from such as Mrs. Charmond and Fitzpiers. Apart from the tendency to decline, already mentioned (a tendency which drags Fitzpiers into the history of·the area, as a representative of an old, decayed family), there is the social rise of

Grace, and the prospering of Melbury's business. For her part, Mrs. Charmond is a purely transient phenomenon, come to her inheritance by marriage alone, and displaced in death by a distant relative, a representative of the long-established traditions of family power and wealth. Her late husband rose through industrial wealth, and is in a sense a precursor of the d'Urbervilles, but the emphasis is all on the new owners' acceptance of old local ways, not upon drastic change consequent on a new 'class' of landlord. There is no suggestion that any changes of a particularly untoward kind are happening: the demolition of Giles' cottage is regretted, but he does not quit the area, and there is no hint that any others are in danger, or that there is an estate policy of destroying the village.[12] Even the emigration of Tim and Suke is carefully placed in its true context; 'they were going to New Zealand. Not but that he would have been contented with Hintock, but his wife was ambitious and wanted to leave; so he had given way.'[13] There is no suggestion of economic necessity in their departure, only of personal choice.

The village itself, the second level of the setting, presents a continuous and unaffected aspect to the events of the novel. The opening description gives a clue to its extent:

> Only the smaller dwellings interested him; one or two houses whose size, antiquity, and rambling appurtenances signified that notwithstanding their remoteness they must formerly have been, if they were not still, inhabited by people of a certain social standing, being neglected by him entirely. . . . Half a dozen dwellings were passed without result.[14]

As the novel proceeds, and we become acquainted with Fitzpiers' house, and the rambling nature of the village, with cottages spread out over the slope of the hill, it begins to appear that it is in fact much larger than might have been supposed from the concentration upon the dwellings of those engaged in the woodland trade. In addition, the references to farms and farmers that crop up from time to time suggest the proximity of other trades and livelihoods. And what of all the young men and women who flock to the Midsummer's Eve rituals? There are not enough men employed by Melbury and Winterborne to provide such a wealth of young people.

The difficulty so far in discussing *The Woodlanders* has been to show how Hardy has encapsulated a particular way of life, and certain events therein, not by totally isolating them from other aspects of the area, but by leaving an undercurrent of permanent community which is never defined, but never falters, above which he then builds the particular world of timber, cider and estate. It is certainly the most sophisticated of all the novels so far discussed in its method of encapsulation.

However, when our attention is turned to the main landscape of the novel, the woodland itself, we are on surer ground in attempting to differentiate between the reality and Hardy's landscape. The buildings, as described, are typical rather than particular, and their relative positions are indefinite. Similarly, the roads and tracks mentioned in the course of the novel — Hintock Hill, the lane below Dr. Fitzpiers', the back road to Ivell — are given no kind of accurate location, extent or character. It is all very similar to *Far from the Madding Crowd*.

But the woodland itself, which characterises this novel, is different from any other landscape so far created by Hardy. It is as atmospherically pervasive as the market scenes in *The Mayor of Casterbridge*, but it permeates the novel far more than those scenes (which are reiterated, but merely lead on to other aspects of the novel, and do not themselves spill over into other sections); it is as apparently self-contained as the Heath in *The Return of the Native*, but has none of the power, or the opposition of man and nature; it is economically as important as the farmland of *Far from the Madding Crowd*, but where the society of the farms is there important, here it is man's individual relationship with the trees around him that matters — Winterborne's empathy with young trees, Marty's skill with spars, South's psychological relationship with the tree, and so on.

The result of the new status is that the woodland seeps into every aspect of life in the novel, only varying in its particular relationship, whether emotional, superstitious, social or economic. From the moment when the hypothetical traveller finds himself 'in the vicinity of some extensive woodlands, interspersed with apple-orchards',[15] to the closing words of Marty South, 'whenever I plant the young larches I'll think that none can plant as you planted; and whenever I split a gad, and whenever I turn the cider wring, I'll say none could do it like you.'[16], there is nothing in *The Woodlanders* which the trees do not touch. The opening description is atomspheric; the view of the village's lights through the bare winter boughs sets the closeness of buildings and trees, as events will show their interdependence. Love and tragedy walk together amongst the plantations: Dr. Fitzpiers meets Grace at the bark-flaying; he is injured by newly-cut underbrush. Even when the characters are elsewhere, the trees seem to follow them: Giles stands beneath his apple tree when he meets Grace at Sherton Market, and they talk of orchards on the journey home; the newly-married Grace meets Giles again in Sherton, with his travelling cider-press; and the members of the search-party that finds the reunited Grace and Fitzpiers at Sherton were 'just as they had come from their work of barking, and not in their Sherton marketing attire'.[17] The woods and orchards in their every aspect greet us at every turn of events.

This is not to say, however, that Hardy portrayed the woodland as all-enveloping. He opens by mentioning that the woods are 'interspersed' with orchards, and there are open spaces around the village; Dr. Fitzpiers watches the gate opposite his house, which gives onto an open field; Suke and he pass the night amongst the new-mown hay of a meadow. Even when the passages deal with the economic state of timber in local life, the scattered nature of the woodland is evident:

> Plodding thoughtfully onward he crossed a glade lying between Little Hintock woods and the plantation which abutted on the park. The spot being open he was discerned there by Winterborne from the copse on the next hill, where he and his men were working.[18]

Elsewhere, the timber merchant follows Fitzpiers down one of the rides of the estate.

All these are features of a mixed woodland and farming area, and of economically-run woodland. But, like the farmers and artisans of Little Hintock, the open spaces and fields, being features that might distract from the importance of the woodland life, are given little attention, and are always described in close proximity to trees of some kind. No open space, field, building or person is allowed to appear as the major feature in any scene – it is always the woodland that predominates.

In this context, the characters themselves are seen (excepting minor characters for the moment) on three levels. At the level most closely involved with the woods and orchards are Giles and Marty, whose work with the trees around them is based on a deep understanding of, and sympathy with, their natural environment—the closest comparison is with Gabriel Oak, whose knowledge and skills are central to *Far from the Madding Crowd*.

He had a marvellous power of making trees grow. Although he would seem to shovel in the earth quite carelessly there was a sort of sympathy between himself and the fir, oak, or beech that he was operating on; so that the roots took hold of the soil in a few days. . . .

Winterborne's fingers were endowed with a gentle conjurer's touch in spreading the roots of each little tree, resulting in a sort of caress under which the delicate fibres all laid themselves out in their proper directions for growth. He put most of these roots towards the south-west; for, he said, in forty years' time, when some great gale is blowing from that quarter, the trees will require the strongest holdfast on that side to stand against it and not fall.[19]

This skill is passed on to Marty, who takes up Giles' equipment and business on his death; and both, as seen in the planting of trees for gales forty years hence, are working for the continuation of man's relationship with nature. The trees they fell were planted by their parents; the trees they plant will be felled by their children. And so it goes on.

But once again the new relationship of man and nature comes through. On the heath, it was a balance of opposing forces; on the farm it was a harmony of growth; in the woods, it is the use and control of nature for man's own ends:

He rose upon her memory as the fruit-god and the wood-god in alternation: sometimes leafy and smeared with green lichen, as she had seen him amongst the sappy boughs of the plantations: sometimes cider-stained and starred with apple-pips, as she had met him on his return from cider making in Blackmoor Vale.[20]

There is harmony, but the man is the dominant force, the 'wood-god', whether in the plantation or in the orchard.

Melbury and Grace are the next on the social scale, and at one remove from the woodlands. For Melbury, it is the economics of life that matter – the title-deeds and shares he shows Grace, and the thriving timber business – but he is not above working with his men, and his own body reminds him, and us, of his past connections:

He knew the origin of every one of these cramps; that in his left shoulder had come of carrying a pollard, unassisted, from Tutcombe Bottom home; that in one leg was caused by the crash of an elm against it when they were felling; that in the other was from lifting a bole.[21]

Grace, the product of her father's ambitions for her, moves on a social level above her origins, but it is her past that comes through when Fitzpiers vanishes. She is seen on the same level as Giles:

> He looked and smelt like Autumn's very brother, his face being sunburnt to wheat-colour, his eyes blue as corn-flowers, his sleeves and leggings dyed with fruit stains . . . Her heart rose from its late sadness like a released bough; her senses revelled in the sudden lapse back to Nature unadorned. The consciousness of having to be genteel because of her husband's profession, the veneer of artificiality which she had acquired at the fashionable schools, were thrown off, and she became the crude country girl of her latent early instincts.[22]

The images are reminiscent of those applied to Bathsheba, but where they flowed naturally through our vision of her, they seem here to leap up from the constraints of earlier imagery, as Grace's heart leaps from its sadness. It is in passages like this that Hardy displays his true skill with the harmonious landscapes of man and nature that were his early vision – yet they are also a reminder that the form has been perfected, is here only being polished and refined, and that such a route does not lead to greater artistic or philosophical truths.

Melbury's other attachment to his woodland world, the family one, links him with Fitzpiers, as Grace's name and social graces also do. Just as the woodland can be seen as atmosphere, economy, setting or power, so the connection with it of the characters can exist validly in different ways. Giles' and Marty's connection, emphasised by their names, is direct – Winterborne is the name of two Dorset streams, and South is obvious as the aspect of sunlight and growth. Melbury's connection, and that of Fitzpiers, is at one remove, via the social dominance of certain local families – here, Melbury is the name of the estate and villages whose location Hardy chose for Hintock in the first edition of the novel; Fitzpiers, whose family connection is supposedly with 'Oakbury Fitzpiers', is named from Okeford Fitzpaine, in the Blackmoor Vale.

However, as Melbury and Grace have different relations to their woodland world, so Fitzpiers moves in a world of higher social values, more cosmopolitan than his family connections suggest. His old connection with Mrs. Charmond, before she made her advantageous marriage, takes him into the social world of the large estate, whose relationship with the woodland is an economic one. If a comparison is made with Sergeant Troy, one can see the same natural connections between the setting and the character; just as Troy, though devastating in his effects, was a part of the farming community, so Fitzpiers, in his family connections with the area, is also a part of the community, and not an outside agent.

The final level, at the top of the economic and social pyramid, is represented by Mrs. Charmond, whose wealth is maintained by people she hardly knows, who are yet closely connected with her via both woodland and human society.

Love, and the economic chain of rural life, are represented in *The Woodlanders* through the pyramid of these characters. Where the other novels avoid the spread of social grades and the wider economic considerations of a community's way of life, here these are explored in detail. The simple three-level society of *The Mayor of Casterbridge* and the single economic unit of the farm in *Far from the Madding Crowd* are expanded and explored, each character interlinking through work and love to each other. The encapsulation of landscape is continued, but the complexities of man's own relationships within a rural community are given their first extensive treatment.

The five novels so far discussed display, in concert, the complex interaction of Man and Nature, and the further complexities within human society, all operating over a time-scale that makes the past an integral part of the present, and the future a concern for all. The minor characters of *The Woodlanders*, whom I set to one side in the discussion of the more powerful figures, are the reminder of this process. For the first time in the novels they are not an active part of the plot, except in very minor ways. Gone are the 'Greek choruses' and the 'third estate' of *The Return of the Native* and *The Mayor of Casterbridge*. Marty and Suke Damson represent the lowest social level.

But despite their relegation to a minor part in the action of the novel, these characters are nevertheless extremely important. Like the trees, they are always there. Just as major characters can escape the trees by entering a house (or occasionally in Sherton), so they can sometimes escape these human watchers, in the lonelier parts of the woodland. But essentially there is a constant presence of humanity, in its social or economic roles, no matter what the events.

So there are various layers of impression to be peeled off before we can get to the bones of the novel. First, and faintest, the village as a whole, with farms and farmers, labourers and maids; then the human presence which overlies that and pervades woods and village alike; then the woods themselves, which are virtually omnipresent; and at last the complexity of human involvement which has its being in this setting. It is as though Hardy had approached his subject from without, focusing on one detail that contains within itself a microcosm of the whole society – the woodland and its people – then inverted his view of it, so that the detail came first, and the broader layers after.

The whole process gives us, at last, yet another landscape of Hardy's world. The emphasis is different, because the subject is different, but the process of selection and emphasis is essentially the same as in, for instance, *The Return of the Native*. There, the heath is perceived visually, in detail and in the mass, and aurally, through the tones of its plant and animal life. Here, the woodland is seen as it truly is, owing its existence to human economics, but imparting of itself to human society. The woods are not as closely encapsulated as the heath or the farm or the town because their relationship with man is more complex, less assured. Yet the landscaping of reality to create a picture of the true situation is as effectively done – with less omission, more selection and emphasis, but with the same end in view.

The Woodlanders was written immediately after the completion of *The Mayor of Casterbridge*, using an idea conceived at the time of the successful reception of *Far from the Madding Crowd*, more than ten years earlier.[23] Hence, no doubt, the similarities to both these earlier novels. It is, as the discussion of the landscape has shown, conceived in the same successful mould as the other Wessex novels, and in many ways represents a more mature version of *Far from the Madding Crowd*.

However, if that were all it represented, it would be a retrograde step in Hardy's development as a novelist. *The Mayor* had already taken the encapsulation technique as far as it could go, and any new setting, however different from those previously used, could only equal the artistic success of that novel, at the very best, or more likely fall short of its ideal.

Of course, Hardy was not averse to writing to fulfil a public demand, rather than in pursuit of an artistic ideal, and in many ways *The Woodlanders* shows his reliance on an established technique. However, it also displays certain radical departures from the style of the 'pastoral' novels.

The most obvious change is the shift of setting, from the Stinsford area, north to the edge of the Blackmoor Vale. There is the practical reason already mentioned for this alteration, in that, although there are extensive woodlands around Stinsford, and cider orchards were attached to most of the larger cottages and farms of the area, and the whole parish lay under the sway of the Kingston Maurward estate (Mrs. Martin's husband being mostly absent from the area, she was often in residence alone), the landscapes of the four previous novels had so effectively covered the area that Hardy would have had great difficulty in using local material to create an entirely fresh setting. But more notably, in choosing a location farther afield from his childhood home, Hardy is following the precedent of his romances and novels of ingenuity, which use Dorset locations (with 'Wessex' names) in much the way that one might expect of ordinary 'regional' novels, describing local settings with accuracy, and utilising landscape to reflect mood,but never allowing it to figure as a major element of the drama.

The Woodlanders, of course, does not use its landscape in such a frivolous manner. It encapsulates and elevates it as seriously as any of the earlier 'pastoral' novels – thus combining, for the first time, major aspects of the previously very distinct styles of Hardy's novels. And this is not the only way in which Hardy seems, for the first time, to be actively seeking to merge the two styles. In the earlier Wessex novels, certain characters emerge as elements of disruption in the self-contained worlds portrayed – in keeping with the general classification of 'Novels of Character and Environment.'[24] But even here, in apparently independent landscapes, Hardy cannot restrain himself from voicing some of the doubts and questions which figure so prominently in the minor novels. References in footnotes and Prefaces to the destruction of individual buildings, or entire communities, carry a more bitter weight than mere nostalgia (as might be expected of an audience looking for an escapist idyll) might warrant. Education of individuals begins to show its disruptive influence within the community: it threatens the courtship of Fancy and Dick, in raising her social standing; it is the status symbol Henchard thrusts on Elizabeth-Jane, which also widens the gap between them; it is the empty dream of the pitiable figure of Clym Yeobright at the end of *The Return of the Native*. The curious stratification of Victorian society shows briefly in the empty-headed would-be brides of Donald Farfrae. And, above all, love and the necessary Victorian consequence of marriage – in all its awful indissolubility – rises to shatter lives and wreck the passing hopes of individuals. From the very start, Hardy displays a remarkable insight of the complexities of human attraction – a far deeper understanding than the simplistic morals and religion of most of his Victorian readers, to whom marriage and duty, if not love, were synonymous. The single-minded passion of Boldwood which, once stirred, cannot be settled, contrasts markedly with the dazzling infatuation of Troy, incapable of feeling as deeply as Boldwood, unable to set others before himself, yet in his own way utterly sincere. And behind them both is the practical affection of Oak, who loves the erstwhile milkmaid 'more than common', and yet is quite prepared to stand aside from his courtship, if it seems better for Bathsheba.

Bathsheba herself, of course, displays all the subtle and complex emotions of a girl in the process of becoming a woman. She is frightened by the depths of Boldwood's passion, fascinated despite herself by Troy's overwhelming displays and, in the end, reliant on the solid support of Oak. She has much in common, emotionally, with the unfortunate Eustacia.

In *Far from the Madding Crowd* love stands as the focus of Hardy's concern. In *The Return of the Native* marriage has entered the lists, complicating the emotional involvements of the central characters. In *The Mayor of Casterbridge* love has retired from the fray, leaving the practical aspects of marriage in the forefront. It is the bond of marriage that brings Susan Henchard to Casterbridge in search of her husband, not the bond of love. She seeks help in a time of distress. It is marriage that has caused Newson to abandon the woman with whom he has spent most of his life, and who bore his child. It is pride, not love, that makes Henchard resent Farfrae's marriage to Lucetta. And in the final marriage of Elizabeth-Jane and Farfrae there is little of what most people would define as 'love'.

The common characteristic of all these novels, however, is that love centres on the character of the individual. The problems of social stratification, differences of education, money and common interest, although mentioned, are no more than barely touched on. Because the landscapes are so independent and self-contained, such problems are less serious or intrusive than individual dissatisfaction or incompatibility. In *The Woodlanders*, Hardy begins to take up these wider social themes in the context of his enclosed world – finally giving the lie to the 'idylls' which, so well-received by his readers, were so far from the whole truth which his Preface to *Under the Greenwood Tree* hints at.

This is not to say, of course, that *The Woodlanders* concentrates on social themes. Its landscape is as carefully drawn as any previously, and love appears as individually as ever before. Giles and Marty are apparently ideally suited:

> . . . alone, of all the women in Hintock and the world, (she) had approximated to Winterborne's level of intelligent intercourse with Nature. In that respect she had formed his true complement in the other sex, had lived as his counterpart, had subjoined her thoughts to his as a corollary.[25]

But 'never would she have been his'. Marty loved Giles with a faithful, unspoken devotion, but he loved only Grace. For her part, Grace was as confused as Bathsheba before her; fascinated by the society of Fitzpiers, and alienated from Giles by her education, she yet retains the underlying need for the simple honesty of Giles' way of life.[26] Fitzpiers, like Troy, is prey to his own moods and needs. Associated with Mrs. Charmond as the actress, his interest is rekindled by her unusual new status, and physical passion rearoused. It is physical desire, too, that leads to his unexpected encounter with Suke; but Grace appeals as a reminder of gentility and refinement in a world which he finds lonely and unsuitable to his outward-looking, enquiring mind. For her part, Felice Charmond, once free of social mores in her acting career, finds herself entrapped by the estate she has inherited from her husband; to her, the lover from the past comes as a welcome reminder of her youth and freedom.

But through all of these complicated emotional interactions runs the theme that was subdued and unvoiced in the earlier novels: these characters are victims, not just of their own natures but of the rules of the society in which they live. And, for the first time at an active level, Hardy sees outside social pressures as having a place in the construction of those rules. Mrs. Charmond is a victim of her social niche, placed there from without, and Grace, sent away by her father to fulfil his own ambition for her, returns to a world that is only half hers; she is caught between her past and her present, swung first one way, then the other, by the social values of the woodland and the social values of Victorian middle-class life.

Very briefly, it seems that there is an answer, provided from above:

> A new court was established last year, and under the new statute, twenty and twenty-one Vic., cap. eighty-five, unmarrying is as

easy as marrying. No more Acts of Parliament necessary: no longer one law for the rich and another for the poor.[27]

No longer are the laws different for rich and poor — but for men and women, there is still no equality. Simple adultery, enough to justify a husband's divorce of his wife, is not it seems enough to allow a wife to rid herself of an unwanted husband.

Hardy, in this novel, pushes the community right into the background, concentrating solely on his main characters. A general undercurrent of village life ties the encapsulated world loosely into the wider world outside, though the encapsulation is, at more obvious levels, still almost complete. However, in uniting the wider canvas of the world with the landscapes of his pastoral novels, he fails to stir the pigments thoroughly, allowing disconnected ideas and themes to stare through the fabric. In concentrating on the main characters, he has still spread the drama over many individuals, without tying it together in the context of a social or other group. The highly confused dating and time-sequence of the novel (discussed at length in a note to the New Wessex Edition) suggests how confused are the ideas Hardy is putting forward, and how confused the new method he uses. Undoubtedly the novel is more successful than *The Hand of Ethelberta* or *A Laodicean*, drawing as it does on the experience of the pastoral novels. But it is also far less effective than *The Mayor of Casterbridge*, which it follows. The tight social grouping and clear-cut issues of that novel are abandoned for wider affairs and at this juncture, it would appear, Hardy's writing was unable to sustain the change.

The confusion of the novel shows too in its landscape. The woodlands, so carefully drawn, are occasionally admixed with or replaced by the orchards of the area. Giles appears in two roles, as woodsman or cider-maker; and outdoor scenes mix, apparently without regard for the differences, a background of copses and apple trees. So different are the scenes that one might be forgiven for expecting associations of mood with each. ' . . . orchards lustrous with the reds of apple-crops, berries, and foliage, the whole intensified by the gilding of the declining sun'[28] contrast strangely with the slightly frightening aspect of the woods at night to Grace: 'If the evening had not been growing so dark, and the wind had not put on its night-moan so distinctly, Grace would not have minded; but she was rather frightened now, and began to strike across hither and thither in random courses.'[29] But the associations are brief, and there is no development of the moods of Nature and Man, nor even a vision of Nature in other than her immediate association with Man.

Places, too, seem at times to have the most tenuous connection with the landscape. Middleton Abbey, and the villages around, mentioned only by name; Sherton Abbas, described in detail that is circumstantial, not merely suited to the character of the novel. All these instances show the difficulty Hardy faced in trying to combine a wider canvas, on which he could denote broader problems, with the very confined and carefully-constructed world which was his forte. The Abbey at Sherton, and the differing hotels, are images of the religious, moral and social problems associated with marriage and love, but in *The Woodlanders* they are too remote, too unconnected with the main landscape to be successfully integrated in the novel. The marks of grafting are all too obvious.

And in the end, the novel shows its inherent weaknesses by its inability to cope with the complex plot. In a community setting, such as *The Return of the Native*, *Far from the Madding Crowd* or *The Mayor of Casterbridge*, the mechanical devices of convenient deaths can be absorbed into the fabric of society, made to seem a part of the wider pattern of Nature. In *The Woodlanders*, death becomes so mechanical, so detached, as to stand out from the patterns of Nature, even when so strongly drawn. Giles' death, for all its ridiculous stretching of credibility, is seen, at the end, to be absorbed by the community. But the novel merely records the utterly unnatural demise of Felice Charmond, in a manner that makes it nothing but a dramatic device and at last, in its attempts to focus on the love of the individual, even withdraws the feeling of Marty for the dead Giles from its context in the community, and elevates it to the status of an heroic passion. With such a conflict of methods and outlooks, the novel cannot but be confused.

6 Wessex Vignettes: *Tess of the d'Urbervilles*

I.

The most obvious aspect of *Tess* that sets it apart from the earlier major novels is the emphasis on movement. Other characters move, of course — Henchard, Farfrae, Oak, Bathsheba — but in none of these cases does the major action of the novel follow the character on his or her travels. Characters may move, but the setting does not. And it is this change more than any other that enables Hardy successfully to make the union of his universal ideas with the enclosed landscapes of his Wessex world.

The obvious and most convenient place to begin is in 'Marlott', home of Tess's family. Yet despite all the references to Hardy's use of Marnhull, north of Sturminster Newton, as the model for this village,[1] (including Hardy's own statement) there is nothing positively to identify the real with the imagined. In fact, there is very little to identify at all in this 'long and broken village': a crooked lane, some assumed cottages (assumed in the mass, and never in the particular), the undescribed 'Pure Drop Inn', and the cursorily described Rolliver's inn and Durbeyfield cottage. Rolliver's has a board outside, 'about six inches wide and two yards long, fixed to the garden palings by pieces of wire, so as to form a ledge',[2] but could otherwise be of any size, shape or architectural style you care to name. The Durbeyfield cottage, we gather, is thatched, with a hedge behind and the road in front. All else to be seen in this Blackmoor Vale village is for the reader's imagination to discern.

Even the position of the village is difficult to discover. The villagers go to the market-day at Shaston ('Sir John' is returning thence in the opening chapter); the view opens before the ascending Tess and Joan as Tess first leaves home, to give a glimpse of the distant town. 'Far away behind the first hills the cliff-like dwellings of Shaston broke the lines of the ridge.'[3] Tess leaves the village for the second time (heading for Talbothays) via Stourcastle[4] — yet the town is unmentioned when she returns along the same roads to help her ailing parents.[5] No accurate description of its whereabouts is ever given.

What is described in detail, however, is the Vale in which the village is set:

> . . . the world seems to be constructed upon a smaller and more delicate scale; the fields are mere paddocks, so reduced that from this height their hedgerows appear a network of dark green threads overspreading the paler green of the grass. The atmosphere beneath is languorous, and is so tinged with azure that what artists call the middle distance partakes also of that hue, while the horizon beyond is of the deepest ultramarine. Arable lands are few and limited; with but slight exceptions the prospect is a broad rich mass of grass and trees, mantling minor hills and dales within the major.[6]

The whole passage reads like the notebook of a painter trying to capture the essential feeling and atmosphere of a particular view, without concern for the exactitude of detail that, in the earlier Wessex novels, is so prominent a feature of each landscape painted in words. It is this general image that is reiterated, as Tess arrives at Talbothays, as she labours at Flintcomb, and as she walks the long road to Emminster.[7] Where one might reasonably expect Tess to remember the cottage in which she was born, or think of parents, friends and incidents of the past, there is a large, impressionistic view of the contrasting natural worlds of 'South Wessex'.

It is early established that Tess is a girl with a larger view of life than the ordinary field-girl, but the author's single-mindedness about this rejection of the particular in favour of the general directs us to that same manipulation of landscape which characterises the earlier novels. Hardy, for some reason as yet undisclosed, is building a specific rural landscape, and contrasting it with another (the second characteristic of each of these descriptions of the Vale is that they are all compared with another landscape – the chalk uplands, or the Froom valley). There is a greater objectivity of description than even a Tess could envisage, so early in her life.

The second major setting of the novel, Trantridge, is just as hard to locate as the first. Tess walks from Marlott to Shaston, takes the carrier's van from there to Trantridge Cross (east of Shaston), and walks from there towards The Chase, on the edge of which Mrs.

d'Urberville's estate is situated. But once again there is no firm indication of where any of these places lies – no distances, specific directions or certain roads – and no descriptions which might make identification possible.

Description here is reserved for 'The Slopes' estate:

> a country-house built for enjoyment pure and simple, with not an acre of troublesome land attached to it beyond what was required for residential purposes, and for a little fancy farm kept in hand by the owner, and tended by a bailiff. . . . Far behind the corner of the house – which rose like a geranium bloom against the subdued colours around – stretched the soft azure landscape of The Chase – a truly venerable tract of forest land, one of the few remaining woodlands in England of undoubted primaeval date, wherein Druidical mistletoe was still found on aged oaks, and where enormous yew-trees, not planted by the hand of man, grew as they had grown when they were pollarded for bows.[8]

In more general terms, 'the soil and scenery differed much from those within Blakemore Vale.'[9]

But once again there is nothing tangible to identify – to say that the estate lies on the edge of 'The Chase' is as helpful to identification as to say that 'Marlott' lies in the heart of the Blackmoor Vale. Either could be 'identified' with half a dozen places; and despite the apparently more detailed description of 'The Slopes', there is little to work on. The house is red-brick, modern, and has a lodge in similar style. It is hardly one of Hardy's fullest accounts of a setting for his novels (compare the lengthy descriptions of the barn, in *Far from the Madding Crowd*, or Hintock House, in *The Woodlanders*).

From Trantridge, after a brief and equally uninformative return to Marlott, Tess goes south to Talbothays, and for the first time in the novel we are on familiar ground. The Froom valley is that fertile lowland which we glimpsed in *The Return of the Native*, on the distant edge of the heath. It borders the farmland of *Under the Greenwood Tree* and reaches up to the very walls of 'Casterbridge'; and it is here, in an area well-known to Hardy,[10] that the main body of the novel is set.

But once more, if we were expecting precise locations, we are doomed to disappointment. The pattern is set when Tess, travelling south, passes through Weatherbury[11] (Puddletown), having accepted a lift there 'instead of travelling in the van by way of

Casterbridge'. Casterbridge, in a manner akin to its banishment in *The Return of the Native*, receives only one more mention in the novel, and we are given the ultimate proof of its 'non-existence' for this story when Clare visits his father at Emminster. Although there is no way of avoiding at least skirting the town on such a journey, it remains unmentioned. This treatment is by no means confined to the unfortunate market-town. Towns and villages alike are excluded from all mention of their existence unless directly relevant to the story – even when working on such a large scale, Hardy does not allow his landscape to take on a life independent of the story.

Having 'lost' the town, Hardy deals almost as cursorily with his beloved Egdon heath:

> The journey over the intervening uplands and lowlands of Egdon, when she reached them, was a more troublesome walk than she had anticipated, the distance being actually but a few miles. It was two hours, owing to sundry wrong turnings, ere she found herself on a summit commanding the long-sought-for-vale . . . (and) . . . descended the Egdon slopes lower and lower towards the dairy of her pilgrimage.[12]

The 'trackless waste' has acquired enough defined tracks to allow of 'sundry wrong turnings'. The endless expanse of furze and heather has become 'but a few miles' across. Hardy, doubtless with an eye to the readers of *The Return of the Native* who would be reading *Tess*, has stretched the heath enough to allow of two hours' journey, but the whole passage bespeaks a determination to reduce the waste to a point where it cannot rival the vale for our attention. It has become a background, a mark on the skyline:

> . . . they went along the level roadway through the meads, which stretched away into gray miles, and were backed in the extreme edge of distance by the swarthy and abrupt slopes of Egdon Heath. On its summit stood clumps and stretches of fir-trees, whose notched tips appeared like battlemented towers crowning black-fronted castles of enchantment.[13]

Its function is the same as that of the chalk scarp above the Blackmoor Vale, to mark and contain the vale below, and allow the observer a suitably objective vantage point.

It is from this vantage point that we are introduced to the Froom valley:

> It was intrinsically different from the Vale of Little Dairies, Blackmoor Vale . . . The world was drawn to a larger pattern here. The enclosures numbered fifty acres instead of ten, the farmsteads were more extended, the groups of cattle formed tribes hereabout; there only families. These myriads of cows stretching under her eyes from the far east to the far west outnumbered any she had ever seen at one glance before.
>
> The birds'-eye perspective before her was not so luxuriantly beautiful, perhaps, as that other one which she knew so well; yet it was more cheering. It lacked the intensely blue atmosphere of the rival vale, and its heavy soils and scents; the new air was clear, bracing, ethereal.[14]

The use of contrasts mentioned earlier is here seen operating to the full; the character of each area is emphasised by comparison with another (or others). The more open nature of the Froom valley, sketched from above, is picked up and reiterated when the story moves to the level meads:

> The secret of Blackmoor was best discovered from the heights around; to read aright the valley before her it was necessary to descend into its midst. . . .
>
> The river had stolen from the higher tracts and brought in particles to the vale all this horizontal land; and now, exhausted, aged, and attenuated, lay serpentining along through the midst of its former spoils.[15]

Yet it remains for the spine of chalk upland linking the two fertile vales to establish clearly the nature of the relationships between the various settings. It appears first as a contrast by which the Blackmoor Vale is defined:

> The traveller from the coast, . . . is surprised and delighted to behold, extended like a map beneath him, a country differing absolutely from that which he has passed through. Behind him the hills are open, the sun blazes down upon fields so large as to give an unenclosed character to the landscape, the lanes are white, the hedges low and plashed, the atmosphere colourless.[16]

When Tess comes at last to this land, it is as a negative aspect of the fertile vales beyond that it appears. It seems almost as though there were no definable character by which the area could be recognised; rather, it impresses by its absolute lack of feature:

> Here the air was dry and cold, and the long cart-roads were blown white and dusty within a few hours after rain. There were few trees, or none, those that would have grown in the hedges being mercilessly plashed down with the quickset by the tenant-farmers, the natural enemies of tree, bush and brake. In the middle distance ahead of her she could see the summits of Bulbarrow and of Nettlecombe Tout, and they seemed friendly. They had a low and unassuming aspect from this upland, though as approached on the other side from Blackmoor in her childhood they were as lofty bastions against the sky. Southerly, at many miles' distance, and over the hills and ridges coastward, she could discern a surface like polished steel: it was the English Channel at a point far out towards France. [17]

But despite the fact this area is defined only by what is around it, Hardy gives no better clue as to the precise location of 'Flintcomb Ash' than he did to the locations of Marlott, The Slopes, or Talbothays. In fact, Hardy makes some slight adjustment to the Flintcomb landscape, altering the real appearance of the area. He does this to obliterate identifiable natural features, which add nothing to the character of the area, but would allow of identification of the real and imagined. Blackmoor and Froom are sufficiently large and featureless to be described exactly. 'The Chase', which might have been identifiable, is so vaguely located as to be impossible to relate to a specific natural place. Flintcomb Ash, however, is established by its various natural features (The Blackmoor Vale, Bulbarrow and Nettlecombe) and by the very specific directions given as to Tess's route to Emminster, as being in the area at the head of the Piddle valley. Hardy has 'smoothed out' this valley, raising the village to be part of an almost featureless 'upland'. In common with his technique in earlier novels, this is not far removed from the reality, as the view from this area excludes the deeper valleys between the bleak heights. [18]

Each setting becomes an arena, its peculiar character contrasted with the others, in which Tess acts out a part of her life. In each arena, as well as the physical differences, the differences of agriculture are

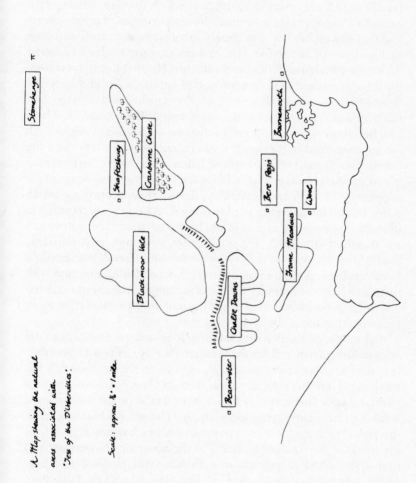

A Map shewing the natural areas associated with "Tess of the D'Urbervilles".

Scale: approx. ¾" = 1 mile.

Stonehenge π

Shaftesbury

Cranborne Chase

Blackmoor Vale

Bournemouth

Wool

Bere Regis

Frome Meadows

Chalk Downs

Beaminster

emphasised: in Blackmoor, Tess works at harvest, digs on the allotment and (to judge from her skill at Talbothays) milks cows; in Froom vale the work is all dairying; at Trantridge it is the poultry, symbol of the 'fancy farm', and at Flintcomb it is swedes, straw and threshing. All are forms of agriculture which overlap, but Hardy is careful to preserve the differences by restricting each to one area.

All of this establishes very clearly that Hardy was creating certain major arenas of action for *Tess*, and inviting the reader to contrast their different characters and atmospheres. The first clue to his reasons for this curious and new construction of landscape lies in the specific descriptions (such as they are) of the Durbeyfield cottage and Rolliver's inn, mentioned at the beginning of this discussion. These two buildings represent the only functions of the village with which we are concerned in the novel: the cottage, a lifehold, represents the family background of Tess, whose father is one of the 'artisan' class whose loss to the village Hardy bemoans;[19] the 'inn' reminds us of the propensity of John Durbeyfield to drink – that propensity which starts Tess on the uncertain road to disaster. All other aspects of life in the village, interesting as they might be, are irrelevant to the story and are therefore discarded, as are all other buildings. It is the same method that Hardy used in *Far from the Madding Crowd*, where certain buildings focus our attention upon the lives of those connected with them, but here the necessity for detail has gone – the community has receded into the background – and the buildings are mere ciphers, set prominently within the arena of action.

At Trantridge, the first such building is obvious: the modern estate, with its fancy farm, reflects the 'modern' family of the d'Urbervilles. It is not, as some critics have said, as alien to the landscape as the mechanical monsters which appear later, but is merely an element of changing agriculture. It may be a 'fancy farm', but it is nonetheless a working farm, employing local labour. The second building set in this arena lies in the 'decayed market-town' of Chaseborough, where the workers go to a dancing party 'at the house of a hay-trusser and peat-dealer who had transactions with their farm. He lived in an out-of-the-way nook of the townlet'.[20] This place serves a dual function, emphasising the 'idiosyncrasy' and 'abiding defect' of Trantridge, that 'it drank hard',[21] and also providing a trigger for the seduction of Tess – both being symptoms of a peculiarly human doom.

In the Froom valley, too, there is no difficulty in recognising the first representative of these symbolic buildings, the dairy. A minor offshoot of this, with much the same relationship to the main building as the rick-field bears to the farm at Flintcomb Ash, is the station where Clare and Tess take the milk. Like the new estate at Trantridge, the railway connection is a sign of changing ways in agriculture, temporarily startling in its newness, but as necessary to the dairying life as the skimmers and butter-churn. The other main building is Wellbridge House, symbol of the d'Urberville connection which alternately endears and alienates Tess and Clare. Like the inn at Marlott and the hay-trusser's house at Chaseborough, it is a symbol of a purely human weakness and prejudice, very different from the working function of the farms.

At Flintcomb, it is the working function that stands alone. The buildings mentioned here are the labourer's cottage in which Tess stays and the barn in which for part of the time she works.

Finally, this specialised use of buildings is carried as far as it can be, in the references to Emminster. Entirely outside the four main arenas, it is nothing more than the home of the Clare family, and their own brands of religion. And in keeping with this function, it is only the church and vicarage which are ever mentioned:

> His father's hill-surrounded little town, the Tudor church-tower of red stone, the clump of trees near the vicarage, came at last into view beneath him, and he rode down towards the well-known gate.[22]

The paucity of this description is shared by almost every other building that appears in the novel, and the only other places mentioned appear simply as marker-posts or sites for certain events: Weatherbury, Stourcastle, Casterbridge and Shaston are reference-points; Nuttlebury is an image of human slumber in the darkened Vale of Blackmoor when Tess returns from Flintcomb;[23] Evershot is a marker and a place to meet the converted d'Urberville. Events and places after Sandbourne are dealt with very differently, but there is one more aspect of the main arenas of action which must be examined first. Earlier, I made mention of the careful differentiation that Hardy preserves between the various modes of agriculture pursued at each location: the arable work of Blackmoor and Flintcomb is separated by an opposition of seasons (how many readers, having been moved by the harshness of the winter at Flintcomb Ash, and being then thrown into the harshness of Tess's work at threshing time, will associate this scene with the friendly atmosphere of the earlier harvesting, near Marlott?). Trantridge, which, despite its 'different soil', must have engaged in some form of dairying and arable work, is rigorously restricted to the poultry-farm, while the superficially similar vales of Blackmoor and Froom are differentiated by a selective description – in Blackmoor it is the harvest-field and allotment which are mentioned (despite its description as 'Vale of Little Dairies'), in Froom the dairy alone appears (although the mill near Woolbridge must, presumably, have had corn supplied from somewhere).

It is here, in the different agricultures, that we come at last to the reason for the careful delineation of the four arenas: each is the setting for a specific aspect of Tess's life, and each is given a character appropriate to its own aspect (bearing in mind that the general nature of each area was the basis for its selection by Hardy; he has merely selected the necessary material to emphasise that nature, and excluded extraneous detail).

In the Blackmoor Vale, as the story commences, nature has a neutral aspect akin to that seen in other novels (*Under the Greenwood Tree, Far from the Madding Crowd*). Man and nature co-exist in a working harmony, of which Tess and her family are a part. The specific weakness of John Durbeyfield, alcohol, is catered for by the mention of Rolliver's Inn and The Pure Drop. For her part, Tess has little conception of the world, and is as yet an unformed feature of the scene,

> . . . a mere vessel of emotion untinctured by experience. The dialect was on her tongue to some extent, despite the village school . . . The pouted-up deep red mouth to which this syllable was native had hardly as yet settled into its definite shape . . .
>
> Phases of her childhood lurked in her aspect still. As she walked along to-day, for all her bouncing handsome womanliness, you could sometimes see her twelfth year in her cheeks, or her ninth sparkling from her eyes; and even her fifth would flit over the curves of her mouth now and then.
>
> . . . to almost everybody she was a fine and picturesque country girl, and no more.[24]

There is none of that rich use of natural imagery common in Hardy's work to describe the unformed Tess, as also there is no specifically human imagery (of society, philosophy, class and so on). She is merely 'a fine and picturesque country girl', quite neutral in her setting; and the Blackmoor Vale, for all its richness and beauty, is equally neutral. Tess's pessimistic flights of fancy to young Abraham are as unformed as her own person, and we can see nothing in the country around to support such a view. Clare puts the correct perspective on Durbeyfield's drunken indolence when he misunderstands what Tess wishes to confess:

> 'I was in the Sixth Standard when I left school, and they said I had great aptness, and should make a good teacher, so it was settled that I should be one. But there was trouble in my family; father was not very industrious, and he drank a little.'
> 'Yes, yes. Poor child! Nothing new.'[25]

The neutrality continues throughout the novel — the Vale impassively accepts Tess's departure and return, the birth and death of her child, the death of her father, the removal of the Durbeyfield family — but the beauty fades a little:

> Instead of the colourless air of the uplands the atmosphere down there was a deep blue. Instead of the great enclosures of a hundred acres in which she was now accustomed to toil there were little fields below her of less than half-a-dozen acres, so numerous that they looked from this height like the meshes of a net. Here the landscape was whitey-brown; down there, as in Froom Valley, it was always green. Yet it was in that vale that her sorrow had taken shape, and she did not love it as formerly. Beauty to her, as to all who have felt, lay not in the thing, but in what the thing symbolized.[26]

That last sentence, in context, means little more than the recession of Blackmoor into the background of Tess's life. It never has a positive influence, in one way or another, nor does it reflect love or disillusion for Tess — it is the scene of her childhood, outside the sphere of adult judgment; it is amoral, in this novel where Hardy for the first time imputes morality to his natural settings (albeit they are mere images and reflections of human morality).

However, when we turn to the other main arenas, that sentence takes on a new, deeper meaning. Beauty lies not in the thing, but in what it symbolises, and Hardy follows this idea into description. At Trantridge, neutrality recedes, to be replaced by a weakly-hinted dissipation.[27] The landscape still reflects little but its own nature, but the village has attained a character lacking in Marlott:

Every village has its idiosyncrasy, its constitution, often its own code of morality. The levity of some of the younger women in and about Trantridge was marked, and was perhaps symptomatic of the choice spirit who ruled The Slopes in that vicinity. The place had also a more abiding defect; it drank hard. The staple conversation on the farms around was on the uselessness of saving money; and smockfrocked arithmeticians, leaning on their ploughs or hoes, would enter into calculations of great nicety to prove that parish relief was a fuller provision for a man in his old age than any which could result from savings out of their wages during a whole lifetime.[28]

Once again, it must be stressed that Hardy is deliberately relating Tess's changed moral appreciation to the locality, choosing a place that fits, and emphasising the elements in it that fit. There is no wanton distortion of nature to reflect every passing mood and fancy of the very slight human figure we are following. Indeed, at Trantridge Tess is little more than another caged bird, whose innocent beauty is at the summons of d'Urberville.

But Tess until now has been virtually a child. It is the seduction and subsequent birth and death of her child that make her a woman, and demand fully-formed images to express her feelings and imagination. Marlott was neutral, Trantridge idiosyncratic. The Froom valley is a new, exciting world:

Either the change in the quality of the air from heavy to light, or the sense of being amid new scenes where there were no invidious eyes upon her, sent up her spirits wonderfully. Her hopes mingled with the sunshine in an ideal photosphere which surrounded her as she bounded along against the soft south wind. She heard a pleasant voice in every breeze, and in every bird's note seemed to lurk a joy.[29]

And in the cattle which symbolise the type of agriculture we see here, and the new participation of Tess in her landscape (neither child nor caged bird nor object of pity), there is a new vibrancy and richness of colour. 'The ripe hues of the red and dun kine absorbed the evening sunlight, which the white-coated animals returned to the eye in rays almost dazzling, even at the distant elevation on which she stood.'[30] Gone is the quiet neutrality of Blackmoor; gone is the pitiful 'excitement' of the Chase; gone is the grey hopelessness of Tess's second sojourn at Marlott, when 'she knew how to hit to a hair's breadth that moment of evening when the light and the darkness are so evenly balanced that the constraint of day and the suspense of night neutralise each other, leaving absolute mental liberty.'[31] Now, in the Froom meadows, Tess steps into a world redolent of sensuality and rich fruitfulness:

> Those of them that were spotted with white reflected the sunshine in dazzling brilliancy, and the polished brass knobs on their horns glittered with something of military display. Their large-veined udders hung ponderous as sandbags, the teats sticking out like the legs of a gipsy's crock; and as each animal lingered for her turn to arrive the milk oozed forth and fell in drops to the ground.[32]

It is in this lush landscape that Tess is to learn the true heights of sensuality and love; and summer, a mere adjunct to the poultry farm, takes on its full-blooded reality. The warmth of love and the warmth of summer step forward together:

> Immediately he began to descend from the upland to the fat alluvial soil below, the atmosphere grew heavier; the languid perfume of the summer fruits, the mists, the hay, the flowers, formed therein a vast pool of odour which at this hour seemed to make the animals, the very bees and butterflies, drowsy.[33]

and together Tess's love and the valley move into autumn – a very different autumn from the weary October in which Tess returned from Trantridge when

> . . . though the sun's lower limb was just free of the hill, his rays, ungenial and peering, addressed the eye rather than the touch as yet. There was not a human soul near. Sad October and her sadder self seemed the only two existences haunting that lane.[34]

This is the reality of the relatively bleaker Trantridge area, just as the relatively warm and receptive October is the reality of Talbothays; but the latter is also the atmosphere of love, as the former was of disillusion:

> . . . during this October month of wonderful afternoons they

roved along the meads by creeping paths which followed the
brinks of trickling tributary brooks, hopping across by little
wooden bridges to the other side, and back again. They were never
out of the sound of some purling weir, whose buzz accompanied
their own murmuring, while the beams of the sun, almost as
horizontal as the mead itself, formed a pollen of radiance over the
landscape. They saw tiny blue fogs in the shadows of trees and
hedges, all the time that there was bright sunshine elsewhere. The
sun was so near the ground, and the sward so flat, that the shadows
of Clare and Tess would stretch a quarter of a mile ahead of them,
like two long fingers pointing afar to where the green alluvial
reaches abutted against the sloping sides of the vale.[35]

But love does not stay forever unchanging. The summer of Tess's
love is ended at Wellbridge, the sun she worships – her Angel
Clare – removed, and winter alone ensues. Once more Hardy shifts
the scene of the action, to an arena more suited atmospherically to the
winter of Tess's love – winter on the chalk uplands, removed from all
contact with the areas of her happiness.

Yet there is a continuity. Marian and Izz work beside Tess, as they
did at Talbothays, and we are reminded that Tess would have left the
dairy, marriage or no, being a victim of the agricultural exigencies of
the day. Flintcomb Ash may be a hard taskmaster, but it is the only
winter work Tess can find. The function of the place as an image of
Tess's mental situation is recalled by the fact that Hardy stipulates he
has ignored a period of relative prosperity and mental inertia:

> . . . she had got through the spring and summer without any great
> stress upon her physical powers, the time being mainly spent in
> rendering light irregular service at dairy-work near Port-Bredy to
> the west of the Blackmoor valley, equally remote from her native
> place and from Talbothays. . . . Mentally she remained in utter
> stagnation, a condition which the mechanical occupation rather
> fostered than checked.[36]

Tess's arrival at Flintcomb Ash is a mixture of emotions – hope
and despair. 'In the middle distance ahead of her she could see the
summits of Bulbarrow and of Nettlecombe Tout, and they seemed
friendly.' 'The stubborn soil around her showed plainly enough that
the kind of labour in demand here was of the roughest kind.' 'The

wall seemed to be the only friend she had.'[37] Winter of love and winter of climate go hand-in-hand, as with summer:

> It was so high a situation, this field, that the rain had no occasion to fall, but raced along horizontally upon the yelling wind, sticking into them like glass splinters till they were wet through. Tess had not known till now what was really meant by that. There are degrees of dampness, and a very little is called being wet through in common talk. But to stand working slowly in a field, and feel the creep of rain-water, first in legs and shoulders, then on hips and head, then at back, front, and sides, and yet to work on till the leaden light diminishes and marks that the sun is down, demands a distinct modicum of stoicism, even of valour.
>
> Yet they did not feel the wetness so much as might be supposed.[38]

Always, no matter how harsh the climate and the work at Flintcomb, there is an element of hope in life. Naturally there in a young woman, it yet parallels the hope Tess nurses for the return of Clare – as winter must always be succeeded by spring. In blinding snow, 'such weather on a dry upland is not in itself dispiriting';[39] outdoor work improves Tess's beauty (Hardy is not of the Victorian school that found beauty in woman's pale fragility). Even the horrifying day spent pulling the rick for threshing is merely transitory.

Only the attentions of d'Urberville are unbearable. It is they alone that change mere winter into a wasteland. And it is for d'Urberville alone that Hardy changes a scene from the reality, vesting it with something beyond its natural effect. Flintcomb Ash, although only a matter of a few miles from the Blackmoor Vale, seems as remote from it as another world, for a curious outcrop of the chalk scarp obscures all view of the Vale, except from the highest fields above 'Flintcomb'. But at 'Cross-in-Hand' the opposite is true: south, the scene is as desolate as Hardy describes; north, there is the whole glorious panorama of the Blackmoor Vale, with the homely farmsteads of Hermitage immediately below. Hardy has chosen this one spot to alter reality and so convey the utter desolation d'Urberville's attentions bring to Tess's mind. 'Of all spots on the bleached and desolate upland this was the most forlorn. It was so far removed from the charm which is sought in landscape by artists and view-lovers as to reach a new kind of beauty, a negative beauty of tragic tone.'[40]

Discussion so far has centred upon the four main arenas of action — Blackmoor, Trantridge, Froom, and Flintcomb. However, there is a large area of action entirely removed from these landscapes and occupying, proportionately, a startlingly small part of the novel; Tess's travels from Sandbourne to Bramshurst Court to Stonehenge to Wintoncester occupy five short chapters, but move us through a whole world of emotion. Each place is seen in a self-contained vignette. Each is utterly different from the others.

The explanation for this sudden change of style in the novel is not difficult to find; but these few chapters mark the complete divorce of Hardy's work from his established rural world. The bulk of the novel, concerned with Tess's struggle to live and love in familiar settings, while under the assault of opposing ideas and ideals, is quite suddenly forsaken, and we follow a Tess and Clare utterly divorced from the society around them, only to see that society demand the sacrifice of their love at the altar of confused ideals.

At Sandbourne, the train which served a function in the agricultural world, but retained a harsh strangeness, now takes up the alien side of its nature, delivering us with Clare at

> . . . a fairy place suddenly created by the stroke of a wand, and allowed to get a little dusty. An out-lying eastern tract of the enormous Egdon Waste was close at hand, yet on the very verge of that tawny piece of antiquity such a glittering novelty as this pleasure city had chosen to spring up. . . .
>
> It was a city of detached mansions; a Mediterranean lounging-place on the English Channel; and as seen now by night it seemed even more imposing than it was.[41]

This alien world is the refuge of d'Urberville with Tess. Its unreality in the solid world around reflects the phantasm of d'Urberville's relationship to Tess, its glittering facade concealing an alien, empty being.

In complete contrast, the empty mansion where Tess and Clare take refuge is the image of Wellbridge, divorced now from the false associations of Tess's family background, speaking only of their love:

> Clare unlatched the door of a large chamber, felt his way across it, and parted the shutters to the width of two or three inches. A shaft of dazzling sunlight glanced into the room, revealing heavy,

old-fashioned furniture, crimson damask hangings, and an enormous four-post bedstead, along the head of which were carved running figures, apparently Atalanta's race.[42]

'A stream of morning light through the shutter-chink fell upon the faces of the pair, wrapped in profound slumber, Tess's lips being parted like a half-opened flower near his cheek.'[43] There is a very distinctive similarity between this beautiful scene and the setting at Wellbridge, before Tess reveals her secret. 'The sun was so low on that short last afternoon of the year that it shone in through a small opening and formed a golden staff which stretched across to her skirt, where it made a spot like a paint-mark set upon her.'[44] Such inconsequential details, in such a very personal setting, are quite as effective as larger similarities in establishing the coincidence.

At Stonehenge, resting in their flight, Tess is caught up in a carefully-constructed 'sacrifice'. Sleeping on the 'altar' at the centre of the circle, the men who symbolise the world of cold 'justice' close in from all sides:

> All waited in the growing light, their faces and hands as if they were silvered, the remainder of their figures dark, the stones glistening green-gray, the Plain still a mass of shade. Soon the light was strong, and a ray shone upon her unconscious form, peering under her eyelids and waking her.[45]

It is the traditional image of sacrifice at Stonehenge — as the first ray of the rising sun touches the victim, she dies. And for Tess, that awakening is death. Clare's part in Tess's sacrifice is not forgotten. Images of her virtual worship of him have been many; at Talbothays and at Flintcomb his role as her sun was made very obvious. And here, at Stonehenge, Clare himself speaks of sacrifice to the sun. Tess's death is nothing to do with God, or Christianity, but a sacrifice to human vanities.

The final vignette of the tragedy is acted without Tess, but the image is all of her and Clare.

> Behind the city swept the rotund upland of St. Catherine's Hill; further off, landscape beyond landscape, till the horizon was lost in the radiance of the sun hanging above it.

Against these far stretches of country rose, in front of the other city edifices, a large red-brick building, with level gray roofs, and rows of short barred windows bespeaking captivity, the whole contrasting greatly by its formalism with the quaint irregularities of the Gothic erections. . . . From the middle of the building an ugly flat-topped octagonal tower ascended against the east horizon, and viewed from this spot on its shady side and against the light, it seemed the one blot on the city's beauty.[46]

Wintoncester is the only place — village or town — so fully described, and it is described in the manner of the four main arenas, as a comprehensive vista. There is one exception — Clare and 'Liza-Lu are leaving this arena, not entering it. 'As soon as they had strength they arose, joined hands again, and went on'.

The allegory is complete:

> They, looking back, all th'eastern side beheld
> Of Paradise, so late their happy seat,
> Waved over by that flaming brand, the gate
> With dreadful faces thronged and fiery arms.
> Some natural tears they dropped, but wiped them soon;
> The world was all before them, where to choose
> Their place of rest, and Providence their guide:
> They hand in hand, with wand'ring steps and slow,
> Through Eden took their solitary way.[47]

Earlier, Tess had thought 'how confidently she would leave them to Providence and their future kingdom! But, in default of that, it behoved her to do something; to be their Providence'.[48] There is no guiding power, no 'President of the Immortals', only the pressures of man and Nature, working together or separately, and the ability or failure of individual or community to deal with them. And the Paradise from which Clare, and 'Liza-Lu, as the image of the unsullied Tess ('she has all the best of me without the bad of me')[49], are cast out is no heaven, but the same human world of vain ideals that demanded the sacrifice. Before them is the world of realistic humanity, to which Clare brings the knowledge he has so bitterly obtained, with all its joy and pain to come. The allegories, having divorced us utterly from the communities of the earlier novels, now deliver us to exactly the same conclusion as those novels: Tess, the individual, is destroyed, but life goes on as before.

2.

It is in Tess's person that we find the major embodiment of the harmony between man and nature that is the focus of the earlier novels. The land itself, and the working of it, is very obviously subservient to Tess herself in this novel, and Hardy therefore allows Tess to take the weight of imagery designed to emphasise the connection between man and nature. In common with the descriptions of the landscape itself, the descriptions of Tess are almost neutral until the moment of her seduction. 'Her mobile peony mouth and large innocent eyes added eloquence to colour and shape'[50] at the club-walking; in the carrier's van returning from Chaseborough, she is 'quite a posy'; [51] and asleep in The Chase, the dark figure of d'Urberville looming over her sees 'this beautiful feminine tissue, sensitive as gossamer, and practically blank as snow as yet'.[52] But as soon as she has been seduced, and that feminine tissue bears the first marks of life's experience, the images begin to change, 'cheeks that were damp and smoothly chill as the skin of the mushrooms in the fields around';[53] 'sad October and her sadder self seemed the only two existences haunting that lane'.[54] And the guilt-laden Tess who haunts the lanes and woods around Marlott at dusk is described, for the first time, in terms of the landscape around her:

> On these lonely hills and dales her quiescent glide was of a piece with the element she moved in. Her flexuous and stealthy figure became an integral part of the scene. At times her whimsical fancy would intensify natural processes around her till they seemed a part of her own story. Rather they became a part of it; for the world is only a psychological phenomenon, and what they seemed they were. The midnight airs and gusts, moaning amongst the tightly-wrapped buds and bark of the winter twigs, were formulae of bitter reproach. A wet day was the expression of irremediable grief at her weakness in the mind of some vague ethical being whom she could not class definitely as the God of her childhood, and could not comprehend as any other.[55]

The great difference between this and earlier descriptions in other novels linking man and nature is that Tess's own fears and emotions seem consciously to pick up the elements of nature and translate them into her own life. However, we are not to be treated to a flood of rhetorical 'natural' imagery, designed to convey all the moods of Tess. As I stated earlier, Tess is a very small part of the world, and her emotions are of no concern to nature:

> . . . this encompassment of her own characterization, based on shreds of convention, peopled by phantoms and voices antipathetic to her, was a sorry and mistaken creation of Tess's fancy – a cloud of moral hobgoblins by which she was terrified without reason. It was they that were out of harmony with the actual world, not she. Walking among the sleeping birds in the hedges, watching the skipping rabbits on a moonlit warren, or standing under a pheasant-laden bough, she looked upon herself as a figure of Guilt intruding into the haunts of Innocence. But all the while she was making a distinction where there was no difference.[56]

The first direct comparison between Tess and the animals around her has been made. And at the same moment Hardy makes his first direct statement of intent. 'She had been made to break an accepted social law, but no law known to the environment in which she fancied herself such an anomaly.'[57] From this point onward, Tess is followed through her development as two opposing elements struggle for dominance within her: the laws of nature and the laws of Victorian morality. There is no one element of social teaching which can destroy her (her resilience at times is quite remarkable), but the process, begun with a Board School education, is pursued inexorably at every turn – by the ideas implanted in Tess, by the animalism of d'Urberville, by the cold ideals of Angel Clare, by the texts of Old Clare's followers – and she is worn inevitably down. We are reminded of this first dual imagery (of nature and of man's false ideals) when Tess once more encounters roosting pheasants, on her way to Flintcomb Ash – but this time as victims of the unintended cruelty of society, counterparts of herself:

> She had occasionally caught glimpses of these men in girlhood, looking over hedges, or peering through bushes, and pointing their guns, strangely accoutred, a bloodthirsty light in their eyes. She had been told that, rough and brutal as they seemed just then, they were not like this all the year round, but were, in fact, quite civil persons save during certain weeks of autumn and winter, when, like the inhabitants of the Malay Peninsula, they ran amuck, and made it their purpose to destroy life – in this case harmless

feathered creatures, brought into being by artificial means solely to gratify these propensities. [58]

There is a very close parallel between this and the seduction scene, with the girl and the birds the victims of the same 'animal' instincts of well-placed men; but the third element – the memory of those quietly-sleeping, innocent birds with which Tess is compared after her seduction – reminds us that there is no rupture of the natural law in being such a victim. The bird that survives such an attack is no less a part of nature for having been attacked.

But a bird too severely wounded is better killed swiftly than left to suffer: and Tess is soon to be injured yet again by d'Urberville. 'I feared long ago, when I struck him on the mouth with my glove, that I might do it someday for the trap he set for me in my simple youth, and his wrong to you through me.'[59] She struck that blow at Flintcomb, when hard-pressed by d'Urberville. In killing him she ends the suffering of which he was a major cause.

All of this, however, concerns the course of Tess's life in the future, and there is much to be seen of Hardy's construction of her character before we reach the final, inevitable stages. At Marlott, the young mother Tess takes to field-work, a part now of a very natural 'religion' – the same harmony between man and nature that marks the earlier novels – in which her sexuality is quite at home:

> The sun, on account of the mist, had a curious sentient, personal look, demanding the masculine pronoun for its adequate expression. . . . One could feel that a saner religion had never prevailed under the sky. The luminary was a golden-haired, beaming, mild-eyed, God-like creature, gazing down in the vigour and intentness of youth upon an earth that was brimming with interest for him.
>
> His light, a little later, broke through chinks of cottage shutters, throwing stripes like red-hot pokers upon cupboards, chests of drawers, and other furniture within; and awakening harvesters who were not already astir.[60]

The image is all of vigour, youth, warmth and freshness, with a pleasant awareness of masculinity in the sun. The image of it breaking through the shutters is the same as that mentioned earlier, in connection with Wellbridge and Bramshurst. In both those cases, the shaft of sunlight marks the bridal chamber in a very gentle sexual reminder. This is taken up again in the picture of Tess:

> From the sheaf last finished she draws a handful of ears, patting their tips with her left palm to bring them even. Then stooping low she moves forward, gathering the corn with both hands against her knees, and pushing her left gloved hand under the bundle to meet the right on the other side, holding the corn in an embrace like that of a lover.[61]

We have already seen that 'a field-woman is a portion of the field; she has somehow lost her own margin, imbibed the essence of her surrounding, and assimilated herself with it,'[62] and now we see Tess, a part of the rich fruitfulness of the field, quite naturally part of a situation that implies sexuality — not the urgent, pressing sexuality of a Lawrence but an assumed, accepted sexuality that is as much a part of the scene as any element of nature, and no more. The open feeding of the baby, fruit of her sexuality, amidst the fruit of the wheatfield is affirmation of the parallel, and two women amongst the workers put the incident into its context (as Clare will put John Durbeyfield's drinking into context):

> 'She's fond of that there child, though she mid pretend to hate en, and say she wishes the baby and her too were in the churchyard,' observed the woman in the red petticoat.
> 'She'll soon leave off saying that,' replied the one in buff. 'Lord, 'tis wonderful what a body can get used to o' that sort in time!'[63]

It is indeed in a more optimistic mood that Tess approaches the Froom Valley, with a paean of praise for nature:

> And probably the half-unconscious rhapsody was a Fetichistic utterance in a Monotheistic setting; women whose chief companions are the forms and forces of outdoor Nature retain in their souls far more of the Pagan fantasy of their remote forefathers than of the systematized religion taught their race at later date.[64]

But once again we are reminded of the insignificance of the individual, no matter how great her problems, in the natural world:

> Tess stood still upon the hemmed expanse of verdant flatness,

like a fly on a billiard-table of indefinite length, and of no more consequence to the surroundings than that fly. The sole effect of her presence upon the placid valley so far had been to excite the mind of a solitary heron, which, after descending to the ground not far from her path, stood with neck erect, looking at her.[65]

The setting is one of natural fruitfulness — the milk oozing from the cows' udders establishes it with a warm, detailed sensuality that reminds us of Tess feeding the baby at Marlott.

In this setting, the images applied to Tess settle down into a quiet regularity, allowing the extremes of great despair and warm fruitfulness to fade, and be replaced by a pleasant sensuality, growing gradually in strength of expression as Tess's love for Clare also grows. When Clare first notices her, she begins 'to trace imaginary patterns on the tablecloth with her forefinger with the constraint of a domestic animal that perceives itself to be watched.'[66] Already she is as much a part of the dairy as any animal, and as naturally so. Their first imaginative encounter works in exactly the same way with Tess, the animal, a part of the natural scene, drawn to the notes of Clare's harp as the cows respond to the songs of the milkmaids. And in this atmosphere, at first, Clare seems as naturally sensual as her:

> The outskirt of the garden in which Tess found herself had been left uncultivated for some years, and was now damp and rank with juicy grass which sent up mists of pollen at a touch; and with tall blooming weeds emitting offensive smells — weeds whose red and yellow and purple hues formed a polychrome as dazzling as that of cultivated flowers. She went stealthily as a cat through this profusion of growth, gathering cuckoo-spittle on her skirts, cracking snails that were underfoot, staining her hands with thistle-milk and slug-slime, and rubbing off upon her naked arms sticky blights which, though snow-white on the apple-tree trunks, made madder stains on her skin; thus she drew quite near to Clare, still unobserved of him.[67]

It is made clearer that Tess's vision, her ability to look beyond the earth and the immediate, is an almost unthinking reaction to her surroundings — a kind of religious ecstasy, akin to the sun-worship mentioned earlier:

> Tess was conscious of neither time nor space. The exaltation

which she had described as being producible at will by gazing at a
star, came now without any determination of hers; she undulated
upon the thin notes of the second-hand harp, and their harmonies
passed like breezes through her, bringing tears into her eyes.[68]

In such an atmosphere, girl and nature become as one in the 'worship'
of the simple joy of living – the ecstatic, unthought joy that is the
counterpart of Hardy's geometric vision of harmony, the pyramid of
earth-rainbarrow-man-sky (*Return of the Native*) in which no part is
complete without any other:

> The floating pollen seemed to be his notes made visible, and the
> dampness of the garden the weeping of the garden's sensibility.
> Though near nightfall, the rank-smelling weed-flowers glowed as
> if they would not close for intentness, and the waves of colour
> mixed with the waves of sound.[69]

At this moment, 'Angel' seems to be the epitome of his name, his harp
the voice of heaven, and as though in confirmation there is a fragment
of day preserved amidst the dusk – the light of his harmony
illuminating the harmony of Tess and the garden: 'The light which
still shone was derived mainly from a large hole in the western bank
of cloud; it was like a piece of day left behind by accident, dusk having
closed in elsewhere.'[70] In this Paradise – this Garden of Eden –
Clare's angelic harmony bespeaks his coming role, as Adam to Tess's
Eve. Like the first Adam, he is her pathway to 'God', to the ecstasy
and understanding of life which she is now beginning to experience.
Like Eve, Tess will worship her lover as pathway to understanding,
but unlike the Christian paradise this one already speaks of paganism
and sun-worship, and ecstasy lies in warm, sensual love, not in the
cold, perverted 'christian' principles ('the last grotesque phase of a
creed which had served mankind well in its time')[71] which argue
back and forth across the bewildered, betrayed Tess later in the novel.
Clare, to Tess, is a sublimation of the direct sensuality of the sun, and
of nature all around.

If any confirmation were needed of this more basic, less 'ideal'
attraction between the two than the perfection of Milton's Adam and
Eve, it is soon made apparent (though, it should be added, Hardy is as
subtle as Milton. He does not avoid an imputation of 'bestiality' in his
sensual love, but allows the sublimity of his description to remind us
of the sublimity of his vision of nature):

The season developed and matured. Another year's instalment of flowers, leaves, nightingales, thrushes, finches, and such ephemeral creatures, took up their positions where only a year ago others had stood in their place when these were nothing more than germs and inorganic particles. Rays from the sunrise drew forth the buds and stretched them into long stalks, lifted up sap in noiseless streams, opened petals, and sucked out scents in invisible jets and breathings. . . .

Thus passed the leafy time when arborescence seems to be the one thing aimed at out of doors. Tess and Clare unconsciously studied each other, ever balanced on the edge of a passion, yet apparently keeping out of it. All the while they were converging, under an irresistible law, as surely as two streams in one vale.[72]

The irresistibility, the Adam and Eve nature of the relationship, is the greater for the proximity, and the two take on the elements of the land around them, as though each personified the beauty of nature:

Whilst all the landscape was in neutral shade his companion's face, which was the focus of his eyes, rising above the mist stratum, seemed to have a sort of phosphorescence upon it. She looked ghostly, as if she were merely a soul at large. In reality her face, without appearing to do so, had caught the cold gleam of day from the north-east; his own face, though he did not think of it, wore the same aspect to her. . . . Or perhaps the summer fog was more general, and the meadows lay like a white sea, out of which the scattered trees rose like dangerous rocks. Birds would soar through it into the upper radiance, and hang on the wing sunning themselves, or alight on the wet rails subdividing the mead, which now shone like glass rods. Minute diamonds of moisture from the mist hung, too, upon Tess's eyelashes, and drops upon her hair, like seed pearls.[73]

The harmony of man and nature, generalised through the communities of earlier novels, becomes here a symbol of personal love; the mist which is beautiful on the meads brings added beauty to Tess, dressing her for the occasion as though she were a lady in society, dressing for her lover. But here there is no calculation involved, and no manufactured lotions; nature beautifies naturally. And we see Tess (and indeed, Clare) through the eyes of love, the tiny details of the face taken in as though all the world around were merely a setting for such a jewel. What more beautiful, or natural, expression of love can there be than through this harmony of man and nature? We see here the whole shift of emphasis in the novel, as Hardy focuses upon the problems and joys of the individual in the setting of the rural community.

But at the same time, there is a deeper, sadder note, as though the dead bell tolled behind the peal. Just as, in the establishment of Tess's harmony in nature, Hardy also foresaw the argument of natural and man-made law, so now, in this harmony of love, he foresees the colder reality of Clare's misguided idealism:

> She was no longer the milkmaid, but a visionary essence of woman — a whole sex condensed into one typical form. He called her Artemis, Demeter, and other fanciful names half teasingly, which she did not like because she did not understand them.
> 'Call me Tess', she would say askance; and he did.[74]

Tess is indeed only a milkmaid: only one individual in a rural world. She lives her life with that knowledge, and it is a part of her tragedy that the word 'd'Urberville' should be of significance to Clare, that he should fail to understand that love and harmony can exist without reference to merely human laws. Four girls fall in love with Clare, all as human as Tess, their love lacking 'everything to justify its existence in the eye of civilisation (while lacking nothing in the eye of Nature)'.[75] All can justify the same harmonious imagery as Tess:

> The rosy-cheeked, bright-eyed quartet looked so charming in their light summer attire, clinging to the roadside bank like pigeons on a roof-slope, that he stopped a moment to regard them before coming close. Their gauzy skirts had brushed up from the grass unnumerable flies and butterflies which, unable to escape, remained caged in the transparent tissue as in an aviary.[76]

It is the whole tenet of the novel that Tess is victim, merely a beautiful young country woman caught up in circumstances which scar her, but able to adapt and adjust. Izz Huett offers herself to Clare when he is married, with the same kind of love that can make Tess kill for 'his wrong to you through me'.[77] It is Tess's very naturalness that appears through the images of her harmony with nature. 'Amid the oozing fatness and warm ferments of the Froom Vale, at a season when the rush of juices could almost be heard below the hiss of fertilisation, it was impossible that the most fanciful love should not grow passionate.'[78] And so Tess's passion grows, and the images grow richer and fuller with her. It cannot be said that the one precedes the other. As a part of this natural harmony, Tess grows; love grows; the images grow.

And as the images grow richer, they grow also more detailed, more intensely human. The vast sweeps of landscape are forgotten, as love focuses the eyes upon the most immediate objects:

> To a young man with the least fire in him that little upward lift in the middle of her red top lip was distracting, infatuating, maddening. He had never before seen a woman's lips and teeth which forced upon his mind with such persistent iteration the old Elizabethan simile of roses filled with snow. Perfect, he, as a lover, might have called them off-hand. But no – they were not perfect. And it was the touch of the imperfect upon the would be perfect that gave the sweetness, because it was that which gave the humanity.
>
> Clare had studied the curves of those lips so many times that he could reproduce them mentally with ease: and now, as they again confronted him, clothed with colour and life, they sent an aura over his flesh, a breeze through his nerves, which well nigh produced a qualm; and actually produced, by some mysterious physiological process, a prosaic sneeze.[79]

The rhapsody of love is tempered by complete humanity. Clare himself is utterly, humanly involved, and we can see how far the reality of human life and love is from the 'idealistic' – what literary hero would sneeze as he considers his loved one's lips?

But it is the selfsame human frailty which will ensure that imperfect Clare, with such a human vision before him, should build it into a 'perfect' ideal, and blind himself to the beauty of imperfection. A sneeze, a seduction – apparent worlds apart, but so close as temporary human frailties. Who can expect perfection of such creatures? More, why should anyone expect it, when imperfection is so much more tangibly beautiful?

It will be obvious by now that the paucity of natural images which marked the neutral days of Tess's life has been more than compensated. Some fifty pages have passed since Tess came to Talbothays, and the images now are as rich and thickly-set as the growth of summer in the Froom valley. It would be impossible to discuss them all individually, but they grow and change with the story, all tending towards the same end, of emphasising Tess's natural humanity.

Then comes the shock. When Tess reveals to Clare her past 'sin', the images stop, die as rapidly as the simply harmony of their love. A single, cold image of Clare's unnatural demands replaces those warm profusions. 'She hardly observed that a tear descended slowly upon his cheek, a tear so large that it magnified the pores of the skin over which it rolled, like the object lens of a microscope.'[80] He too is human, but would deny his own imperfection, freeze the humanity of his tears with the cold logic of 'reason', and study human imperfection beneath a scientist's lens. Only one image stands to remind us of the fact that life will not wait upon Clare's 'ideals'; that Tess, like the world around her, must grow or die: 'new growths insensibly bud upward to fill each vacated place'.[81]

It is on the road to Flintcomb that the images return. But they are very different now from the rich phrases of Talbothays:

> Thus Tess walks on; a figure which is part of the landscape; a fieldwoman pure and simple, in winter guise; a gray serge cape, a red woollen cravat, a stuff skirt covered by a whitey-brown wrapper, and buff-leather gloves. Every thread of that old attire has become faded and thin under the stroke of raindrops, the burn of sunbeams, and the stress of winds. There is no sign of young passion in her now.[82]

The love story of Tess is following a seasonal pattern, as did the story of *Under the Greenwood Tree*, but this story is far subtler in its use of the seasons as images of love. Hardy selects the appropriate season for the mood (though it must be remembered that this second level of arrangement, after the choice of arena, applies only to Talbothays and Flintcomb) but then both season and mood are treated completely naturally, complementing each other simply by their coincidence of atmosphere. It is worth quoting the first description of fieldwork at Flintcomb, since it so closely parallels the description of Tess standing upon the level Froom meads:[83]

> Every leaf of the vegetable having already been consumed, the whole field was in colour a desolate drab; it was a complexion without features, as if a face, from chin to brow, should be only an expanse of skin. The sky wore, in another colour, the same likeness;

a white vacuity of countenance with the lineaments gone. So these two upper and nether visages confronted each other all day long, the white face looking down on the brown face, and the brown face looking up at the white face, without anything standing between them but the two girls crawling over the surface of the former like flies.[84]

In case any reader should think that Tess is any the less a part of this scene than of that at Talbothays, this single image assures us of Hardy's determination that the two settings should be equally natural, Tess's involvement equal in each. Only the mood and season differ.

And in case the image of the 'flies' should detract from the humanity which Hardy has been so carefully constructing as an element of natural harmony,[85] there follows a reminder of another, earlier image: 'The pensive character which the curtained hood lent to their bent heads would have reminded the observer of some early Italian conception of the two Marys.'[86] This vision recalls Clare's early observation: 'the mixed, singular, luminous gloom in which they walked along together to the spot where the cows lay, often made him think of the Resurrection hour. He little thought that the Magdalen might be at his side.'[87] Hardy is not assuming a religious connotation for Tess, but approaching his Victorian readers at a level they understand – the level of that unforgiving 'christianity' which the novel condemns, the 'last grotesque phase' of the creed. His images remind us (as he reminds elsewhere) that a 'fallen' woman is no less capable of worshipping love; that Jesus was more than capable of forgiveness. It is not the act that matters, as Hardy tells us over and over again, but the intent. In his 'religion' of nature, Hardy implies, there are all the true principles of christianity; it is the organised creed that has gone astray. Jesus, after all, was the image of Man.

As at Talbothays, the 'huge' experiences of Tess's life, already put into an overall context by the 'fly' image, are contrasted with some of the vastness of experience in nature, and sexual 'transgressions' are relegated to their true status of unimportance:

. . . strange birds from behind the North Pole began to arrive silently on the upland of Flintcomb-Ash; gaunt spectral creatures with tragical eyes – eyes which had witnessed scenes of cataclysmal horror in inaccessible polar regions of a magnitude such as no human being had ever conceived, in curdling temperatures that no man could endure; which had beheld the crash of icebergs and the slide of snow-hills by the shooting light of the Aurora; been half blinded by the whirl of colossal storms and terraqueous distortions; and retained the expression of feature that such scenes had engendered. These nameless birds came quite near to Tess and Marian, but of all they had seen which humanity would never see, they brought no account. The traveller's ambition to tell was not theirs, and, with dumb impassivity, they dismissed experiences which they did not value for the immediate incidents of this homely upland – the trivial movements of the two girls in disturbing the clods with their hackers so as to uncover something or other that these visitants relished as food.[88]

The implication is obvious – that nature in all its parts, from the most prosaic to the most spectacular, is equally a part of life; there is no intrinsic reason why any more importance should be attached to blinding blizzards (or sexual activities) than to the searching-out of food.

This mechanical production continues, in images which mingle Tess (and the other human beings around her) indiscriminately with natural features and aspects of cultivation, at reed-drawing, turnip-slicing, and threshing. Finally, back at Marlott to care for her ailing parents, we see Tess and 'Liza-Lu together on the allotment, the young girl introduced with the same kind of natural neutrality first associated with Tess. 'Liza-Lu's part in the book is brief, but in this one image the two girls are mingled as one in the natural work they perform, woven together by the wreaths of smoke from the bonfires around. It is an image which establishes the younger sister, even before Tess's statement, as the 'future' of Tess and, fittingly, is the last such image before the novel moves into its final, allegorical phase. In the smoke of the allotment the spirit of Tess in her natural state of harmony is passed unbroken to her sister:

As soon as twilight succeeded to sunset the flare of the couch-grass and cabbage-stalk fires began to light up the allotments fitfully, their outlines appearing and disappearing under the dense smoke as wafted by the wind. When a fire flowed, banks of smoke, blown level along the ground, would themselves become illuminated to an opaque lustre, screening the work-people from one another; and the meaning of the 'pillar of cloud', which was a wall by day and a light by night, could be understood.[89]

Once again Hardy resorts to the Biblical images which have stressed throughout his attitude to the established religion. His concept of the harmony between man and nature as the true basis of 'religion' comes through here as the pillar of cloud, the Biblical guide, comes not from 'the Lord' but from the smoke of man's working relationship with nature.

But how do Clare and d'Urberville, the only other major characters, fit into this pattern? We have already seen that Clare, at Talbothays, imbibes with Tess some of that harmony in nature which marks their love as natural and untainted. Images involving them both treat him as naturally as her — with one exception. Clare idealises. In the most simple, natural setting, he cannot resist the personification of 'Artemis' and 'Demeter' in Tess.

We are introduced to Clare in a logical exposition of his early life, a study of his beliefs and tendencies which has little relation to the simple, unassumed, animal-like Tess we first meet. They are two worlds apart:

> He spent years and years in desultory studies, undertakings, and meditations; he began to evince considerable indifference to social forms and observances. The material distinctions of rank and wealth he increasingly despised. Even the 'good old family' . . . had no aroma for him unless there were good new resolutions in its representatives. As a balance to these austerities, when he went to live in London to see what the world was like, and with a view to practising a profession or business there, he was carried off his head, and nearly entrapped by a woman much older than himself, though luckily he escaped not greatly the worse for the experience.[90]

He has done nothing socially untoward, but in this brief passage we see an almost precise parallel, in his world, of the course of Tess's life.[91] Even their concept of life is similar, albeit his is considered (intellectually of course, rather than on the basis of personal experience) and hers unplanned:

> 'What is the good of your mother and me economizing and stinting ourselves to give you a University education, if it is not to

be used for the honour and glory of God?' his father repeated.

'Why, that it may be used for the honour and glory of man, father.'[92]

Yet Clare's logic, however good in principle, has still to be tried in practice. For the moment (and for most of the novel) he is an element of those social values imposed from without on a natural rural world, which disrupt by their unsuitability. What works independently in each world cannot be transplanted unaltered. Like the simple philosophies of which Tess partook at school, which did so much to give her an unwarranted pessimism in life, Clare's attitudes come unprepared to the natural world of Talbothays. For all his apparent acceptance of this new life — 'it was with a sense of luxury that he recognised his power of viewing life here from its inner side, in a way that had been quite foreign to him in his student-days'[93] — for all this, he yet fails to understand the natural processes of love which have grown between him and Tess. Nor does he understand the power of her worship of him, taking him as symbol of all the joy of life. As we have seen from the images, he is a part of this; but as we are also aware, he does not understand his own passion. 'Clare knew that she loved him — every curve of her form showed that — but he did not know at that time the full depth of her devotion, its single-mindedness, its meekness; what long-suffering it guaranteed, what honesty, what endurance, what good faith.'[94] He sees her animal form, but not the spiritual; and in himself, he sees the spiritual, but not yet the animal. 'Clare's love was doubtless ethereal to a fault, imaginative to impracticability. With these natures, corporeal presence is sometimes less appealing than corporeal absence; the latter creating an ideal presence that conveniently drops the defects of the real.'[95] Clare, of course, can never be the same as Tess. They have grown up in different cultures, been stamped with different philosophies. But Hardy does see a growing-together, through experience and contact, of these two representatives of two worlds:

> Cynical things he had uttered to himself about her; but no man can be cynical and live; and he withdrew them. The mistake of expressing them had arisen from his allowing himself to be influenced by general principles to the disregard of the particular instance.
> But the reasoning is somewhat musty; . . . Clare had been harsh towards her . . . Men are too often harsh with women they love

or have loved; women with men. And yet these harshnesses are
tenderness itself when compared with the universal harshness out
of which they grow; the harshness of the position towards the
temperament, of the means towards the aims, of to-day towards
yesterday, of hereafter towards to-day.[96]

That first paragraph speaks it all of Clare – his musty reasoning has
been tempered by the passion of love. His intellect does not change –
he reasons with the passion – but however worded, it is the passion
that has changed him. The second paragraph reminds us once more
that these characters, for all their personal tragedy, are as nothing to
life. This is the reasoned argument that is Clare's version of the images
of Tess, the 'fly' upon the bare earth. Still they are parallel; the same
yet not quite the same. But in life, such differences are as nothing.

It is Clare, of course, who makes the most of Tess's d'Urberville
descent. To Tess, as to most of the characters around her, it is little
more than curious. To 'Sir John' it is an excuse to justify his own
indolence. To Alec d'Urberville, it is a name in the British Museum,
the seal upon his family's commercial success. Two comments can
perhaps sum up as well as any the relative importance of the name in
its rural environment. Of the Stoke family's annexation of the name,
Hardy says 'it must be admitted that this family formed a very good
stock whereon to regraft a name which sadly wanted such re-
novation.'[97] And when Tess obtains a job at The Slopes, John asks
'"What's her trump card? Her d'Urberville blood, you mean?"
"No, stupid; her face – as 'twas mine."'[98] The implicit irony of
Joan's reply (is it fortune to have married a drunkard?) reflects the
irony that Tess's own beauty is far from a benefit to her. Yet it is
frequently stressed in the novel that she is no more beautiful than
some of those around her; and Clare's love for her, prompted by her
beauty, is yet assured by her outlook, and fertilised by the natural
passions of summer. Her d'Urberville descent, to him, becomes first
a half-hearted romantic repudiation of his parents' doubts as to her
suitability; then it becomes a ghastly condemnation of his choice:

> . . . he caught sight of one of the d'Urberville dames, whose
> portrait was immediately over the entrance to Tess's bedchamber.
> In the candlelight the painting was more than unpleasant. Sinister
> design lurked in the women's features, a concentrated purpose of
> revenge on the other sex – so it seemed to him then. The Caroline

bodice of the portrait was low – precisely as Tess's had been when
he tucked it in to show the necklace; and again he experienced the
distressing sensation of a resemblance between them.[99]

But the d'Urberville connection is never a strong influence in their
affairs. References to the d'Urberville coach are made; Alec
d'Urberville rises from the tomb at Kingsbere, like the modern spirit
of the once-powerful family laying waste those around. But these are
romantic fancies, mere frivolities of the imagination. The true place
of this family name comes through when Clare, returning from
Brazil, pays the debt on John Durbeyfield's stone. The power of the
name is buried with him, and in the allegories that follow it is the
absence of the name that figures. The mansion, that counterpart of
Wellbridge, is deliberately stripped of all such connections, and Clare
and Tess find happiness in being together at last, without en-
cumbrance of this or any other 'ideal' name ('Artemis' or 'Demeter').

This obsession with a name, like the Board-School philosophies, is
merely one more element in the damaging invasion of ideas from a
different world into the rural communities. Conceived in the mind of
Parson Tringham, it reaches full power in the mind of Clare – a man
from the same world. Alone it is weak, but combined with the many
other invasions of ideas it promotes in the mind of a Tess such a
confusion of ideas that trouble can ensue.

Alec d'Urberville, the 'Satan' figure in the Eden of Clare and Tess,
represents another aspect of this invasion. It is not as an outsider,
representative of a strange family and new culture, that he appears
(that is refuted in the already-quoted description of the Stoke family
as a 'good stock', and the easy assimilation of the estate into local life).
He threatens Tess as an unfeeling representative of the animal lust
present in the other society from which he, Clare and Tringham all
spring.

In a sense, all are victims, mere products of the worlds in which
they live. The damage is done when the different worlds are
unthinkingly mixed. Neither world, in its own context, demands
perfection: Clare and the older woman in London, talked of in social
terms; or Tess and Alec, sexuality for the former being a natural state.
But Tess, imbibing philosophies and morals from another world,
cannot realise that they are flexible in context; and Joan fails to teach
of the natural imperfections of her own world. Even then, with a less
thoughtful girl than Tess, adjustments of personal morality could
no doubt have been made. Even she is slightly flexible (there is no such

state as perfection). But Tess, in search of perfect purity and love, rejects all compromise, and as pressure piles on pressure, she does not fall but is destroyed – a sacrifice to a false philosophy.

It is in Tess's destruction that we see the coming-together of this novel with the earlier ones. Nature has receded into the background, with each arena serving a new function as a 'moral image'. The community of men has also receded. Characters revolve around Tess; yet the harmony of man and nature, the working community, still exists as strongly. Marian and Retty and Izz are all treated with the same natural imagery as Tess. Agricultural work goes on behind the action of the novel:[100]

> The wide acreage of blank agricultural brownness, apparent where the swedes had been pulled, was beginning to be striped in wales of darker brown, gradually broadening to ribands. Along the edge of each of these something crept upon ten legs, moving without haste and without rest up and down the whole length of the field; it was two horses and a man, the plough going between them, turning up the cleared ground for a spring sowing.[101]

To the fore has come the personal relationship between man and nature, and the effect upon the individual's mind of introducing purely human philosophies into that relationship without adjustment. The effect, as we have seen, is the destruction of Tess; but more, behind and beyond that destruction we see the continuance of others. Marian and Izz find new employment; Talbothays and Trantridge and Flintcomb go on unconcerned. Tess at Talbothays was expendable even without her marriage, despite her skills – she was there, as everywhere, no more than an ordinary country girl. And at Marlott, time closes over the heads of the Durbeyfield family without a ripple:

> The house in which Tess had passed the years of her childhood was now inhabited by another family who had never known her. The new residents were in the garden, taking as much interest in their own doings as if the homestead had never passed its primal time in conjunction with the histories of others, beside which the histories of these were but as a tale told by an idiot. They walked about the garden paths with thoughts of their own concerns entirely uppermost, bringing their actions at every moment into jarring collision with the dim ghosts behind them, talking as

though the time when Tess lived there were not one wit intenser in story than now. Even the spring birds sang over their heads as if they thought there was nobody missing in particular.[102]

Nothing can stand still, if it would survive. 'New growths insensibly bud upward to fill each vacated place.' In the end, it is the same position as in the other novels, with those who can bend and adapt surviving, those who cannot going under. Even with all that happened to Tess, it is still her own purity of mind that contributes to her end. She cannot practise the social deceits of Clare's world on her lover, nor can she live in social deceit with d'Urberville; but she cannot either practise the more natural deceits of a Joan or an Izz. In part it is ignorance, the fault of school and mother; but in part, too, it is her own reluctance to practise deceit in the few simple philosophies she has imbibed.

Change, of course, cannot be averted. Hardy may have relegated the natural, organic processes of change in the rural community to a very minor place in this novel — but that is only because he is concentrating on the effects of change on the individual. Change is present throughout the novel, at every level. After all, that superficial note of hope, the unformed 'Liza-Lu hand-in-hand with the wiser, sadder Clare, reminds us above all of one fact: life goes on, and there is another generation of Tesses waiting to be formed or destroyed; but the world, for all the depth of this one tragedy, has not changed enough. Tess herself exhibits, particularly in the early stages of the novel, the same familiarity with local traditions as her fellows; though possibly her more sensitive nature might be said actually to make her more prone than they to fear or belief, despite Hardy's stated vision of her as a modern girl beside her 'Jacobean' mother's beliefs. She takes part in the Club walking with the other village girls, and when returning from Trantridge, she pricks her chin on the thorn of one of d'Urberville's roses; 'like all the cottagers in Blackmoor Vale, Tess was steeped in fancies and prefigurative superstitions; she thought this an ill omen — the first she had noticed that day.'[103] Which suggests that she was on the look-out for such omens — something never suggested of other characters in the novel, despite several references to this 'characteristic' of the villagers.

It is, in fact, very much an aspect of Tess's own personality that brings fears and beliefs to the fore in her mind. Indeed, compared with the carefully understated superstitions of the minor characters, her attitudes are given a curious weight of imagery:

THY, DAMNATION, SLUMBERETH, NOT

Against the peaceful landscape, the pale, decaying tints of the copses, the blue air of the horizon, and the lichened stile-boards, these staring vermilion words shone forth. They seemed to shout themselves out and make the atmosphere ring. Some people might have cried 'Alas, poor Theology!' . . . But the words entered Tess with accusatory horror.[104]

Her wedding dress seems to accuse her, to threaten change of colour at her dishonour, and in the gruesome history of Cross-in-Hand her own imagination feels the poetic force of the association with d'Urberville: 'it was put up in wuld times by the relations of a malefactor who was tortured there by nailing his hand to a post and afterwards hung. The bones lie underneath. They say he sold his soul to the devil, and that he walks at times.'[105]

At one level, of course, such emphasis on Tess's fears and beliefs is another aspect of the change to a concentration on the central figure, rather than the landscapes and the communities within them. However, the images also reflect very clearly the personal sensitivity of Tess to the formation of ideas. She is the unformed poet and philosopher who represents Mankind's involvement with the universe at a higher level than the physical; she is, in modern form, the representative of those who originated the superstitions and beliefs which her contemporaries treat so lightly, yet which once expressed a feeling belief in Man's comprehension of things beyond the tangible present:

> The trees have inquisitive eyes, haven't they? – that is, seem as if they had. And the river says, – 'Why do ye trouble me with your looks?' And you seem to see numbers of to-morrows just all in a line, the first of them the biggest and clearest, the others getting smaller and smaller as they stand farther away; but they all seem very fierce and cruel and as if they said, 'I'm coming! Beware of me! Beware of me!'[106]

Clare, though failing to understand fully himself, accurately places her thoughts as 'sensations which men and women have vaguely grasped for centuries.'[107]

In fact, Angel Clare's involvement with senseless, debased ideas is far closer that Tess's, who, even when using words or ideas derived from her parents and friends, clothes them with the real feelings of her soul. For his part, he has developed a cold, incisively logical dislike of 'ancient families'; on the surface it is a patently absurd idea, but Clare owes more to emotion than he will, in most of the novel, allow. His 'reasoned' condemnation of such heredity as the d'Urbervilles', set aside for his passionate involvement with Tess, is revealed in its true light by his reaction to the gloomy family associations of Wellbridge, and his shock at discovering Tess's association with Alec. In an instant, the semi-pagan attitude with which he hung mistletoe over their bed is dissolved into an unreasoning hate which conceals, deeper still, the love that is expressed in his sleep-walk.

Clare is, in many ways, a type of the Victorian rationalism, scholarship and philosophical exploration which, while purporting to free the human mind from the shackles of human superstition and darkness, only served to mask and distort true feeling and the inexpressible wonder of the human mind. In convincing his parents of the wisdom of his association with Tess, Clare uses logic and cold reason, as much to smooth his own doubts at the sheer passion of his feelings as to convince them. He will not allow himself to believe that passion and comprehension can be synonymous.

But Tess understands some things almost too well. The images of her traditional involvement, already moulded and revitalised by her far-seeing spirit, are gradually replaced by images of a basic involvement between Man and his universe, before the mechanics of everyday life have translated them into rules of conduct and keys to social ciphers. The unformed idea first expressed by Grace Melbury above the orchards of the Blackmoor Vale, 'in all this proud show some kernels were unsound as her own situation, and she wondered if there were one world in the universe where the fruit had no worm, and marriage no sorrow'[108] is refined and translated by the still childlike Tess: 'They sometimes seem to be like the apples on our stubbard-tree. Most of them splendid and sound – a few blighted.'[109] But she is to undergo far more than poverty and drunken parents before her soul grasps just how difficult life can be for the human being who tries to understand it.

The first image in fact passes unrecognised by Tess:

The sun, on account of the mist, had a curious sentient, personal look, demanding the masculine pronoun for its adequate expression. His present aspect, coupled with the lack of human forms in the scene, explained the old-time heliolatries in a moment. One could feel that a saner religion had never prevailed under the sky.[110]

But as she leaves Marlott, walking south to a 'new' life at Talbothays, she finds words – albeit from a standard source – to express the harmony she senses, singing the Benedicite, 'O ye Sun and Moon . . . O ye Stars . . . ye Green Things upon the Earth . . . ye fowls of the Air . . . Beasts and Cattle . . . Children of Men . . . bless ye the Lord, praise Him and magnify Him forever!'[111]

Tess understands that, despite her 'education', she has not learnt anything of the paradoxes by which Man lives, and which he seems only to gloss over in his attempts to see the universe as logical (in the manner of Clare):

> What's the use of learning that I am one of a long row only – finding out that there is set down in some old book somebody just like me, and to know that I shall only act her part; making me sad, that's all. The best is not to remember that your nature and your past doings have been just like thousands' and thousands'. . . . I shouldn't mind learning . . . why the sun do shine on the just and the unjust alike.[112]

She has, however, discovered the paradox whereby men are tied to their bodies, and to the same frailties as those who have gone before them, while their minds, set free by nature, can rise to the stars:

> I don't know about ghosts . . . but I do know that our souls can be made to go outside our bodies when we are alive . . . lie on the grass at night and look straight up at some big bright star; and, by fixing your mind upon it, you will soon find that you are hundreds and hundreds o' miles away from your body, which you don't seem to want at all.[113]

The human being has been given the ability to experience, to comprehend, and to relate; yet, paradoxically, he has not even the freedom of the birds of the air. When the 'gaunt spectral creatures' arrive from the North, the things they have seen are material for the greatest human mind to work upon. Yet 'with dumb impassivity, they dismissed experiences which they did not value for the immediate incidents of this homely upland.'[114] Tess, the brown figure bound to the earth by her bodily needs, has the soul to appreciate the wonder of what these birds have seen. But it is the unquestioning creatures which see.

How then does Man overcome this paradox, of mental liberty and physical enslavement? Hardy has already indicated, in *The Return of the Native*, *The Mayor of Casterbridge* and *The Woodlanders* the way to his mind such an impossible contradiction must tend: to death, as the only release. In *The Return of the Native*, the question was without words until briefly, in one chapter heading, came the precursor of the quotation that is to toll through the endless quest of Jude for an answer: 'Wherefore is Light given to him that is in Misery?'.[15]

In *The Mayor of Casterbridge*, Elizabeth-Jane, stoically facing the future at the bedside of her dying mother, put the first tentative words to the thought:

> asking herself why she was born, why sitting in a room and blinking at the candle; why things around her had taken the shape they wore in preference to every other possible shape. Why they stared at her so helplessly, as if waiting for the touch of some wand that should release them from terrestrial constraint; what that chaos called consciousness, which spun in her at this moment like a top, tended to, and began in.[116]

And in *The Woodlanders*, the thought is clothed. It is in portraying Grace that the doubt first seems to arise, reminding us of the image of Eustacia atop the Rainbarrow; ' . . . to precisely describe a human being, the focus of a universe, how impossible!'[117] But Grace is never fully developed and it is Felice Charmond who actually voices the question:

> Sorrow and bitterness in the sky, and floods of agonised tears beating against the panes. I lay awake last night, and I could hear the scrape of snails creeping up the window glass; it was so sad! My eyes were so heavy this morning that I could have wept my life away. I cannot bear you to see my face; I keep it away from you purposely. O! why were we given hungry hearts and wild desires if we have to live in a world like this? Why should Death alone lend what Life is compelled to borrow — rest?[118]

The passage borrows heavily from the imagery of the *Book of Job*: and it picks up the image of the dead Eustacia, for whom final rest was the first occasion of real fulfilment. This paradox of Man, hinted at but never explored, is in *The Woodlanders* at last given statement. Now, sleeping on the sacrificial stone within Stonehenge, Tess lies like an offering to the sun which, as giver of life on the earth, first created the beauty of human form and first enslaved the human mind. Dawn comes like the lifting of a curtain of darkness in the understanding, and as the tiny human figures gather round the sacrifice there seems, for the first time, to be a glimpse of possibilities, as tantalisingly unformed and beyond definition as once was the paradox itself:

> The uniform concavity of black cloud was lifting bodily like the lid of a pot, letting in at the earth's edge the coming day, against which the towering monoliths and trilithons began to be blackly defined . . . All waited in the growing light, their faces and hands as if they were silvered, the remainder of their figures dark, the stones glistening green-gray, the Plain still a mass of shade. Soon the light was strong, and a ray shone upon her unconscious form, peering under her eyelids and waking her.[119]

The whole scene becomes an image of Man. His face and hands in light, he can understand and build – yet his body, still in darkness, hampers his every effort and, in the inevitable end, drags him once more into the darkness. The sun touches the sleeping 'lesser creature', rouses it to understanding, and delivers it over to the sacrifice of death.

In this brief, brilliant vignette of human existence, Hardy encapsulates all that has gone before, encompasses all the questions and doubts, formed and unformed, of the earlier novels, and delivers them, upon the sacrificial stone, to the greatest question of all, 'Wherefore is light given to him that is in Misery, and life unto the bitter in soul?' Yet the terribly brief span of the 'sacrifice' by which Tess's life is compassed cannot entirely remove the sense of lingering beauty in the short moments of her love for Clare. Driven beyond human rationale by the power of her love Tess reaches at last, no madness, but a sublimity that far transcends her understanding. Her life is, after all, not so pointless as the sacrifice might make it seem, for she has, in a few short years, risen through love to a grasp of her own brilliant transience. The trials and experiences of life work upon the basic material of comprehension until all the complexities of her situation which have driven her like some hunted creature through Wessex, and tangled her ever more thoroughly in the snares of emotion and idea, prove to be mist before the dawn of her understanding.

7 Landscapes of the Mind: *Jude the Obscure*

I.

In *Tess*, Hardy brings the enclosed landscape to its artistic and thematic end. The future for the rural world was inevitable; it was about to be changed, whether it would or no, by education, by technological advance, by theorising and planning, by the decay of an outworn paternal order, and the coming of a new breed of landowner fresh from the industrial midlands, with concerns on the scale of an Empire not of a county. But what of the individuals who would once, like Henchard, have perished dumbly in their search for an escape from the blind acquiescence of their world? The new light flooding in brought to such as Tess, not answers or explanations, but new learning as mechanical as the old, theories empty of reality and ideas and morals that contradicted each other and life.

But how can the individual, his mind suffused with the strange light of existence, discover even such knowledge for himself until he has searched? In *Jude the Obscure*, his last novel, Hardy follows a man in this complex search.

The new landscapes are completely divorced from the enclosed landscapes of the five early novels, and the associated arena of *Tess*. Even the final vignettes of that novel are abandoned, remaining unique in Hardy's Wessex. However, the rural community continues as flourishing as ever, an undercurrent to the large landscapes of *Jude*. At Marygreen, Christminster, Aldbrickham, Stoke-Barehills or Shaston, communities live and work as effectively, unheedingly and uncrushably as ever they did in the earlier novels. It is simply Hardy's portrayal of them that has changed, from involvement and sympathy at various levels to a rather bleak objectivity. We occasionally drift, with Jude, into the fringes of these communities, but there is never any sense of personal involvement for Jude, Hardy or the reader.

The new landscapes of the novel are ones of the mind – the

author's, the reader's, and Jude's — involving individual perceptions of places. Christminster changes and evolves in Jude's eyes, as his search for a way of life that to him seems real and worthwhile, whether study, religion or love, changes his perception of its role and reality in life. It changes, too, for Hardy, as he questions its reality first as a place of study, then as an architectural expression of man's skill, then as a heart of the changing nineteenth century society and culture, then as simply a living town, finally as a symbol of division, unfairness, tragedy, pleasure and transience. It even changes for the reader, as characters give differing perspectives upon it without authorial judgement, and as Hardy's own comments contradict or amend themselves.

In a sense, it is Christminster that is the heart of the novel, all other physical settings being extremely sketchy by comparison. Yet to see novel or settings in merely physical terms would be a gross simplification of the facts. We follow Jude, as we once followed Tess, from place to place, yet now it is Jude who matters, in his stumbling search for a definitive 'reality' in his life, not the interaction of particular communities with the individual.

The dream city is changed and changed again, seen from many sides at once, and perceptions of it changed even by the contact of Jude, Hardy and the reader with other places and other ideas (Melchester and religion, for example). There is no longer any simple definition of 'landscapes'. There is, perhaps, no definition at all. The landscape has finally become, what it was gradually evolving into through the course of Clym's, Elizabeth-Jane's, Grace's, Mrs. Charmond's and Tess's musings, the entire canvas of individual human life, defined only by that question, 'wherefore is light given to him that is in misery?' In their own ways, each preceding character has asked the same question, and now in *Jude the Obscure* Hardy, Jude and the reader search both understanding and environment for some kind of answer.

The quest begins at one of Hardy's farthest-flung settings, Marygreen (based on Great Fawley in Berkshire); and it is no coincidence that we are so far removed from the South Dorset world of the early Wessex novels, and even from the landscapes of *The Woodlanders* and *Tess of the d'Urbervilles*. Like Jude himself, we are plucked from 'Mellstock, down in South Wessex'[1] and transported to a world that, while apparently similar, is alien to our understanding of Wessex life. We have been used, even in *Tess* to see the community in all its diverse forms as the compass of an individual's

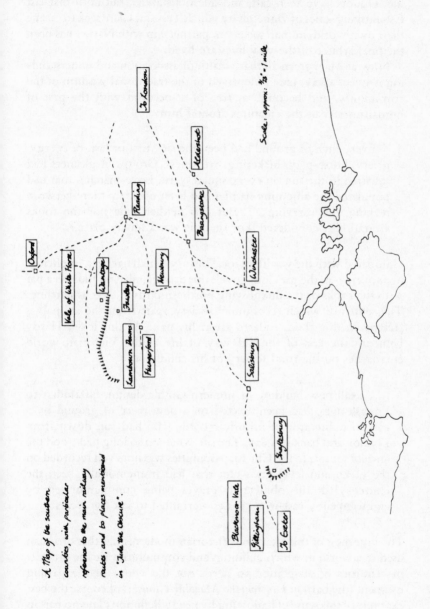

A Map of the southern counties, with particular reference to the main railway routes, and to places mentioned in "Jude the Obscure".

Scale: appox: ⅔ = 1 mile

life. Doubts have been cast, and questions asked, but until that last fast-moving series of vignettes by which Tess and Clare seek to escape their own world, human society in partnership with Nature has been the final arbiter of the way lives are lived.

Now at Marygreen all that wealth of association and understanding is swept away; Jude is deprived of the traditional wisdom of the community, and becomes as free of association with the past of human society as the creatures around him:

> Every inch of ground had been the site, first or last, of energy, gaiety, horse-play, bickering, weariness. Groups of gleaners had squatted in the sun on every square yard. Love-matches that had populated the adjoining hamlet had been made up there between reaping and carrying . . . But this neither Jude nor the rooks around him considered. For them it was a lonely place. [2]

Compared with the wealth of local history which has been implicit — or explicit — in the previous novels this passage, placing Jude on a par with the rooks or the unknowing northern birds in *Tess*, is startling. The sentience which sets human society apart from the animals is lacking in this child, isolated from his past. At this level, Hardy bemoans the loss of the old way of life as the Victorian world encroaches on the rural society of his childhood

> . . . a tall new building of modern Gothic design, unfamiliar to English eyes, had been erected on a new piece of ground by a certain obliterator of historic records who had run down from London and back in a day. The site whereon so long had stood the ancient temple to the Christian divinities was not even recorded on the green and level grass-plot that had immemorially been the church-yard, the obliterated graves being commemorated by eighteenpenny cast-iron crosses warranted to last five years. [3]

The bitterness of this attack on Victorian modernism is that of a man used to a world in which buildings and communities are the product of centuries of adaptation to need, not the whim of the passing moment (the barn in *Far from the Madding Crowd* is of course the best example of this sense of hallowing by need). Religion plays no part in this association, Christianity being deliberately regarded in the detached manner of the classical religions, with a 'temple' and 'divinities'. But, as with the church in *Under the Greenwood Tree*, Hardy was always aware of the deep emotional need in human society for such visible manifestations of faith in the innate order of the universe. Like the rural society itself, such a building was the tangible compromise that represents the struggle of Man to survive and prosper.

Yet, as *Tess* has shown us, Hardy had long ago realised the fundamental conflict betweeen society and the human instinct of certain individuals to seek greater truths, greater understanding. At this level, Marygreen becomes the dried carcase of a society that can never offer fulfilment to a man such as Jude. Its anonymity takes on a cruel, inhuman aspect, in which the animal law of survival of the fittest takes precedence over all else. Farmer Troutham beats Jude for allowing the crows to feed. Jude's courtship of Arabella commences with the receipt on his ear of a pig's penis, the most basic, unspiritual association possible for the act of procreation. Arabella herself is virtually pure animal. '(She) was a fine dark-eyed country girl, not exactly handsome, but capable of passing as such at a little distance, despite some coarseness of skin and fibre . . . She was a complete and substantial female animal – no less.'[4] Her marriage to Jude is based on a false assumption of pregnancy. And the 'high point' of cottage life – of their married life – is the killing of the pig, now a matter of horror, not of daily need:

> The animal's note changed its quality. It was not now rage, but the cry of despair; long-drawn, slow and hopeless. . . . The blood flowed out in a torrent instead of in the trickling stream she had desired. The dying animal's cry assumed its third and final tone, the shriek of agony; his glazing eyes riveting themselves on Arabella with the eloquently keen reproach of a creature recognizing at last the treachery of those who had seemed his only friends.[5]

The doubts were first expressed by Gabriel Oak, as he regarded the necessary death of those lambs he tended with such care – but Oak was a true countryman, part of his environment, with no desire to change. Tess was surrounded by elements of sheer brutality – the drunken women fighting in the fields on their way home; her father too drunk to work – but still the country ways seemed fundamental to life. But now, Marygreen and its way of life has become a symbol of all that is lowest in Man; a symbol of the paradox that all of Man's sophisticated social world is based on the cruel requirements of life on this earth. The cottages may be modern, the church an interloper, but Marygreen is still a thriving community with customers for Jude's bakery round and Vilbert's potions, children for a school, farms and labourers, tranters and all the other aspects of an efficient rural society. But certainly, in the changing environment of the rural world at the time of *Jude*, there is no sense of beauty in Man's partnership with Nature:

> Nature's logic was too horrid for him to care for. That mercy towards one set of creatures was cruelty towards another sickened his sense of harmony. As you got older, and felt yourself to be at the centre of your time, and not at a point in its circumference, as you had felt when you were little, you were seized with a sort of shuddering, he perceived. All around you there seemed to be something glaring, garish, rattling, and the noises and glares hit upon the little cell called your life, and shook it, and warped it.[6]

This dreadful, barren atmosphere is common to all of Marygreen's natural surroundings. 'The fresh harrow-lines seemed to stretch like the channellings in a piece of new corduroy, lending a meanly utilitarian air to the expanse, taking away its gradations, and depriving it of all history beyond that of the few recent months.'[7] 'Here the ploughed land ended, and all before him was bleak open down.'[8] Buildings are sparse, mostly undescribed, and given the most cursory mention when absolutely necessary – 'the corner by the rectory-house',[9] 'this being one of the few old houses left',[10] 'a weather-beaten old barn of reddish-gray brick and tile',[11] 'the cottage post-office',[12] 'a small homestead, having a garden and pig-sties attached',[13] 'an inn of an inferior class',[14] 'a lonely roadside cottage'.[15] Everything tends to a view of the utterly functional nature of the area, unrelieved by any hint of human spirituality.

Between the world of Marygreen and the world of Christminster is set a yawning gulf, unbridged by any natural or human feature. The plain below the 'Brown House', visible 'to a distance of forty or fifty miles'[16] has 'a bluer, moister atmosphere' than the open downs, and it is in the plain that Alfredston, where Jude works for a stonemason, lies and where much of his courtship of Arabella takes place. Yet those events, so much a part of Marygreen life for Jude, are never connected with Christminster. The tiler says to Jude, 'Christminster is out across there, by that clump. You can see it – at least you can on a clear day. Ah, no, you can't now.'[17] Nor can any of the minor characters ever see it. It appears to Jude's eyes, a haze of light at dusk, or a glimpse of some fabled city as the setting sun strikes it:

> The air increased in transparency with the lapse of minutes, till the topaz points showed themselves to be the vanes, windows, wet roof slates, and other shining spots upon the spires, domes, freestone-work, and varied outlines that were faintly revealed. It was Christminster, unquestionably; either directly seen, or mir-aged in the peculiar atmosphere.[18]

The images are striking in their freshness and intensity, set as they are amongst the bleakness of the Marygreen landscape, but they are 'miraged in the peculiar atmosphere' – an atmosphere within Jude's own mind, that takes the distant reality and translates it into a child's imaginings of fabled promise. To the inhabitants of the cold Marygreen world, Christminster is a city in a story, a matter of hearsay, unconnected with ordinary folk:

> You know, I suppose, that they raise pa'sons there like radishes in a bed? And though it do take – how many years, Bob? – five years to turn a lirruping hobble-de-hoy chap into a solemn preaching man with no corrupt passions, they'll do it, if it can be done . . . I've never been there, no more than you; but I've picked up the knowledge here and there, and you be welcome to it. . . . A friend o' mine, that used to clane the boots at the Crozier Hotel in Christminster when he was in his prime, why, I knowed him as well as my own brother in his later years.[19]

The fable is ridiculed by the imprecise musings of a rural figure devoid of all the sympathy and nobility of innocence that once marked such characters in Hardy's work. The picture of a man claiming knowledge on the basis of an acquaintance with a retired boot-boy is redolent of the disillusion in Hardy's vision of his rural world – the disillusion of a man once criticised for making his labourers too lucid of expression. But to Jude, and to us, as the repeated emphasis upon its unseen virtues or barely-glimpsed spires contrasts with bare, terse descriptions of the local landscape, Chris-tminster 'acquired a tangibility, a permanence, a hold on his life.'[20]

The gap between the two worlds is carefully maintained when, three years after his marriage to Arabella, Jude enters the city. We join him 'at a point a mile or two to the south-west of it', leaving

Marygreen without ceremony or comment. We do not, however, walk immediately into a city made concrete by Jude's arrival. On the contrary, our vision of it remains as mystic and imprecise as Jude's. He pauses to look across to where it lies, 'grey stoned and dun-roofed', 'within hail of the Wessex border'. 'The buildings now lay quiet in the sunset, a vane here and there on their many spires and domes giving sparkle to a picture of sober secondary and tertiary hues.'[21] The image is no more than a closer realisation of Jude's first distant dream; and, though guided by a map, Jude sees the ancient city in his first evening there in the light of his own vision: ' . . . then he began to be encircled as it were with the breath and sentiment of the venerable city. When he passed objects out of harmony with its general expression he allowed his eyes to slip over them as if he did not see them'.[22] He peoples the city with shades of his own imagining, until the voice of a lone policeman comes as an intrusion upon the reality of his muddled procession of poets, philosophers, divines, historians, statesmen, scientists, philologists and official men.[23] But even in the mellow warmth of Jude's mind, there is no escape from the tactile reality of the buildings and – by association – the men they house:

> High against the black sky the flash of a lamp would show crocketed pinnacles and indented battlements. Down obscure alleys, apparently never trodden now by the foot of man, and whose very existence seemed to be forgotten, there would jut into the path porticoes, oriels, doorways of enriched and florid middle-age design, their extinct air being accentuated by the rottenness of the stones. It seemed impossible that modern thought could house itself in such decrepit and superseded chambers.[24]

Darkness and shadow, neglect and desertion, crumbling stone-work and outmoded design – Christminster seems to reek of decay in mind and body. Yet Jude continues to regard the city in an inspirational light:

> From his window he could perceive the spire of the Cathedral and the ogee dome under which resounded the great bell of the city. The tall tower, tall belfry windows, and tall pinnacles of the college by the bridge he could also get a glimpse of by going to the staircase. These objects he used as stimulants when his faith in the future was dim.[25]

The self-delusion of Jude is all too apparent in the horridly prosaic necessity of going to the staircase to catch a glimpse of windows and pinnacles. The colleges have irrevocably taken on an air of 'something barbaric'[26] and Jude, the mason, is gradually coming to an understanding, in despite of himself, of the tangible aspects of his ethereal world. 'The numberless architectural pages around him he read, naturally, less as an artist-critic of their forms than as an artizan and comrade of the dead handicraftsmen whose muscles had actually executed those forms.'[27] Jude the dreamer, the seeker after wisdom, subverts the skills and hopes of Jude the artisan, in the hopeless search for man-made answers to the riddles of life. But the curious juxtapositions of Marygreen, whereby Jude's Christminster opposed the Christminster of the older villagers, which left us in doubt as to which was the more dream-like, are now replaced by an all too concrete realisation of the actual situation. We can see, as could Jude if he would allow himself to, the degenerate, outworn buildings which are symbols of the philosophies within. But there is a curious muddle here to Hardy's own vision: ' . . . here in the stoneyard was a centre of effort as worthy as that dignified by the name of scholarly study within the noblest of the colleges.'[28] On the face of it, the brief illumination granted to Jude is entirely in the mould of William Morris and the Arts and Crafts Movement of Victorian society. Yet the 'scholarly study' which is the comparison of merit for this work is held up to ridicule. And as for the masonry of the colleges, the replacement of which is such a noble pursuit, 'They were marked by precision, mathematical straightness, smoothness, exactitude: there in the old walls were the broken lines of the original idea; jagged curves, disdain of precision, irregularity, disarray.'[29] Yet those 'broken lines' are condemned as 'rottenness';[30] and the gothic originals were once as precise as these repairs. Morris's vision of craftsmanship was based not on a mere revivalism but a revitalisation of the mediaeval spirit of art, craft and science combined in the human expression of the individual — head and hands combining together in one man. But Hardy does not agree:

He did not at that time see that mediaevalism was as dead as a fern-leaf in a lump of coal; that other developments were shaping in the world around him, in which Gothic architecture and its associations had no place. The deadly animosity of contemporary logic and vision towards so much of what he held in reverence was not yet revealed to him.[31]

But even this is not a simple statement of fact. In this curious double-edged weapon of praise and condemnation we see a simple principle in operation — that it is the thing we have not achieved which is ideal. At Marygreen the dream of Christminster was a thing of splendour, occasionally ridiculed by local people, but always seen as the brilliant ideal (albeit a very imprecise ideal) which lightens the primitive darkness of life at the animal level. Marriage to Arabella seems a tragic disruption of a promising future.

Yet no sooner have we entered Christminster than the dream is shattered. It may take Jude, self-deluded, a little longer to realise it, but the very first encounter — the first moment of real contact — has destroyed the dream. Hardy describes it as Jude's 'form of the modern vice of unrest'.[32] But is it? In immediate terms, his unrest and dissatisfaction may seem almost capricious, but the words of Tess, refined by personal suffering, seem to recur: 'sensations which men and women have vaguely grasped for centuries'.[33] In Jude's search for better things, more logical answers than the cruelty of Nature's scheme, there seem to echo the hopeless strivings of Henchard, Clym, and Tess herself. Troy, Wildeve and Fitzpiers, seeking their own escapes from a deadening certainty of life, can be glimpsed in the unambitious 'ambitions' which were the dream of boy who could not accept his world.

But still, behind all this, runs the concept of a society in which all men have a place:

> his gaze travelled on to the various spires, halls, gables, streets, chapels, gardens, quadrangles, which composed the ensemble of this unrivalled panorama. He saw that his destiny lay not with these, but among the manual toilers in the shabby purlieu which he himself occupied, unrecognized as part of the city at all by its visitors and panegyrists, yet without whose denizens the hard readers could not read nor the high thinkers live.[34]

The dream is fled; Jude, unable to accept less, and unwilling to humble the pride of his vision, now changes the direction of his search. But the undercurrent of a thriving community, the tapestry of human life, larger now than anything ever before conceived, runs through the novel from this moment onwards:

> It had more history than the oldest college in the city. It was literally teeming, stratified, with the shades of human groups, who

had met there for tragedy, comedy, farce; real enactments of the intensest kind. At Fourways men had stood and talked of Napoleon, the loss of America, the execution of King Charles, the burning of the Martyrs, the Crusades, the Norman Conquest, possibly of the arrival of Caesar. Here the two sexes had met for loving, hating, coupling, parting; had waited, had suffered, for each other; had triumphed over each other; cursed each other in jealousy, blessed each other in forgiveness.[35]

This is the material of which Casterbridge was built (and which echoed faintly across the bleak fields of Marygreen) — but now there are no artistic restrictions, and the threads of wider history are mingled with the affairs, petty or great, of each community.

But for Jude, the exception who cannot accept his place in this rich tapestry, there must be some personal justification of existence. Christminster, as an intellectual hope, is dead. Sue has gone, and the blossoming of love is thwarted by the barrier of his first marriage. Drink, briefly, provides escape — but Jude, in the awful parody of the drunken Latin creed, realises the emptiness of such a path; and he turns to the only other available dream, religion. 'It was a new idea — the ecclesiastical and altruistic life as distinct from the intellectual and emulative life.'[36] To us, with foreknowledge, the example of Clym's self-destructive dreams is all too clear; but Jude is, once more, blind to all but the ideal.

The bare landscape of Marygreen, brightened only by the dreamlike vision of Christminster, gave way to the crumbling reality of that city. Yet still there has been no firm, identifiable landscape, in the manner of the previous Wessex novels. There were no suburbs described in the city — Jude fled before he could come to realise the concrete reality of his life there. Even the colleges, like the anonymous scholars they contain, stood indistinguishable, with no connection between the names and the vision. The city never clothed itself in the flesh and bones of reality.

Now, in his new course, Jude once more sees only what he wants to at the town of his dreams. Melchester cathedral becomes the misty symbol of the new idea: 'The lofty building was visible as far as the roof-ridge; above, the dwindling spire rose more and more remotely, till its apex was quite lost in the mist drifting across it.'[37] Like Christminster before it, it is real enough to be considered a goal, yet far enough removed to make it desirable and imprecise. Within the precincts of his dream, Jude establishes himself in a fashion that is almost a parody of his concept of religion – and a parody of certain Victorian attitudes:

> His combined bed and sitting room was furnished with framed photographs of the rectories and deaneries at which his landlady had lived as trusted servant in her time. . . . Jude added to the furniture of his room by unpacking photographs of the ecclesiastical carvings and monuments that he had executed with his own hands . . . As a relaxation from the Fathers, and such stock works as Paley and Butler, he read Newman, Pusey, and many other modern lights. He hired a harmonium, set it up in his lodging, and practised chants thereon, single and double.[38]

All sense of reality is removed from this scene, as the masonry becomes an enshrined symbol of religious belief – bringing with it its own atmosphere of decay, gathering the hierarchy of the Church into itself by association and, with an utter seriousness of language, reflecting Jude's own seriousness of purpose, reducing theological literature to the level of a cheap harmonium – a kind of mechanical parody of ideas and music that once conveyed true passion and concern. Like the Greek and Latin texts before them, it is these objects that become symbols of the new endeavour.

It is at Melchester, however, that a building first takes on an aspect outside this mirroring of Jude's dreams and understandings. The Melchester Normal School, in some ways similar to the crumbling colleges, and associated with the same round condemnation of the Gothic, appears in an almost neutral guise – but leans just perceptibly to the imprisoning image which soon becomes apparent, as Sue's free spirit is fettered. 'It was an ancient edifice of the fifteenth century, once a palace, now a training-school, with mullioned and transomed windows, and a courtyard in front shut in from the road by a wall.'[39] And in the undescribed Wardour Castle we realise, for the first time, that the slight, spiritual figure of Sue has already trodden the paths which Jude now follows in the blinkers of idealism. 'It was evident that her cousin deeply interested her, as one might be interested in a man puzzling out his way along a labyrinth from which one had one's self escaped.'[40]

Jude's next step along the labyrinthine ways is taken when Sue marries Phillotson. The news of his aunt's illness, and an offer of work at Christminster, take him back to the city of his early dreams. But now, shorn of its intellectual associations, it appears in its visual light, as to a passing stranger:

> The City of learning wore an estranged look, and he had lost all feeling for its associations. Yet as the sun made vivid lights and shades of the mullioned architecture of the facades, and drew patterns of the crinkled battlements on the young turf of the quadrangles, Jude thought he had never seen the place look more beautiful.[41]
>
> . . . college after college, in picturesqueness unrivalled except by such Continental vistas as the Street of Palaces in Genoa; the lines of the buildings being as distinct in the morning air as in an architectural drawing.[42]

It might be a passage from the diary of some gentleman on the Grand Tour, for all the involvement implicit in the crisp lines and clear shadows of the colleges. But within this city of detached observation lie the seeds of a new involvement. In words almost as detached as those describing the colleges, Jude sees the new interior of the inn where he once before 'had a wet'. But the old association, and the imminent presence of Arabella, are enough to remind us of the dangers inherent in this simple picture (as the training school quietly announced the reality of its influence on Sue):

> The bar had been gutted and newly arranged throughout, mahogany fixtures having taken the place of the old painted ones, while at the back of the standing-space there were stuffed sofa-benches. . . . On the inside of the counter two barmaids leant over the white-handled beer-engines, and the row of little silvered taps inside, dripping into a pewter trough.[43]

The scene has become attractively neutral in its moral tone, but the vivid image of beer dripping into the pewter trough seems to flash briefly upon our minds with an intensity that bodes ill for the customer at this deceptively innocent tavern. Having, for the moment at least, put Christminster behind him, Jude throws himself with renewed vigour into a further ideal – the chastising of the flesh. To this end, he sees the proximity of Shaston, with the now-married Sue, and Melchester as a suitable subject for internal warfare: a fit manner in which to keep at bay the tempting despair of that seductively attractive public house. Arabella and his own lower aspects have become no longer an object of loathing but a warm attraction – their candidacy for a future path in the labyrinth of life has been announced.

Meanwhile, Shaston becomes the new 'city of a dream': [44]

> Vague imaginings of its castle, its three mints, its magnificent apsidal Abbey, the chief glory of South Wessex, its twelve churches, its shrines, chantries, hospitals, its gabled freestone mansions – all now ruthlessly swept away – throw the visitor, even against his will, into a pensive melancholy, which the stimulating atmosphere and limitless landscape around him can scarcely dispel. . . . it is hardly accessible . . . but by a sort of isthmus on the north-east, that connects it with the high chalk table-land on that side.
>
> Such is, and such was, the now world-forgotten Shaston or Palladour. [45]

Like Christminster before it, it is not the tangible reality its description at first seemed to promise; the past, imagined and real, presses heavy on this island in the sky. The present, it seems, is more of a dream than the past. Sue, in Old-Grove Place, is oppressed physically and mentally by the very real nature of the house she occupies

> whose walls were lined with wainscoting of panelled oak reaching from floor to ceiling, the latter being crossed by huge moulded beams only a little way above her head. The mantelpiece was of the same heavy description, carved with Jacobean pilasters and scroll-work. The centuries did, indeed, ponderously overhang a young wife who passed her time here. [46]

There is none of the mellow harmony of man and his creation which characterised the Jacobean darkness of Weatherbury Farm, in this house. It stands out from the 'vague imaginings' of Jude's new dream-city with a clarity that emphasises the ponderousness of man-made things closing upon the free spirit of the woman within. The city, with all its history and close community of life, becomes a burden on her soul.

But neither Jude nor Sue can for long survive their respective actions. After his aunt's death, Jude abandons all profession of his vocation to the Church, burning his books in a symbolic gesture as typical as any of his previous actions. He and Sue join together and leave their homes at Melchester and Shaston, to live in the anonymity of Aldbrickham, a town of 'sixty or seventy thousand inhabitants'. [47]

Anonymity is indeed the overriding characteristic of the town. Undescribed at any point, it is no more than a setting for the next stage in the relationship of Jude and Sue. There are no dreams, no houses old or new, there is no crumbling masonry or shining Gothic improvement. Not until the young couple seek out the Registrar's Office is any feature portrayed:

> The day was chilly and dull, and a clammy fog blew through the town from 'Royal-tower'd Thame'. On the steps of the office there were the muddy footmarks of people who had entered, and in the entry were damp umbrellas. . . . Law books in musty calf covered one wall, and elsewhere were Post-Office Directories, and other books of reference. Papers in packets tied with red tape were pigeon-holed around, and some iron safes filled a recess; while the bare wood floor was, like the doorstep, stained by previous visitors. [48]

Like the sudden clarity of the interior of Old-Grove Place, the intrusion of this drearily precise picture into a hitherto characterless setting draws an enormous weight of attention upon an otherwise slight passage. There is nothing drastically upsetting in the image of a foggy day, a muddy floor, and a bare office; yet these features stand out as distasteful beacons in an empty landscape, forcing an assumption of distaste in the reader at the circumstance of the proposed marriage.

In the wandering anonymity of this time and the period that follows, two places stand out – Stoke-Barehills and Kennetbridge. The former is a bare (as the name implies), characterless mixture of old and new – in its attenuated description, very similar to Marygreen:

> There is in Upper Wessex an old town of nine or ten thousand souls; the town may be called Stoke-Barehills. It stands with its gaunt, unattractive, ancient church, and its new red brick suburb, amid the open, chalk-soiled cornlands . . . The most familiar object in Stoke-Barehills nowadays is its cemetery, standing among some picturesque mediaeval ruins beside the railway; the modern chapels, modern tombs, and modern shrubs, having a look of

intrusiveness amid the crumbling and ivy-covered decay of the ancient walls. [49]

There is the same air of barrenness about the town as there was about the village; and the tired, uninteresting details seem to echo the dreary interior of the Registrar's Office. The town is seen from without, a mere tourist-stop on the railway, with no character or community. And even in the cemetery, as at Marygreen, there is a gaunt anonymity and disharmony in death. But death is now the dominant feature. There is nothing regenerative or harmonious in the new buildings among the old — eighteenpenny crosses or red-brick villas are not a sign of fresh life — and the terrible, stagnant air of village and town emerges from the realms of Jude's childhood to become a feature of the world at large. The only life in the town is provided by the fair — no longer a working gathering, but a day of anonymous pleasure for everyone within reach of the railway — and even here it is the impermanence that is emphasised:

> Rows of marquees, huts, booths, pavilions, arcades, porticoes — every kind of structure short of a permanent one — cover the green field for the space of a square half-mile, and the crowds of arrivals walk through the town in a mass, and make straight for the exhibition ground. [50]

Kennetbridge, mentioned once before as the home of the composer of the hymn 'The Foot of The Cross', is as characterless as Stoke-Barehills, though no attempt is made to reiterate a sense of desolation about the place. Its fair, also barely described, does however pick up an aspect of the earlier occasion which, as we are so well accustomed with Jude, stands as a symbol of his present trend of thought. At Stoke-Barehills it was a 'model of Cardinal College, Christminster; by J. Fawley and S. F. M. Bridehead', [51] at Kennetbridge it is 'windows and towers, and pinnacles', executed in pastry. [52] 'Christminster is a fixed vision with him' says Sue, 'He still thinks it a great centre of high and fearless thought, instead of what it is, a nest of commonplace school-masters whose characteristic is timid obsequiousness to tradition.' [53] But in fact Jude's vision when he left Christminster was of neither aspect. He saw the cold beauty of the place, and the real life in its streets. His return now to the city, on 'Remembrance Day', is made in the same spirit of inspired self-chastisement that led him to follow Sue to Melchester, and then to

Shaston. He is too weak to utterly shun the fallen dream; yet Christminster is no 'fixed vision'. In the bustle of Remembrance Day the city, for the first time, comes to life as to its indigenous population. Gown is seen clearly from without, as the colleges appeared in their 'Grand tour' light before:

> They turned in on the left by the church with the Italian porch, whose helical columns were heavily draped with creepers, and pursued the lane till there arose on Jude's sight the circular theatre with that well-known lantern above it, which stood in his mind as the sad symbol of his abandoned hopes . . . To-day, in the open space stretching between this building and the nearest college, stood a crowd of expectant people. A passage was kept clear through their midst by two barriers of timber, extending from the door of the college to the door of the large building between it and the theatre. . . . carriage after carriage drew up at the lower door of the college, and solemn stately figures in blood-red robes began to alight.[54]

The real opposition within the town has now emerged, and the colleges become tangible objects looming horribly within the living mass that throngs the narrow back-lanes of the city:

> At some distance opposite, the outer walls of Sarcophagus College – silent, black and windowless – threw their four centuries of gloom, bigotry, and decay into the little room she occupied, shutting out the moonlight by night and the sun by day.[55]

The city seems at last to have been revealed in its true light, its darkness of spirit, and for a time we could almost forget the bare anonymity of the towns and villages elsewhere; the weight of the dead past at Shaston; and the unreasoning bigotry of Aldbrickham. But the landscape of Christminster has one last twist with which to warp our dreams and reduce the healthy openness of the new vision to a yet more dreadful darkness:

> The floor-cloth deadened his footsteps as he moved in that direction through the obscurity, which was broken only by the faintest reflected night-light from without. High overhead, above the chancel steps, Jude could discern a huge, solidly constructed

Latin cross – as large, probably, as the original it was designed to commemorate. It seemed to be suspended in the air by invisible wires; it was set with large jewels, which faintly glimmered in some weak ray caught from outside, as the cross swayed to and fro in a silent and scarcely perceptible motion. Underneath, upon the floor, lay what appeared to be a heap of black clothes, and from this was repeated the sobbing that he had heard before. It was his Sue's form, prostrate on the paving.[56]

This, one of the very rare occasions when a church is seen as more than a simple building, seems to contain within the horrific vision of darkness the nearest approach to a sense of real evil ever to be found in Hardy's work. The capriciousness of fate, the vagaries of character, the visions of poverty and crime, are all familiar features to readers of the novels; but in this image the sickly ray of night-light from the darkness of the world is caught and refracted in an awful glimmer by the massive, dominating symbol of the cross, towering above the crumpled figure below.

It is the supreme symbol – of the system Man has created for himself in the world, and also of the system by which Man was created. And it presses down with the full weight of its darkness – lightened only enough to perceive, not to question or understand – upon the pitiful figure of the lone human being.

2.

In the context of such a drastic alteration of landscape function as we have seen Hardy make in *Jude the Obscure*, it is hardly surprising to remark that he has also changed the role of his minor characters in the novel. They have never performed an exactly similar function in any two of the Wessex novels, but they were always, even in *Tess*, an associated part of the rural landscapes, in one form or another (entirely apart from any direct dramatic purpose they may have had).

Now, in *Jude*, these characters are introduced in huge numbers, apparently without reference to their role in any particular landscape. Apart from the pool of recurring figures – notably Vilbert, Tinker Taylor, Mrs. Fawley and the Widow Edlin – there is a plentiful supply of unrepeated references to people unconnected with the main drama, or even with the particular landscape. At Marygreen there are Farmer Troutham, Mrs. Williams, Belinda, Caroline, the blacksmith, the farm bailiff, the rector, the miller at Cresscombe, 'a man', two tilers, 'a carter, a second man, and a boy', the local policeman, the villagers on Jude's bread-round, a stone-mason at Alfredston, Arabella's two companions at the washing of the chitterlings, a maidservant at the inn, 'a neighbour', Challow the slaughterer, and a broker — all of these characters being of no relevance to the plot, and having no personalities or appearances ascribed to them. In all cases, they could have been omitted altogether, or their parts given to developed characters, in the manner of the earlier novels.

The fact is, however, that these people now serve a very different purpose from their forerunners in the Wessex novels. Locations are scattered from Stoke-Barehills to Exonbury, and in the case of Cresscombe, Alfredston, Lumsdon, Kennetbridge, and Leddenton — all of which are featured in the action of the novel, not merely as names — they are undescribed. Both characters and locations are designed to preserve the anonymity of the settings and their inhabitants, and in particular to destroy any sense of communal effort or support. Major landscapes are enclosed in a similar way to the earlier novels, even though they also serve symbolic purposes, or develop according to the line of Jude's own perception; but these lesser settings are used in a manner that could not differ more from the landscapes of Hardy's Wessex world. When Phillotson is visited by Jude and Sue at Lumsdon, the anonymous location negates any possible connection with the communities of Marygreen or Christminster; when he needs advice from an old friend, it is to Leddenton that he goes — a place that is nothing but a name to us. The married life of Jude and Arabella stretches across Marygreen, Cresscombe and Alfredston, the last two being undescribed and undeveloped; and the Kennetbridge where Jude seeks out the hymn's composer is no more than a small town a dozen miles from Marygreen. Our attention is scattered across numberless anonymous places and characters, and any possibility of association prevented. Jude and Sue are doomed to wander beyond hope of succour from any community or family links.

However, in small groups these minor characters are occasionally used to fulfil a function symbolic of a wider social attribute. Notably, the unmarried Jude and Sue see their life at Aldbrickham destroyed by the empty gossip and self-righteous attitudes of the nameless figures around them. The Artizans' Mutual Improvement Society, which should, like the masonry trade which might almost have ennobled Jude's life as a working man, have been the refuge of a man

of misfortune, proves itself as narrow and bigoted as the old women
who secured his dismissal from church repairs:

> Some ordinary business was transacted, and it was disclosed that
> the number of subscriptions had shown a sudden falling off for that
> quarter. One member – a really well-meaning and upright man –
> began speaking in enigmas about certain possible causes: that it
> behoved them to look well into their constitution; for if the
> committee were not respected, and had not at least, in their
> differences, a common standard of conduct, they would bring the
> institution to the ground.[57]

In other words, freedom of thought and action is permissible, as long
as it conforms to accepted standards. These well-meaning, upright
people form, in their amorphous mass, part of the new landscapes of
the mind. They are the bigotry of society at large, which survives by
destroying all incipient aberration within itself.

It is another group of minor characters which, from the time of
Jude's return to Christminster, provides the foil to the dark
degeneracy of the colleges. But it is not as representatives of some
human ideal that they appear; the lesson of the mason's yard has
already destroyed the concept of the noble working man, and the
betrayal of the Artizans' Society reduced all levels of this world to a
common intolerance. The reunion of Jude and Arabella is celebrated
in a fashion that jars horribly on the sensibilities we have come to
associate with Jude:

> Their eyes followed the movements of the little girl as she spread
> the breakfast-cloth on the table they had been using, without
> wiping up the slops of the liquor. The curtains were undrawn, and
> the expression of the house made to look like morning. Some of the
> guests, however, fell asleep in their chairs.[58]

It is a far cry from the wedding randies of earlier novels – even from
the quietened celebrations which attended more thoughtful brides,
such as Elizabeth-Jane and Tess. Like the settings themselves, the
situation has had all beauty removed, leaving only a grotesque
imitation of pleasure in its place – as though we could see the grin of
the skull through the too transient flesh of the moment.

The more prominent among the minor figures partake also of this
mood. Tinker Taylor and Arabella's father are mere emanations of

the animal spirit of this underworld. Vilbert, the travelling quack, is a parody of the characters in other novels – Conjurer Minterne, or the much-respected Wide-O, or even Diggory Venn:

> Vilbert was an itinerant quack-doctor, well known to the rustic population, and absolutely unknown to anybody else, as he, indeed, took care to be, to avoid inconvenient investigations. . . . Jude had one day seen him selling a pot of coloured lard to an old woman as a certain cure for a bad leg, the woman arranging to pay a guinea, in instalments of a shilling a fortnight, for the precious salve, which, according to the physician, could only be obtained from a particular animal which grazed on Mount Sinai, and was to be captured only at great risk to life and limb.[59]

All the pleasant inconsequentiality of Mrs. Penny's witch-book, the serious belief of Susan Nunsuch's pins, and the curious superstition of Joan Durbeyfield's *Compleat Fortune Teller*, has gone from this man's actions. He is a fraud, so callous of human misery as to swindle an old woman of a large sum of money. He is not actively malicious, but he uses other people to his own ends.

For their part, Mrs. Fawley and the Widow Edlin have none of the close involvement of previous relatives and family friends, such as Mrs. Yeobright and Melbury. Advice has degenerated into gossiping tales about past family problems; and the family itself has become nothing more than a reminder of the human frailty we all inherit at birth:

> Your father and mother couldn't get on together, and they parted. . . . Your mother soon afterwards died – she drowned herself, in short . . . It was the same with your father's sister. Her husband offended her, and she so disliked living with him afterwards that she went away to London with her little maid. . . . A little further on – where the road to Fensworth branches off . . . A gibbet once stood there not onconnected with our history.[60]

The individual is affected, despite him or herself, by the inheritance of flesh; and in particular, as is the nature of society at the time, by the tricks of fate which decree that the silent witnesses of the past shall speak out and brand the living person as of high or low degree, lucky or unlucky in love, criminal or honest. Society is changing, anonymity everywhere, yet this paradox stands as one of the rules by which men choose to live. As with all else in this barren world of *Jude*, Hardy sees the good aspects of each law being cast aside, the bad retained. All the major characters are doomed to wander, cut off from their original homes, yet branded irrevocably by the mistakes of their own lives, and even by the mistakes of others.

Arabella, of course, is the survivor. From beginning to end her life is one of self-care and constant avoidance of sacrifice. We have seen her described initially in animal images that make her seem the genius loci of unspiritual Marygreen. Yet most of our acquaintance with her is centred elsewhere. She was a barmaid before she married, and accepts easily the prospect of emigration with her parents to Australia, where she marries bigamously, first having abandoned the child of her marriage to Jude with her unfortunate parents.

Her only weakness is a jealousy for the happiness she sees in Jude's relationship with Sue which, despite her relative success in life, she has never attained. A temporary resort to religion, after the death of Cartlett, is cast aside as easily as it was taken up:

> 'I've reached a more resigned frame of mind' . . . (said) the widow, from the serene heights of a soul conscious not only of spiritual but of social superiority. 'I make no boast of my awakening, but I'm not what I was. After Cartlett's death I was passing the chapel in the street next ours, and went into it for shelter from a shower of rain. I felt a need of some sort of support under my loss, and, as 'twas righter than gin, I took to going there regular, and found it a great comfort.'[61]

In many ways Arabella is a symbol of the hyprocrisies and self-interest of society. She cannot leave Jude and Sue alone, but must probe and chafe, awaiting any opportunity to regain something that, once removed from her grasp, becomes infinitely more desirable than before.

Yet there is no real malice or evil in her. Like the well-meaning citizens of Aldbrickham, she believes in an adherence to accepted social forms; doubtless she would have echoed the sentiment of Phillotson's friend, Gillingham, regarding Sue, 'I think she ought to be smacked, and brought to her senses.'[62] Arabella may have married bigamously, but in every other way she conforms to social ideals, and is therefore better, in the eyes of society, than Jude and Sue, who are honest in their refusal to conform.

From Jude's lust for Arabella sprang Father Time, the symbol of two paradoxes – the natural paradox, that the passing desire of the flesh should shackle the spirit with unwanted new life, and burden a new soul with existence in a world he did not ask to enter, and which his parents did not seek to bring him into; and the social paradox, that the action of a moment should, by the rules of society, haunt a man forever, and destroy his hopes in any future course. Behind it all, at the marriage of Jude and Arabella and the remarriage of Sue and Phillotson, stands the anonymous figure of the rector, uttering empty platitudes of joy at the subjection of these people to their social and religious yoke.

Phillotson stands out from this sorry picture as the only ordinary man who can appreciate and accept the concept of personal happiness being more important than social conformity. He has his dreams – of a degree at Christminster, and his book on Romano-British antiquities; but he accepts failure without struggle, allowing the dead weight of his humble background to limit him to a predestined niche in society (the schoolmaster's level of himself and Gillingham). But unlike other such figures in the novel he is aware of the faults of society, and aware too of the realities of love and self-sacrifice – the very attributes which help to advance the human spirit from its animal state. He sacrifices his love, his desire, his career, to the spiritual needs of Sue. Because he is honest enough to give her liberty, instead of playing the outraged husband, he is condemned by society at large. But his love for Sue is one of the few dreams that have illuminated his life; even if it was a reflected light:

> She went to where a swing-glass stood, and taking it in her hands carried it to a spot by the window where it could catch the sunshine, moving the glass till the beams were reflected into Phillotson's face.
> 'There – you can see the great red sun now!' she said.[63]

Sue, in contrast to Arabella's very clear animal beauty, with all its attendant frowsiness of physical imperfection (for what human body is perfect?) is ephemeral, changing, beautiful in the perception of the soul within, rather than in any perception of bodily appearance:

> She looked right into his face with liquid, untranslateable eyes,

that combined, or seemed to him to combine, keenness with tenderness, and mystery with both, their expression, as well as that of her lips, taking its life from some words just spoken to a companion, and being carried on into his face quite unconsciously. . . . There was nothing statuesque in her, all was nervous motion. She was mobile, living, yet a painter might not have called her handsome or beautiful.[64]

Her appearance accords well with her own disposition towards classical rather than Christian concepts and beliefs; 'He went up to seize her hand, and found she was clammy as a marine deity, and that her clothes clung to her like the robes upon the figure in the Parthenon frieze.'[65] But, as with all the characters, physical description is kept to a minimum. The true scope of the novel lies within her mind.

Jude, too, is scantily described for such an important figure. Until he reaches Christminster, he is purely a mind, no face or figure being visible for our study — a contrast with the coarsely physical aspect of Marygreen and Arabella. But at Christminster, where the dream becomes flesh, he appears:

Jude would now have been described as a young man with a forcible, meditative, and earnest rather than handsome cast of countenance. He was of dark complexion, with dark harmonizing eyes, and he wore a closely trimmed black beard of more advanced growth than is usual at his age; this, with his great mass of black curly hair, was some trouble to him in combing and washing out the stone-dust that settled on it in the pursuit of his trade.[66]

The characteristic of this and Sue's descriptions is its neutrality of physical aspect. There is nothing in either of them at first to suggest, in the way of Arabella's beauty, the nature of the being. But in both of them there is a fragility of countenance that contrasts — in a muted way — with the coarseness of their physical surroundings:

The fevered flush on his face from the debauch of the previous evening lessened the fragility of his ordinary appearance, and his long lashes, dark brows, and curly black hair and beard against the white pillow, completed the physiognomy of one whom Arabella, as a woman of rank passions, still felt it worth while to recapture.[67]

Compared with the grossly physical aspect of Sue's remarriage to Phillotson ('A man could be heard snoring in the room opposite' and 'I must drink to the dregs.') the delicacy of Jude's physical bearing sets him well apart from the common mass of humanity – the animal run of the species. But, no matter how delicate his appearance, Man is a prisoner of the flesh.

It is an already established paradox in Hardy's work that the thinking human creature cannot be happy, either in search or in discovery. In *Tess of the d'Urbervilles* there was a brief moment of pure joy, when time seemed to stop, the world recede, and all life to focus on the two lovers, Clare and Tess, in the limbo of their New Forest hideaway. Similarly Jude and Sue seem to find, in the brief period at Aldbrickham, a happiness in their life together. 'We gave up all ambition, and were never so happy in our lives till his illness came.'⁶⁸ But even in the limbo of unthinking joy, no mind can really deny its own awareness:

> 'I feel that we have returned to Greek joyousness, and have blinded ourselves to sickness and sorrow, and have forgotten what twenty-five centuries have taught the race since their time . . . There is one immediate shadow, however, – only one.' And she looked at the aged child.
> . . . ' I am very, very sorry, father and mother,' he said. 'But please don't mind! – I can't help it. I should like the flowers very very much, if I didn't keep on thinking they'd all be withered in a few days'.⁶⁹

Father Time becomes another symbol, of mortality. Children are borne who are both the future of the race and the ever-present reminder of the passing of the years which wipes clean the briefly-marked slate of one thinking life. To poor Sue, torn between the pleasure of love and its animal effects, and aware too keenly of what life means to the thinking individual, the birth of a child is something too great to be trusted to a passion; 'it seems such a terribly tragic thing to bring beings into the world – so presumptuous that I question my right to do it sometimes!'⁷⁰

Sue remains throughout something of an enigma, her actions never fully explained, her thoughts often private, yet in certain ways she emerges very clearly as the victim of the body in which she is trapped, and the mores of the society which guards that body. Her education was liberal and informal, her knowledge of the classics coming from the translations recommended by the Christminster graduate with whom, for a time, she lived:

> I have no respect for Christminster whatever, except, in a qualified degree, on its intellectual side . . . And intellect at Christminster is new wine in old bottles. The Mediaevalism of Christminster must go, be sloughed off, or Christminster itself will have to go.[71]

She despises the religion which surrounds her, rejects its imprisoning idolatries; she is the leader who sees Jude still groping down labyrinthine ways; to her, marriage is like the sacrifice of heifers 'in old times.'[72] Yet she trembles at her temerity in buying the figures of Venus and Apollo; she runs without thinking from the training school; she marries Phillotson; she vacillates childishly; in the end, she turns blindly to the dark security of religion and self-chastisement when events are too strong for her.

On the face of it, she is a curious figure. But one weakness Hardy never admitted to his novels was the portrayal of an embodied ideal. Men and women are frail, contradictory creatures, swept by emotions and thoughts too powerful for their weak bodies or the characters they have so brief a life to build. Jude is searching always for an ideal, and so is puzzled by the contradictions of his love-dream, forgetting that she, too, is flesh.

In the end, of course, there is no such thing as an ideal. To perceive beauty we must know ugliness; to love we must hate; to laugh we must cry. Life is built on opposites. Man is the tormented soul who can perceive but cannot change the apparent chaos that is his world.

But even the chaos is not real – Nature is ordered; society is ordered. We must have the learning and experience of twenty-five centuries at our fingertips, if we are to begin to change our world. If each new generation had to learn afresh, we should once more be animals – and in that, the brief span of happiness allowed to Jude and Sue is an illusion. It is as animal as the lusts which brought together Arabella and Jude, because it admits of no attempt to understand.

Jude is the central figure of the novel, the only one we are permitted to communicate with through thought. Even Sue is no more than a figure seen through Jude's life. And his life is no more than a process of searching. One after another, he builds his dreams; one after another he seems to grasp them, only to see them turn to clay and crumble in his arms. Intellect, religion, love, craft, even a lingering faith in the human species in the mass, are reduced to cold, degenerate reality — crumbling stone, doomed flesh, wilting flowers, drunkenness and lust.

Hardy throws out ideas as the novel proceeds — a vision of a Christminster cleansed of its wealth, patronage, mediaevalism, returned to an 'original' concept of education for such as Jude; a future more tolerant of deviation from the social norm; a matriarchal society — but all are swept away before the onrush of Man's mortality. In the final chapter the dreadful beauty of life and death, standing in their eternal juxtaposition, brings home to us the strength of a well-established order, with all its social divisions, its barriers of class, wealth, religion and intellect, which so favours the beauty of the moment, and mocks the man who would be different:

> The powerful notes of that concert rolled forth through the swinging yellow blinds of the open windows, over the house-tops, and into the still air of the lanes. They reached so far as to the room in which Jude lay; and it was about this time that his cough began again and awakened him. . . . While he remained, his face changing, shouts and hurrahs came from somewhere in the direction of the river.

The living excitement of Remembrance Day rolls heedlessly over the dying words of Jude:

> (Hurrah!)
> 'Why died I not from the womb? Why did I not give up the ghost when I came out of the belly? . . . For now should I have lain still and been quiet. I should have slept: then had I been at rest!'
> (Hurrah!)
> 'There the prisoners rest together; they hear not the voice of the oppressor. . . . the small and the great are there; and the servant is free from his master. Wherefore is light given to him that is in misery, and life unto the bitter in soul?'[73]

The dust of mortality is on the 'old, superseded' and 'dog-eared'[74] volumes that were the symbols of a dream; but life in the ordered landscapes of the world around goes joyously, unheedingly, eternally on. In the end it is obvious that the rules by which we live, whatever their weaknesses and injustices, are stronger than all the hopes and dreams of the individual. From Mellstock to Christminster, no matter what their differences, all Hardy's landscapes have that in common: they are beyond the power of one man to change or alter in any degree. In the course of six novels we have watched many characters struggle blindly against the sheer dead weight of the human landscapes by which they are inevitably trapped; in the seventh novel we have been given insight, to follow the contours of the individual's own mental landscape as he struggles. But in the end there is still no resolution of the conflict, no 'justification', no description of the human 'focus of a universe', no 'saner religion', not even forgetfulness. There is only life, and death, and all the blind rigidity of society by which the irreconcileable mind and body of man are held in uneasy balance for so long as it takes him to pass from the state of awareness to the silence of the grave. The landscapes are the same; only our perception has altered.

Notes

CH. 1—TOWNSCAPE: *THE MAYOR OF CASTERBRIDGE*

1. Throughout his life Hardy retained a fascination with the historical links of family names, and it is an interesting point of speculation that his childhood acquaintance with a man rumoured to be connected in some way with the poet might have planted the seeds of an interest in John Keats that lasted until Hardy's death. In the collection of Hardy's books at the Dorset County Museum is a first edition copy of Keats' poetry, presented by close friends to a man who was then the Grand Old Man of literature, to whom most gifts would have been of passing interest.
2. *The Life of Thomas Hardy* (London 1965), ch. 1.
3. Ibid., ch. 2.
4. *The Mayor of Casterbridge* (New Wessex Edition. London 1974), p.59.
5. Ibid., p. 59.
6. Sir Frederick Treves *Highways and Byways in Dorset* (London 1935), ch. 22.
7. The walls themselves were largely demolished in the eighteenth century, and the Walks laid out along the old ramparts.
8. *The Mayor of Casterbridge*, p. 59.
9. See Thomas Hardy 'Some Romano-British Relics found at Max Gate, Dorchester', *Proceedings of the Dorset Natural History and Archaeological Society*, 11.
10. See C. D. Drew and K. C. Collingwood Selby, 'First and Second Interim Reports on the excavations at Colliton Park, Dorchester', *Proceedings of the Dorset Natural History and Archaelogical Society*, 59 & 60.
11. *The Mayor of Casterbridge*, p. 161.
12. See *Proceedings of the Dorset Natural History and Archaeological Society*, 59 & 60.
13. *The Mayor of Casterbridge*, p. 59.
14. Ibid., p. 72.
15. Ibid., p. 63.
16. Ibid., p. 92.
17. Ibid., pp. 167—8.
18. Ibid., p. 61.
19. Ibid., p. 100.
20. Ibid., p. 100.
21. Ibid., p. 101.
22. Ibid., p. 132.
23. Ibid., p. 285.
24. See *Elizabeth Ham by herself, 1783—1820*, ed. E. Gillett (London, 1945).
25. New thatching had been banned in the town in 1776, following the latest of several serious fires.

26. *The Mayor of Casterbridge*, p. 91.

27. Daniel Defoe, *A Tour through the Whole Island of Great Britain*, Letter 3 (London, 1962).

28. *The Mayor of Casterbridge*, p. 92.

29. It was not until the large-scale sale of Duchy land for speculative building, in the late 1870s, that Dorchester seriously outgrew its Roman form.

30. *The Mayor of Casterbridge*, p. 59.

31. Ibid., p. 90.

32. Ibid., pp. 91–2.

33. Ibid., pp. 60–1.

34. Ibid., p. 92.

35. Ibid., pp. 279–80.

36. Ibid., p. 255.

37. Ibid., p. 256.

38. Ibid., p. 329.

39. Ibid., p. 147.

40. Ibid., pp. 278–9.

41. Ibid., p. 72.

42. Ibid., pp. 302–4.

43. Ibid., p. 149.

44. Ibid., p. 161.

45. Ibid., pp. 56–7.

46. Ibid., p. 354.

47. Ibid., p. 190.

48. Ibid., pp. 267–8.

49. Ibid., p. 85.

50. Ibid., p. 186.

51. Ibid., p. 195.

52. Ibid., pp. 247–8.

53. Ibid., p. 215.

54. Ibid., p. 340.

55. Ibid., p. 353.

CH. 2—THE VILLAGE COMMUNITY: *UNDER THE GREENWOOD TREE*

1. M. R. Skilling, *Hardy's Mellstock on the Map* (Dorchester 1968), p. 9.

2. *Under the Greenwood Tree* (New Wessex Edition, London, 1974), p. 57.

3. The date is indicated by reference to Hardy's preface to the 1896 edition: 'the villages of 50 or 60 years ago'. In addition, William talks of 'a' empty house, as befell us in the year thirty-nine and forty-three'. The school referred to was built in 1848. The imaginative 'reality' of the novel is based on Hardy's own childhood experiences, and on his mother's tales of the village in the days of his father's early manhood, hence the relatively wide spread of the dating.

4. *Under the Greenwood Tree*, p. 57.

5. Ibid., p. 111.

6. Ibid., p. 111.

7. Ibid., p. 56.

8. Cf. Dickens' similar use of imagery.
9. *Under the Greenwood Tree*, p. 88.
10. Ibid., p. 142.
11. Ibid., p. 168.
12. *The Mayor of Casterbridge*, p. 210.
13. *Far from the Madding Crowd*, p. 273.
14. *Under the Greenwood Tree*, p. 34.
15. *Far from the Madding Crowd*, p. 89.
16. *Under the Greenwood Tree*, pp. 43–4.
17. Ibid., p. 43.
18. *Far from the Madding Crowd*, p. 41.
19. *Under the Greenwood Tree*, p. 43.

CH. 3—THE FARMING COMMUNITY: *FAR FROM THE MADDING CROWD*

1. Cf. the local rhyme, based on the 'Old Cat' public house:

> Into Church,
> Out of Church,
> Into Cat,
> Out of Cat,
> Into Piddle.

2. Cf. *The Life of Thomas Hardy*, ch. 38.

'He recalled how, crossing eweleaze when a child, he went on hands and knees and pretended to eat grass, in order to see what the sheep would do. Presently he looked up and found them gathered around in a close ring, gazing at him with astonished faces.'

3. *Far from the Madding Crowd* (New Wessex Edition, London, 1974), p. 154.
4. Gustav Holst, Opus 47, *Egdon Heath*, 1927.
5. *Far from the Madding Crowd*, p. 106.
6. Ibid., p. 152.
7. Ibid., pp. 176–7.
8. Ibid., p. 89.
9. With the two extraneous exceptions of the Workhouse and the Barracks.
10. *Far from the Madding Crowd*, p. 123.
11. Ibid., pp. 46–7.
12. Ibid., p. 134.
13. Ibid., pp. 157–8.
14. Ibid., p. 329.
15. Ibid., p. 47.
16. Ibid., p. 64.
17. Ibid., p.61.
18. Ibid., pp. 62–3.
19. Ibid., p. 70.

20. Ibid., p. 90. Cf. p. 56. 'He heard what seemed to be the flitting of a dead leaf upon the breeze, and looked. She had gone away'. Also *The Mayor of Casterbridge*, p. 88. 'innumerable tawny and yellow leaves skimmed along the pavement, and stole through people's doorways into their passages with a hesitating scratch on the floor, like the skirts of timid visitors.'
21. *Far from the Madding Crowd*, p. 135.
22. *The Return of the Native*, p. 41.
23. *Far from the Madding Crowd.*, p. 135.
24. Ibid., pp. 278–9.
25. Ibid., p. 284.
26. Ibid., p. 64.
27. Ibid., p. 56.
28. Ibid., p. 53.
29. Ibid., p. 223.
30. Ibid., p. 109.
31. Ibid., p. 158.
32. Ibid., p. 89.
33. Ibid., p. 87.
34. Ibid., p. 187.
35. Ibid., p. 177.
36. Ibid., p. 75.
37. Ibid., p. 50.
38. Ibid., p. 174.
39. Ibid., pp. 272–3.
40. Ibid., pp. 357–8.
41. Ibid., p. 99.
42. Ibid., p. 267.
43. Ibid., pp. 226–7.
44. Ibid., p. 102.
45. Ibid., p. 92.
46. Ibid., p. 387.
47. Ibid., p. 137.
48. Ibid., p. 313.
49. Ibid., p. 266.
50. Ibid., p. 273.
51. Ibid., p. 288.
52. Ibid., p. 344.
53. Ibid., p. 193.
54. Ibid., p. 266.
55. Ibid., p. 216.

CH. 4—THE LANDSCAPES OF 'THE GREAT HEATH': *THE RETURN OF THE NATIVE*

1. *The Return of the Native* (New Wessex Edition, London, 1974), p. 36.
2. The soil here is of the Reading Type, quite different from all other soils in the supposed area of Egdon Heath, except on the small spine of Affpuddle Heath. See J. Percival *Report on the soils of Dorset* (Reading 1906).

3. H. Lea, *Thomas Hardy's Wessex* (London 1969), p. 75, and D. Kay-Robinson, *Hardy's Wessex Re-appraised* (Newton Abbott 1972), p. 59. Lea identifies Blooms-End as Bhompston Farm, but my own research indicates that the site of the fictional house corresponds most closely to that of Hardy's own cottage at Higher Bockhampton. Kay-Robinson, too, states that 'Hardy's own map for *The Return* appears to identify the site with his birthplace'. Diggory Venn, appearing from the darkness at Rainbarrow (p. 59), is directed to take his van from the Anglebury road (beyond the Quiet Woman, as we meet it shortly afterwards, approaching the inn) by a roundabout route, up a rough track that runs beside the Rainbarrow ridge. This can only correspond with the track to the west of the ridge, and since Bhompston Farm lies well down the valley from there, it is immediately excluded as a potential site for Blooms-End. In addition, although the description of the house may have been taken from Bhompston (as Lea asserts), the farm's situation by rich river meadows, virtually screened from the bulk of the heath by the low grassy knoll to the north-east, is utterly different from the described setting, facing up the valley to the heath itself, and backing onto grassland — a setting which admirably reflects that of Hardy's cottage in the nineteenth century. As with other heath settings in *The Return of the Native*, the accuracy of this assertion becomes self-evident in the course of the novel.

4. *The Return of the Native*, p. 379.

5. Ibid., cf. p. 99. Johnny Nunsuch returning home at night by this track:

> Only unusual sights and sounds frightened the boy. The shrivelled voice of the heath did not alarm him, for that was familiar. The thorn bushes which arose in his path from time to time were less satisfactory, for they whistled gloomily, and had a ghastly habit after dark of putting on the shapes of jumping madmen, sprawling giants, and hideous cripples.

6. Hardy often walked the heath road by night, as a child.

7. Ibid., p. 69.

8. Ibid., p. 84.

9. Ibid., pp. 134–5.

10. Ibid., p. 299.

11. Ibid., p. 33.

12. Ibid., p. 81.

13. Ibid., pp. 213–14.

14. Ibid., p. 312.

15. Ibid., p. 113. See S. C. S. Brown, 'The Rape of Bournemouth', *Dorset Magazine*, 52. An article discussing the widespread slaughter of both rare and common wildlife in the Bournemouth heath area in the early nineteenth century, by Lord Malmesbury and others.

16. Ibid., p. 64.

17. Ibid., p. 84.

18. Ibid., p. 41.

19. Ibid., p. 41.

20. Ibid., p. 41.

21. *Far from the Madding Crowd*, p. 135.

22. *The Return of the Native*, p. 36.

23. Ibid., p. 82.

24. Ibid., pp. 43–4.
25. Ibid., p. 45.
26. Ibid., p. 45.
27. Ibid., p. 379.
28. Ibid., p. 37.
29. Ibid., p. 379.
30. Ibid., p. 173.
31. Ibid., p. 250.
32. Ibid., p. 65.
33. Ibid., pp. 93–4.
34. Ibid., p. 94.
35. Ibid., p. 83.

CH. 5—TRANSITION: *THE WOODLANDERS*

1. A less obvious connection – though one that has relevance when the other novels are considered,– is the Hardy family: with Woolcombe Farm (on his father's side); the marriage of his parents at Melbury Osmond; and the residence of his mother's family there and at nearby Stockwood. There is such a family connection for the location of every major novel (more complete details are given in Robert Gittings' *Young Thomas Hardy*. London 1975).

2. As a point of speculative interest, the description of Mrs Charmond's house, so unlike Melbury Sampford, is, architecturally at least, very close to the appearance of the old Stinsford manor house. This is an unspoilt Elizabethan house, abandoned complete for the grandeur of Kingston House, its manorial successor, which stands less than a quarter of a mile away.

3. *The Woodlanders* (New Wessex Edition, London, 1974), p. 35.
4. Ibid., p. 39.
5. Ibid., p. 76.
6. Ibid., p. 54.
7. Ibid., pp. 54–5.
8. Ibid., p. 55.
9. Ibid., pp. 88–9.
10. Ibid., p. 55.
11. Ibid., p. 142.
12. Cf. p. 215, 'according to the landlords' principle at this date of getting rid of cottages whenever possible'. But this 'principle' has no place in the context of Giles' circumstances.
13. Ibid., p. 364.
14. Ibid., p. 39.
15. Ibid., p. 35.
16. Ibid., p. 393.
17. Ibid., p. 389.
18. Ibid., p. 258.
19. Ibid., pp. 93–4.
20. Ibid., pp. 305–6.
21. Ibid., p. 61.
22. Ibid., pp. 235–6.

23. *The Life of Thomas Hardy*, ch. 7.
24. General Preface to the Wessex Edition of Hardy's Works, 1912.
25. *The Woodlanders*, p. 357.
26. Ibid., pp. 235–6.
27. Ibid., pp. 298–9.
28. Ibid., p. 234.
29. Ibid., p. 269.

CH. 6—WESSEX VIGNETTES: *TESS OF THE D'URBERVILLES*

1. See Robert Gittings, *Young Thomas Hardy*.
2. *Tess of the d'Urbervilles* (New Wessex Edition, London, 1974), p. 53.
3. Ibid., p. 80.
4. Ibid., p. 138.
5. Ibid., pp. 393–4.
6. Ibid., p. 39.
7. Ibid., pp. 139, 327, 343.
8. Ibid., pp. 66–7.
9. Ibid., p. 110.
10. See Robert Gittings, *Young Thomas Hardy*. The Hardy Talbothays connection.
11. *Tess of the d'Urbervilles*, p. 138.
12. Ibid., pp. 139 and 141.
13. Ibid., p. 226.
14. Ibid., pp. 139–40.
15. Ibid., pp. 141–2.
16. Ibid., p. 39.
17. Ibid., pp. 326–7.
18. By personal observation I have satisfied myself that Hardy based the 'Flintcomb' description on the village and farms of Alton Pancras. It is, however, no more than a curiosity that the area Hardy made most amorphous is in fact most readily identifiable in this novel: the overall effect of his descriptions is to make these arenas sufficiently large to be identifiable but not precise.
19. *Tess of the d'Urbervilles*, p. 401.
20. Ibid., p. 95.
21. Ibid., p. 94.
22. Ibid., p. 197.
23. Ibid., p. 393.
24. Ibid., pp. 42–3.
25. Ibid., p. 229.
26. Ibid., p. 343.
27. Ibid., p. 83. 'behind, the green valley of her birth, before, a gray country of which she knew nothing.'
28. Ibid., p. 94.
29. Ibid., p. 140.
30. Ibid., p. 139.
31. Ibid., p. 120.

32. Ibid., p. 143.
33. Ibid., p. 209.
34. Ibid., p. 114.
35. Ibid., p. 235.
36. Ibid., p. 318.
37. Ibid., p. 327.
38. Ibid., p. 332.
39. Ibid., p. 335.
40. Ibid., p. 357. These are many instances in the novel of very personal interpretation of particular views or scenes, but this is the only instance of an alteration of the real scene on which the arena of action is based, in order to convey a certain idea to the reader's mind. In all other cases, the arenas are made appropriate to the general mood by a process of selection and emphasis – here, the 'selection' is of which way to look from Cross-in-Hand.

   A minor use of this type of blinkered selection – a process very similar to that used in the earlier novels – is the athletic railway line at Wellbridge, which appears or disappears apparently at will. When milk is put on the London train, it is there. When Clare works at the mill, in an atmosphere of cold reality, it is there. When the couple walk in silence by the river, and when a sleeping Clare carries Tess to the ruined Abbey, it has vanished.
41. *Tess of the d'Urbervilles*, p. 426.
42. Ibid., p. 440.
43. Ibid., p. 442.
44. Ibid., p. 260.
45. Ibid., p. 447.
46. Ibid., p. 449.
47. John Milton, *Paradise Lost*, Book 12.
48. *Tess of the d'Urbervilles*, p. 406.
49. Ibid., p. 446.
50. Ibid., pp. 41–2.
51. Ibid., p. 73.
52. Ibid., p. 107.
53. Ibid., p. 113.
54. Ibid., p. 114.
55. Ibid., p. 120.
56. Ibid., pp. 120–1.
57. Ibid., p. 121.
58. Ibid., p. 324.
59. Ibid., p. 436.
60. Ibid., p. 122.
61. Ibid., p. 124.
62. Ibid., p. 123.
63. Ibid., p. 126.
64. Ibid., p. 141.
65. Ibid., p. 142.
66. Ibid., p. 158.
67. Ibid., pp. 161–2.
68. Ibid., pp. 162.
69. Ibid., p. 161.

70. Ibid., p. 162.
71. Ibid., p. 115.
72. Ibid., p. 168.
73. Ibid., pp. 170–1.
74. Ibid., p. 170.
75. Ibid., p. 187.
76. Ibid., p. 183.
77. Ibid., p. 436.
78. Ibid., p. 189.
79. Ibid., pp. 190–1.
80. Ibid., p. 273.
81. Ibid., p. 289.
82. Ibid., p. 326.
83. Ibid., p. 142.
84. Ibid., p. 331.
85. Cf. *The Return of the Native.*, p. 41.
86. *Tess of the d'Urbervilles*, p. 332.
87. Ibid., p. 170.
88. Ibid., p. 334.
89. Ibid., p. 395.
90. Ibid., pp. 154–5.
91. Cf. p. 43. When the three brothers arrive at Marlott: 'the appearance of the third and youngest would hardly have been sufficient to characterise him.'
92. Ibid., p. 154.
93. Ibid., p. 209.
94. Ibid., p. 255.
95. Ibid., p. 287.
96. Ibid., pp. 389–90.
97. Ibid., pp. 67–8.
98. Ibid., p. 82.
99. Ibid., p. 277.
100. As do the normal activities of rural life: the changes from dairy to winter work; the vast removals of Lady Day; the markets and fairs.
101. *Tess of the d'Urbervilles*, p. 361.
102. Ibid., p. 422.
103. Ibid., p. 73.
104. Ibid., pp. 114–15.
105. Ibid., p. 359.
106. Ibid., p. 163.
107. Ibid., p. 163.
108. *The Woodlanders*, p. 234.
109. *Tess of the d'Urbervilles*, p. 59.
110. Ibid., p. 122.
111. Ibid., pp. 140–1.
112. Ibid., p. 165.
113. Ibid., p. 158.
114. Ibid., p. 334.
115. Book five, chapter one. From *Job*. III. 20.
116. *The Mayor of Casterbridge*, p. 147.

117. *The Woodlanders*, p. 69.
118. Ibid., pp. 226–7.
119. *Tess of the d'Urbervilles*, pp. 446–7.

CH. 7—LANDSCAPES OF THE MIND: *JUDE THE OBSCURE*

1. *Jude the Obscure* (New Wessex Edition, London, 1974), p. 32.
2. Ibid., p. 34.
3. Ibid., p. 31.
4. Ibid., p. 59.
5. Ibid., pp. 84–5.
6. Ibid., pp. 37–8.
7. Ibid., p. 33.
8. Ibid., p. 38.
9. Ibid., p. 29.
10. Ibid., p. 32.
11. Ibid., p. 39.
12. Ibid., p. 49.
13. Ibid., p. 58.
14. Ibid., p. 66.
15. Ibid., p. 79.
16. Ibid., p. 39.
17. Ibid., p. 39.
18. Ibid., p. 41.
19. Ibid., pp. 44–5.
20. Ibid., p. 42.
21. Ibid., p. 97.
22. Ibid., p. 98.
23. Ibid., pp. 99–100.
24. Ibid., p. 98.
25. Ibid., pp. 106–7.
26. Ibid., p. 103.
27. Ibid., p. 103.
28. Ibid., p. 104.
29. Ibid., p. 104.
30. Ibid., p. 98.
31. Ibid., p. 104.
32. Ibid., p. 104.
33. *Tess of the d'Urbervilles*, p. 163.
34. *Jude the Obscure*, p. 136.
35. Ibid., p. 137.
36. Ibid., p. 148.
37. Ibid., p. 150.
38. Ibid., pp. 154–5.
39. Ibid., pp. 150–1.
40. Ibid., p. 157.
41. Ibid., pp. 197–8.
42. Ibid., p. 205.

43. Ibid., pp. 198–9.
44. Ibid., p. 220.
45. Ibid., pp. 220–1.
46. Ibid., p. 227.
47. Ibid., p. 258.
48. Ibid., pp. 302–3.
49. Ibid., pp. 308–9.
50. Ibid., p. 309.
51. Ibid., p. 314.
52. Ibid., p. 331.
53. Ibid., p. 332.
54. Ibid., p. 343.
55. Ibid., p. 352.
56. Ibid., p. 369.
57. Ibid., pp. 323–4.
58. Ibid., pp. 402–3.
59. Ibid., p. 46.
60. Ibid., pp. 90–1.
61. Ibid., p. 332.
62. Ibid., p. 253.
63. Ibid., p. 270.
64. Ibid., p. 109.
65. Ibid., p. 164.
66. Ibid., p. 96.
67. Ibid., p. 398.
68. Ibid., p. 332.
69. Ibid., p. 316.
70. Ibid., p. 331.
71. Ibid., p. 170.
72. Ibid., p. 306.
73. Ibid., pp. 423–4.
74. Ibid., pp. 427–8.

Bibliography

Abbreviation – D. N. H. & A. S.: Dorset Natural History & Archaeological Society

Abercrombie, L., *Thomas Hardy – a critical study* (London, 1919).
Anderson, R. C. and J. M., *Quicksilver. 100 years of coaching 1750–1850* (Newton Abbot, 1973).
Atkins, N. J., *The Country of The Mayor of Casterbridge* (Dorchester, 1974).
Atkinson, C. T., *History of the Dorsetshire Regiment* (Oxford, 1947).
Bailey, J. O., *Thomas Hardy and the Cosmic Mind* (Oxford, 1956).
Barnes, W., *A glossary of the Dorset dialect* (Guernsey, 1970).
Barrie, J. M., 'Thomas Hardy, the historian of Wessex', *Contemporary Review*, July 1939.
Bartelot, R. G., 'Stinsford and the Hardy family', *Somerset & Dorset Notes & Queries*, March, 1928.
——, *The History of Fordington* (Dorchester, 1915).
Begg, E. J., 'Cases of witchcraft in Dorsetshire'. *Folklore* Vol. 52.
Benfield, E., *Dorset* (London, 1950).
Bettey, J. H., *Dorset* (Newton Abbot, 1974).
Bjork, L. A., *The literary notes of Thomas Hardy* (Goteborg, 1974).
Blunden, E., *Thomas Hardy* (London, 1957).
Boundaries Commission, *Report on the borough of Dorchester* (London, 1832).
Brocklebank, J. and Kindersley, B., *A Dorset book of folk songs* (London, 1948).
Brown, D., *Thomas Hardy* (London, 1961).
Buckingham, J. A., *A summer trip to Weymouth & Dorchester* (Weymouth, 1842).
Burnett, D., *A Dorset Camera (1855–1914)* (Stalbridge, 1974).
Carter, K., *Thomas Hardy Catalogue* (Dorset Library) (Dorchester, 1973).
——, *Dorset Catalogue* (Dorset Library) (Dorchester, 1975).

Cecil, D., *Hardy the novelist* (London, 1943).

Chesney, K., *The Victorian Underworld* (London, 1970).

Child, H., *Thomas Hardy* (London, 1916).

Chiplen, R. F. J., *The rural landscape of the Vale of Blackmore c.1840* (Unpublished thesis, Exeter University, 1969).

Clark, G. and Thomson, W. H., *The Dorset landscape* (Edinburgh, 1935).

Clarke, E. D., *A tour through the South of England* (London, 1793).

Clegg, A. L., *A history of Dorchester, Dorset* (London, 1972).

Cochrane, C., *The lost roads of Wessex* (Newton Abbot, 1969).

Cockburn, E. O., *The almshouses of Dorset* (Dorchester, 1970).

Coleman, S. J., *Traditional tales of Dorsetshire* (Douglas, 1954).

Cox, J. S. (ed.), *Dorset folk remedies of the 17th and 18th centuries* (Guernsey, 1970).

——(ed.), *The peasantry of Dorsetshire* (Beaminster, 1963).

——(ed.), *Monographs on the life of Thomas Hardy – bibliography* (Beaminster, 1963).

——, *Hardy's Wessex* (Guernsey, 1973).

Cox, R. G. (ed.), *Thomas Hardy – the critical heritage* (London, 1970).

Cox, R. H., *Green roads of England* (London, 1948).

Cox, T., *A Complete history of Dorsetshire* (London, 1716).

Dacombe, M., *Dorset up along and down along* (Dorchester, 1971).

Danielson, H., *The first editions of the writings of Thomas Hardy and their values* (London, 1916).

Darton, F. J. H., *The marches of Wessex* (London, 1922).

Davie, D., 'The traditional basis of Thomas Hardy's fiction'. *Southern Review*, Vol. 6.

Defoe, D., *A Tour through the whole island of Great Britain* (London, 1962).

Dewar, C. D., *The excavations at Colliton Park, Dorchester, 2nd interim report.* (Dorchester, 1939).

Dewar, H. S. L., *The Giant of Cerne Abbas* (Guernsey, 1963).

——, 'The Dorset Ooser'. *Proceedings 84,* D. N. H. & A. S.

Dorset Constabulary, *Dorset constabulary 1856–1956* (Dorchester, 1956).

Dorset County Chronicle (Weekly newspaper 1824–1957).

Dorset County Magazine (occasional).

Dorset Evening Echo (daily newspaper).

Dorset Natural History and Antiquarian Field Club, *Proceedings* 1877–1928.

D.N.H. & A.S., *Proceedings* 1928 –
——, *Short notes on the Roman house, Colliton Park* (Dorchester, 1960).
——, Sir James Thornhill of Dorset (Dorchester, 1975).
Dorset Year Book
Drabble, M. (ed.), *The Genius of Thomas Hardy* (London, 1976).
Duffin, H. C., *Thomas Hardy: a study of the Wessex novels* (Manchester, 1937).
Fagersten, A., *The place names of Dorset* (Uppsden, 1933).
Fiennes, C., *The journeys* (ed. C. Morris) (London, 1949).
Firor, R. A., *Folkways in Thomas Hardy* (London, 1962).
Fisher, C. M., *Life in Thomas Hardy's Dorset* (Beaminster, 1965).
Fowler, P., *Wessex* (London, 1967).
Frampton, M., *The Journal, 1779–1820* (ed. H. G. Mundy) (London, 1886).
Garwood, H., *Thomas Hardy: an illustration of the philosophy of Schopenhauer* (Philadelphia, 1911).
General Register Office, Census returns for Dorset 1841, 1851, 1861.
Geological Survey and Museum, *Geology of the country around Dorchester* (Clement Reid), (London, 1899).
——, *Geology of the country around Weymouth, Swanage, Corfe and Lulworth* (W. J. Arkell), (London, 1968).
Gittings, R., *Young Thomas Hardy* (London, 1975).
Gomme, G. L., *The handbook of folklore* (London, 1890).
Good, R., *The old roads of Dorset* (Dorchester, 1940).
Gosse, E., *Thomas Hardy* (ed. R. Knight) (Upminster, 1968).
Graham, E., 'Dorset in the 17th & 18th centuries.' Lecture, 1925.
Gregor, I., *The Great Web* (London, 1974).
Grinsell, L. V., *The archaeology of Wessex* (London, 1958).
Guerard, A. J., (ed.), *Hardy: a collection of critical essays* (New York, 1963).
——(ed.), *Thomas Hardy, the novels and the stories* (Oxford, 1950).
Haggard, H. Rider, *Rural England* (London, 1902).
Halliday, F. E., *Thomas Hardy – his life and work* (Bath, 1972).
Ham, E., *Elizabeth Ham by herself, 1783–1820* (ed. E. Gillett) (London, 1945).
Hansford, F. E., 'When Edmund Kean played', *The Schoolmaster*. 24/11/27.
Hardy, E., *Thomas Hardy – a critical biography* (London, 1954).

Hardy, F. E., *Life of Thomas Hardy* (London, 1965).

Hardy, Thomas, *Desperate Remedies* (London, 1912).

    Under the Greenwood Tree (London, 1872 (1st edition)); 1912 (Wessex edition); 1974/5 (New Wessex).

    A Pair of Blue Eyes (London, 1912).

    Far from the Madding Crowd (London, 1874, 1912, 1974/5).

    The Hand of Ethelberta (London, 1912).

    Return of the Native (London, 1878, 1912, 1974/5).

    The Trumpet Major (London, 1912).

    A Loadicean (London, 1912).

    Two on a Tower (London, 1912).

    The Mayor of Casterbridge (London, 1886, 1912, 1974/5).

    The Woodlanders (London, 1887, 1912, 1974/5).

    Wessex Tales (London, 1912).

    A Group of Noble Dames (London, 1912).

    Tess of the d'Urbervilles (London, 1891, 1912, 1974/5).

    Life's Little Ironies (London, 1912).

    Jude the Obscure (London, 1896, 1912, 1974/5).

    The Well Beloved (London, 1912).

    The Dynasts (London, 1903–8).

    A Changed Man (London, 1913).

    The Famous Tragedy of the Queen of Cornwall (London, 1923).

    Our Exploits at West Poley (Oxford, 1952).

    Letters of Thomas Hardy (ed. C. J. Weber), (Maine, 1954).

    Thomas Hardy's notebooks (ed. E. Hardy), (London, 1955).

    Dearest Emmie (letters to his first wife, ed. C. J. Weber), (London, 1963).

    The architectural notebook of Thomas Hardy (Dorchester, 1966).

    Personal writings (ed. H. Orel) (London, 1967).

    A Rare Fair Woman (Hardy-Henniker letters, ed. E. Hardy and F. B. Pinion) (London, 1972).

    An indiscretion in the life of an heiress (London, 1976).

    The Complete Poems (London, 1976).

Harper, C. G., *The Hardy country* (London, 1925).

Harrod, J. G., Postal and commercial directory of Dorset (London, 1865).

Harvey, O. D., *Puddletown* (Puddletown, 1968).

Hawkins, D., *Hardy the novelist* (Newton Abbot, 1966).

Holland, C., *Thomas Hardy's Wessex scene* (Dorchester, 1948).

Hopkins, R. T., *Thomas Hardy's Dorset* (London, 1922).

Howe, I., *Thomas Hardy* (London, 1968).

Hutchings, M., *Wessex reflections* (Sherborne, 1972).

——, *Hardy country of Dorset* (Exmouth, 1962).

——, *Hardy's river* (Sherborne, 1967).

Hutchins, J., *The history and antiquities of the county of Dorset* (London, 1861–1873).

Jackman, D., *300 years of Baptist witness in Dorchester, 1645–1945* (Dorchester, 1945).

Johnson, L., *The Art of Thomas Hardy* (London, 1894).

Kay-Robinson, D., *Hardy's Wessex re-appraised* (Newton Abbot, 1972).

Kerr, B., 'The Dorset agricultural labourer 1750–1850', *Proceedings 84*, D. N. H. & A. S.

——, *Bound to the soil* (London, 1968).

Knott, O. *Witches of Wessex* (Milborne Port, 1974).

——, *Blackmore Vale villages* (Milborne Port, 1972).

——, *Dorset with Hardy* (Dorchester, 1968).

Kramer, D., *Thomas Hardy, forms of Tragedy* (London, 1975).

Lawrence, D. H., *Phoenix* (London, 1936).

Lea, H., *Some Dorset superstitions* (Guernsey, 1968).

——, *Thomas Hardy's Wessex* (London, 1969).

Legg, R., *Dorset Ghosts* (Bournemouth, 1969).

Lerner, L. and Holmstrom, J. (eds.), *Thomas Hardy and his readers* (London, 1968).

Lloyd, D. W., *The Buildings of Dorchester* (Dorchester, 1968).

Lovelace, M., *Thomas Hardy's use of legend in Tess of the D'Urbervilles* (Unpublished thesis, University of Newfoundland, 1977).

Mantle, G., *A brief history of Kingston Maurward House* (Kingston Maurward, 1968).

Maxwell, D., *The landscape of Thomas Hardy* (London, 1928).

Mee, A. (ed.), *Dorset: Thomas Hardy's country* (London, 1967).

——, *Dorset* (London, 1967).

Michael, T. N., *Place names in Dorset* (Bournemouth, 1969).

Millgate, M., *Thomas Hardy: his career as a novelist* (London, 1971).

Moule, H., *Old Dorset* (London, 1893).

——, *Paupers, criminals and cholera at Dorchester in 1854* (Guernsey, 1968).

Newman, J. and Pevsner, N., *The Buildings of England: Dorset* (London, 1972).

Okeden, D. O. P., *A letter to the members in Parliament for Dorsetshire on the subject of poor relief and labourers' wages* (Blandford, 1830).

Palmer, K., *Oral folktales of Wessex* (Newton Abbot, 1973).

Percival, J., *Report on the soils of Dorset* (Reading, 1906).

Piggott, A. M., *A Traveller's notes* (London, 1866).

Pigot & Co. Ltd., *Directory of Dorsetshire* (London, 1842).

Pinion, F. B., *A Hardy Companion* (London, 1968).

——, *Thomas Hardy. Art and Thought* (London, 1977).

——(ed.), *Thomas Hardy and the Modern World* (Dorchester, 1974).

Pitt-Rivers, M., *Dorset* (London, 1966).

Purdy, R. L., *Thomas Hardy: a bibliographical study* (Oxford, 1968).

Purves, J., 'Mr. Thomas Hardy's rustics.' *Time*, June 1885.

Royal Commission on Historical Monuments, *Dorset* Parts 1—4 (London, 1952—72).

Ruegg, L. H., 'Farming of Dorsetshire', *Journal of Royal Agricultural Society*, vol. 15.

Sherren, W., *The Wessex of Romance* (London, 1908).

Sherry, D., *Dorset Crafts and Trades* (Swanage, 1974).

Simon, J. S., *Methodism in Dorset:* a sketch (Weymouth, 1870).

Skilling, J. P., *The Country of Far from the Madding Crowd* (Dorchester, 1973).

——, *The Country of The Return of the Native* (Dorchester, 1972).

——, *The Country of The Woodlanders* (Dorchester, 1973).

——, *The Country of Tess of the D'Urbervilles* (Dorchester, 1972).

Skilling, M. R., *Hardy's Mellstock on the map* (Dorchester, 1968).

Southerington, F. R., *Hardy's Vision of Man* (London, 1971).

Southern Newspapers, *What's in a name?* (Southampton, 1969).

Stevenson, W., *General view of the Agriculture of the county of Dorset* (London, 1815).

Stewart, J. I. M., *Thomas Hardy: a critical biography* (London, 1971).

Summer, H., *Cranborne Chase* (Bournemouth, 1934).

Syers, B. B., *Folklore in Thomas Hardy's major Wessex novels* (Unpublished thesis, University of Texas, 1933).

Taylor, C., *Dorset* (London, 1970).

Thomas Hardy Festival Society, *Official Handbook* (Dorchester, 1968).

Thomas Hardy Year Book (ed. J. S. Cox), (Guernsey, 1970—   ).

Thurley, G., *The Psychology of Hardy's Novels* (Queensland, 1975).

Treves, F., *Highways and Byways in Dorset* (London, 1935).

Udal, J. S., 'Christmas mummers in Dorsetshire', *Folklore Record* vol. 3.

——, *Dorsetshire folklore* (Hatford, 1922).

Victoria History of the County of Dorset (ed. W. Page), 2 vols. (London, 1900 and Oxford, 1968).

Vigar, P., *The Novels of Thomas Hardy* (London, 1974).

Watt, I. (ed.), *The Victorian Novel* (Oxford, 1971).

Weber, C. J., *Hardy of Wessex* (Oxford, 1940).

Webster, H. C., *On a darkling plain* (Chicago, 1947).

Weinstock, M. B., *Old Dorset* (Newton Abbot, 1967).

——, *Studies in Dorset History* (Dorchester, 1953).

Western Gazette (weekly newspaper).

Whitehead, R. A., *The century of service: an illustrated history of Eddison Plant Ltd.* (Grantham, 1968).

Wightman, R., *The Wessex heathland* (London, 1953).

——, *Portrait of Dorset* (London, 1965).

Wightman, T. R., *The Country of Jude the Obscure* (Dorchester, 1975).

Wildman, W. B., *A short history of Sherborne* (Sherborne, 1911).

Williams, M., *Thomas Hardy and rural England* (London, 1972).

——, *A Preface to Hardy* (London, 1976).

Williams, R., *The Country and the City* (London, 1973).

Winchcombe, A. D., *The Country of Under the Greenwood Tree* (Dorchester, 1973).

Windle, B. C. A., *The Wessex of Thomas Hardy* (London, 1925).

Young, E. W., *Dorchester, its ancient and modern history; principal buildings and institutions* (Dorchester, 1886).

Index